Lecture Notes
in Business Information Processing

316

More information about this series at http://www.springer.com/series/7911

Raimundas Matulevičius · Remco Dijkman (Eds.)

Advanced Information Systems Engineering Workshops

CAiSE 2018 International Workshops
Tallinn, Estonia, June 11–15, 2018
Proceedings

 Springer

Editors
Raimundas Matulevičius
University of Tartu
Tartu
Estonia

Remco Dijkman
Eindhoven University of Technology
Eindhoven, Noord-Brabant
The Netherlands

ISSN 1865-1348 ISSN 1865-1356 (electronic)
Lecture Notes in Business Information Processing
ISBN 978-3-319-92897-5 ISBN 978-3-319-92898-2 (eBook)
https://doi.org/10.1007/978-3-319-92898-2

Library of Congress Control Number: 2018944435

Printed on acid-free paper

This Springer imprint is published by the registered company Springer International Publishing AG
part of Springer Nature
The registered company address is: Gewerbestrasse 11, 6330 Cham, Switzerland

Preface

For 30 years, the Conference on Advanced Information Systems Engineering (CAiSE) has been the primary yearly event for discussing the latest developments in the area of information systems engineering. The conference has a long tradition of hosting workshops that are focused on particular areas of information systems engineering and, as such, provide ideal forums for researchers to discuss their work with others who are active in the same area. Workshops provide ample time for discussing early-stage research ideas as well as work that is suitable for discussing in a smaller, more focused, setting.

This year the CAiSE workshop program consisted of the following workshops:

- The 5th Workshop on Advances in Services Design Based on the Notion of Capability (ASDENCA)
- The First Workshop on Business Data Analytics: Techniques and Applications (BDA)
- The First Workshop on Blockchains for Inter-Organizational Collaboration (BIOC)
- The 6th Workshop on Cognitive Aspects of Information Systems Engineering (COGNISE)
- The Second Workshop on Enterprise Modeling
- The 14th Workshop on Enterprise and Organizational Modeling and Simulation (EOMAS)
- The First Workshop on Flexible Advanced Information Systems (FAiSE)
- The 4th Workshop on Socio-Technical Perspective in IS Development (STPIS)

The workshops were selected from a total of ten submissions, based on their fit with the CAiSE conference and their potential to attract papers.

Each of the workshops established its own program, in collaboration with the workshop chairs. All workshops allowed papers to be submitted for consideration for the workshop program and selected a number of them for presentation and discussion. The papers of the ASDENCA, BDA, BIOC, COGNISE, Enterprise Modeling, and FAiSE workshops are published in these proceedings. EOMAS and STPIS publish their own proceedings. In total, 49 papers were submitted to the workshops that are published in these proceedings; 22 of these papers were accepted. In addition to paper presentations, keynote presenters were invited to speak on the workshop topics and discussion sessions were planned.

We would like to use this opportunity to thank the workshops chairs of the respective workshops for their hard work in organizing their workshops. Of course we would also like to thank the work of the reviewers. Reviewing is an incredibly important scientific service and we appreciate the time they took to read the workshop submissions and provide feedback.

April 2017

Raimundas Matulevičius
Remco Dijkman

Contents

COGNISE – Cognitive Aspects of Information Systems Engineering

Workshop on Enterprise Modeling

FAiSE – Flexible Advanced Information Systems

ASDENCA – Advances in Services Design Based on the Notion of Capability

The 5th International Workshop on Advances in Service Design Based on the Notion of Capabiliy – ASDENCA

Preface

Lately, the notion of capability is gaining an increased presence within the field of information systems engineering, due to a number of factors: the notion directs business investment focus, it can be used as a baseline for business planning, and it leads directly to service specification and design. Historically, it has been examined in economics, sociology, and management science. More recently, it has been considered in the context of business–IT alignment, in the specification and design of services using business planning as the baseline.

Capability is commonly seen as an ability or capacity for a company to deliver value, either to customers or to shareholders, right beneath the business strategy. It consists of three major components: business processes, people, and physical assets.

Thus it is an abstraction away from the specifics of how (process), who (agent), and why (goals), i.e., with a focus on results and benefits. The same capability should allow for fairly straightforward integrations with the aforementioned established bodies of knowledge and practices, such as goals (through "goal fulfilment"), processes (through "modeling"), and services (through "servicing").

The idea for the ASDENCA workshop came from the academic and industrial community gathered in the EU/FP7 project "CaaS." In its fifth year, ASDENCA placed the focus on discussing (a) business domain-related problems and (b) data-management problems that could be solved by using the notion of capability to embody software service solutions by integrating business architecturing with IS design able to cope with changes in the environment at the run-time.

The Program Committee selected four high-quality papers for presentation at the workshop, which are included in the CAiSE 2018 Workshops proceedings volume. In addition, a discussion panel was organized. The workshop was organized under the scope of the EMMSAD++ conference.

We owe special thanks to the Workshop Chairs of CAiSE 2018, Raimundas Matulevičius and Remco Dijkman, for supporting the ASDENCA workshop, as well as for providing us with the facilities to publicize it. We also thank the Program Committee for providing valuable and timely reviews for the submitted papers.

April 2018

Oscar Pastor
Peri Loucopoulos
Jelena Zdravkovic

ASDENCA Organization

Organizing Committee

Jelena Zdravkovic   Stockholm University, Sweden
Pericles Loucopoulos   University of Manchester, UK
Oscar Pastor   University of Valencia, Spain

Program Committee

Janis Grabis, Latvia
Giancarlo Guizzardi, Brazil
Martin Henkel, Sweden
Tharaka Ilayperuma, Sri Lanka
Janis Kampars, Latvia
Dimitris Karagiannis, Austria
Evangelia Kavakli, Greece
Marite Kirikova, Latvia
John Krogstie, Norway
Raimundas Matulevičius, Estonia
Andreas Opdahl, Norway
Geert Poels, Belgium
Jolita Ralyte, Switzerland
Gil Regev, Switzerland
Irina Rychkov, France
Kurt Sandkuhl, Germany
Monique Snoeck, Belgium
Pnina Soffer, Israel
Janis Stirna, Sweden
Francisco Valverde, Spain
Hans Weigand, The Netherlands
Eric Yu, Canada

Validation of Capability Modeling Concepts: A Dialogical Approach

Jānis Grabis[1], Janis Stirna[2(✉)], and Lauma Jokste[1]

[1] Institute of Information Technology,
Riga Technical University, Kalku 1, Riga, Latvia
{grabis,lauma.jokste}@rtu.lv
[2] Department of Computer and Systems Sciences,
Stockholm University, PO Box 7003, 164 07 Kista, Sweden
js@dsv.su.se

Abstract. Involvement of potential users in early stages of elaboration of development methods is needed for successful method adoption in practice. This paper reports on activities of introduction and assessment of the Capability Driven Development (CDD) methodology with a group of industry representatives. This was performed in an interactive workshop and the main evaluation objectives were to assess the relevance of the CDD concepts and their recognizability as well as to identify potential use cases for CDD application. A dialogical approach was used to convey the CDD methodology to the participants and to entice discussions. The main findings are that the participants easily recognized the modeling constructs for capability design. They found that adjustments are particularly useful for the purpose of identification capability steering actions. The use cases described by the participants were later formalized as capability models.

Keywords: Enterprise modeling · Capability modeling · Capability design

1 Introduction

Capabilities are used in strategic management to define core competencies possessed by enterprises [1]. Several enterprise architecture and management frameworks identify capabilities as a starting point of defining enterprise services, processes and supporting technologies, c.f., for instance [2, 3]. Despite the importance of this concept, there is a disagreement on its meaning. Zdravkovic et al. [4] identify that frameworks that use the concept of capability and require capability modeling often lack methodological guidance for capability elicitation and development. Furthermore, only a few of them integrate capability with information systems (IS) solutions. Thus, the capability concept seems to be better elaborated at the strategic level while there is limited understanding of how to go about the actual implementation of capabilities once they have been identified on the strategic level.

The Capability Driven Development (CDD) methodology [5] operationalizes capabilities by defining their associations with other concepts used in enterprise modeling (EM) and IS development as well as by elaborating processes for developing

R. Matulevičius and R. Dijkman (Eds.): CAiSE 2018 Workshops, LNBIP 316, pp. 5–14, 2018.
https://doi.org/10.1007/978-3-319-92898-2_1

information systems enabling capability delivery. The objective of the CDD is to create IS providing the expected performance in various circumstances. The expected performance is characterized by enterprise goals and indicators and the circumstances are specified using contextual information. The process of capability development includes stages of design and delivery. During the delivery stage, adjustments are invoked to adapt the capability delivery to the specific context situation. Capability delivery knowledge in a form of patterns is used to suggested solutions for coping with context situations encountered.

Development of the CDD methodology was motivated and guided by requirements of three in industrial use cases [6]. These use cases were provided by companies participating in a consortium involved in a joint research project. In order to validate the methodology beyond the boundaries of the project consortium, several workshops with other representatives from industry were also organized. The CDD methodology was presented and its potential for wider application areas were identified.

This paper reports the course of action and results of one of the workshops with industry representatives.

From the scientific perspective, the workshops were aimed at validating the concepts used in the CDD methodology. From the practical perspective, companies were introduced to the methodology and new potential application areas were identified. The specific research questions explored at these workshops were:

- Do industry representatives recognize concepts used in capability modeling?
- Are they able to define capabilities and identify goals, context, and adjustments?
- Are there common patterns emerging across cases? .

Representatives of companies were actively involved in explorative activities following the principles of dialogical action research [7].

The rest of the paper is organized as follows. The theoretical foundations of this work are discussed in Sect. 2. Section 3 describes the research method. The main findings are presented in Sect. 4. Section 5 concludes.

2   Background

The capability meta-model [8] provides the theoretical background for designing the workshop with practitioners, and the related work highlights some of the challenges associated with promoting and introducing new development methods in practice.

2.1   Capability Modeling

A simplified overview of the key elements used in capability modeling is provided in Fig. 1. Goals are business objectives the capability allows to achieve. They are measured by Key Performance Indicators (KPI). Each capability is designed for delivery in a specific context defined using context elements. The context elements represent factors affecting the capability delivery while context situations refer to combinations of context element values at runtime. A process element specifies a capability delivery solution. In order to ensure that capability is delivered as expected in different

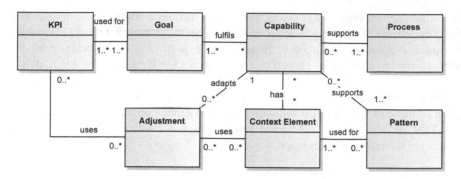

Fig. 1. A fragment of the capability model focusing on adjustments

contextual situations, adjustments are used to adapt capability delivery [9]. The adjustments take the context data and KPIs as input and evaluate potential changes in capability delivery according to an adaption algorithm. Reusable knowledge of capability delivery is represented using patterns. They are used to streamline capability delivery (i.e., what kind of adjustments could be incorporated in the capability design if specific context situations are expected) as well as to suggest capability delivery modifications (e.g., are there any patterns suggesting appropriate actions in the observed context situation). The patterns are intended for application in specific context situations.

2.2 Related Work

Concerning related work, three dimensions are relevant to this investigation, namely, role of capabilities in development of supporting information systems, validation of modeling concepts, and acceptance of new development methodologies.

The capability concept is used in different areas of business and IS development [10]. For example, ArchiMate defines capability as an ability possessed by an active structural element [3]. There are various ways of realizing the capability by combining elements of enterprise architecture. TOGAF [2] advocates capability-based planning to engineer and deliver strategic business capabilities. As an architectural framework, it focuses on structural elements required to deliver the capabilities. Differences among frameworks and their support for capability based development is analyzed in [4].

Although capabilities ought to improve business and IT alignment, empirical evidence is required to prove this assumption [11]. Mohd Salleh et al. [12] show that appropriate information systems are vital to enact capabilities. Capabilities are also identified as important for linking motivation and implementation [13] or strategic planning process and enterprise architecture [14].

Capabilities and capability-based development approaches are novel propositions to many practitioners, and therefore evidence that new modeling and development methods are better perceived if users are involved in early stages of elaboration and adoption should be provided [15]. If modeling methods are viewed through the prism of new product development, customer focused idea generation and early feedback also feature among the critical success factors of the method's adoption, as discussed in [16]. The process of selecting an appropriate EM method is analyzed by in [17] and it is concluded that method adoption facilitators and experts play an important role. The method adoption also can be viewed as a process of knowledge transfer. Methods also should be suitable for the needs of a particular enterprise or project team [18] and should provide a balance between the effort required and results achieved [19]. Evaluation of methods is preformed following multiple generation and enactment activities [20]. That includes internal, theoretical and empirical evaluation activities. This paper focuses on the empirical evaluation.

3   Research Methods

The investigation was a part of the CaaS research project that followed the principles of Design Science Research (DSR) [21] with CDD methodology and environment being the main design artifacts. The research process consisting of several use case driven design-evaluation iterations, i.e., the theoretical concepts of capability driven development were elaborated according to the needs identified by the industrial use-case partners involved in the project [6]. This information was used to refine the capability meta-model, to develop the CDD methodology, and to apply it at the use case companies. The use case partners had a good understanding of the methodology and an immediate access to additional experts which lead to good results of applying CDD to solve the business cases of the use case companies as well as generally good appreciation of the methodology. Somewhat contrary, initial presentations of the CDD methodology to a wider industrial community showed that much time had to be spent on general discussions about the meaning of various concepts, such the difference between the concepts of capability and service, and limited insights were made about the actual applications of the methodology. The industry representatives were also involved mainly as passive observers. These presentations were made as part of the first industry CDD workshop held in 2015.

The second industry workshop was organized in 2016 to spark active participation of the industry representatives. The workshop was organized as the diagnostics phase of the action research cycle [22]. In particular, the dialogical approach was chosen to involve industry representatives in an open discussion about capabilities and their role in enterprise evolution. To achieve this the capability modeling concepts were conveyed in terms familiar to the industry representatives and the presentation of the CDD methodology focused on the benefits, assumptions, and examples rather than on methodological procedures. The workshop agenda was as follows (duration of the workshop was three hours and one hour for post-meeting discussions):

1. Overview of CDD
2. Exploration of travel management case; step-by-step capability model development;
3. Summary of key elements of the capability model using a tabular template;
4. Identification of use cases;
5. Description of the use- case following the tabular template;
6. Discussion of the use cases.

The tabular template for capability definition includes fields for naming the capability as well as defining KPI, context, and adjustments. Its purpose was to highlight the crucial aspects of capability development, i.e., the interplay among goals, context, and delivery mechanisms, and to abstract from intricacies of the capability meta-model by hiding specific aspects of representing these concepts.

The meeting was attended by representatives from five companies. Their positions at the companies were board member, chief information officer, and system architect. Their companies has only limited experience with EM techniques. Their areas of interest used as precursors for the use case and capability identification were:

1. Logistics (Postal terminals)
2. Wholesale (Spare parts of agricultural machinery)
3. IT management (Incident management)
4. Software development
5. IT infrastructure management

The concepts defined in the interactive section were later confirmed with the company representatives. Preliminary, capability models were developed after the meeting. Some of them were subsequently used to explore possibilities for future collaborative capability development activities.

4 Results

During the workshop a number of use cases were suggested according to the profiles of the involved industry representatives although they were free to choose their own use cases. The selected use cases were briefly discussed and the industry representatives filled out the template and clarifications were made as necessary. The identified capabilities are described in Table 1. In the first two cases the most important capability was easily identified by the experts. The Incident management and User satisfaction management capabilities were selected as one of many related capabilities in the third and fourth cases. For example, in the IT management use case, provisioning of computational resources and help desk services possessed similar importance and characteristics. In the case of IT infrastructure management, the expert mainly focused on consumer value of the services provided. However, he found difficult to clearly separate capabilities of the service provider and the service consumer, probably, due to the wide scope of the capability definition.

The capabilities identified were further elaborated by defining associated concepts. The participants easily recognized the concepts to define the capabilities. Definitions for KPIs were readily available while they recognized that in part they have not attempted to think about the problem in terms of context and adjustments. Identification of context seemed somewhat natural and sometimes perceived as an organic part of the business. However, the participants acknowledged that explicit representation of the context becomes important when quantitative context measurements are to be taken into account. Previously, much of the contextual information has been addressed in an intuitive manner.

Table 1. Identified capabilities

Name	Use case area	Description
Automatic parcel delivery	Logistics	A company operates automatic parcel delivery machines to ensure speedy and accessible deliveries. Its ability is to provide last mile logistics services and capacity is parcels delivery lockers
Spare parts management	Wholesale	A company supplies spare parts for agricultural machinery to ensure continuous operations. Its ability is inventory management of slow moving and critical parts and its capacity is a distribution network
Incident management	IT management	A company support users of large-scale enterprise applications to ensure reliable service delivery. Its ability is to provide application support and its capacity is support infrastructure
User satisfaction management	Software development	A company develops e-government systems and aims to improve user acceptance and usage intentions
E-health service provisioning	IT infrastructure management	A company develops un runs data processing and networking solutions for large organizations. Its ability is development of scalable data processing infrastructure and its capacity is computational resources

The participants found the adjustment concepts of particular value because it provoked thinking about potential solutions for different contextual situations. In particular, they were willing to think about adjustments in relation to context and KPIs even though identification of the relations was beyond the scope of the session. It was noted that despite numerous discussions at companies about decision-making policies, these kind of response mechanisms to changes in the context situation have not been formalized.

The results of capability identification are summarized in Table 2. In the case of Automatic parcel delivery, the company is interested in processing as many parcels as possible within the required delivery timeframe and it is not interested to maintain many empty lockers or to have parcels that are not retrieved by customers. Predictable events such as the Holiday Season can be accounted for up-front in the systems design while context-based adaption is mainly important for unexpected events. For instance, beginning of the gardening season can vary by as much as a month and may overlap with other contextual factors. The contextual elements have varying degrees of predictability and data availability. Clients share information about the number of parcels in transition and this information comes from various sources and requires context processing. The clients' marketing campaigns are often not shared with the company and data can be obtained using context monitoring facilities. The Buffer warehouse adjustment implies that parcels are stored in intermediate facilities if lockers are full and these facilities are often identified in a dynamic manner. Clients dispatch parcels only if there are free lockers in the case of the Storage at the client side adjustment.

Table 2. Capability description

Name	KPI	Context	Adjustment
Automatic parcel delivery	Terminal load percentage Late deliveries Returns to warehouse Number of parcels processed	Calendar events Season Number of parcels in transition Clients marketing campaigns	Buffer warehouse Storage at the client side Transfer of portable storage modules Variable storage size
Spare parts management	Order fulfillment rate Delivery time Demand Delivery cost Fixed cost	Shipments transit time from manufacturers Data accuracy Season	Dynamic stock planning Direct shipment Transshipment among warehouses
Incident management	Number of new/open incidents Resolution within SLA	Irregular events Seasonal events	Resource allocation Scheduling of services
User satisfaction management	User satisfaction level Number of logged user errors Number of helpdesk request	Computational load Irregular events Seasonal events	Provisioning of computational resources Automated recommendations
E-health service provisioning	Treatment waiting time Treatment success rate Number of customers requests Customer request response time	Season Irregular events	Dynamics resource planning

That does not incur direct costs but might lead to the loss of client's goodwill. The Transfer of portable storage modules and Variables storage size adjustments dynamically change physical dimensions of stations and lockers, respectively.

The CDD approach envisions that best practices defined as patterns can be identified and used to deal with various unexpected contextual situations including usage across various related patterns. E.g. context elements such as season and events are present in several of the identified capabilities. However, it has to be acknowledged that they are measured very differently from case to case. Hence, the response mechanisms (i.e., adjustments) are transferable only at the high level. The common adjustments are resource allocation and used of various advanced inventory management policies.

The results of the workshop were processed and initial capability model was created for the Automatic parcel delivery capability (Fig. 2).

The model shows KPI (identified by suffix "KPI"), context (identified by suffix "Ctx" and adjustments (identified by suffix "Adj") discussed at the workshop. According to the CDD methodology, context elements are associated with capability by using a

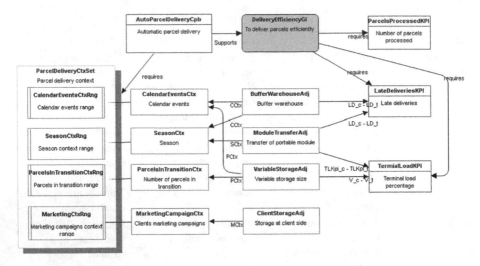

Fig. 2. Initial capability model of automatic parcel delivery

bundle of related context elements or context set. This aspect was not explicitly discussed during the workshop. The goals are kept at a relatively high level of abstraction because they were not explicitly discussed at the workshop. The associations among the elements are introduced. They show, for example, the *VariableStorageAdj* uses *CalendatEventsCtx* and *ParcelsTransitionCtx* context elements and attempts to improve *LateDeliveryKPI* and *TerminalLoadKPI*. *ParcelsTransitionCtx* is not used in *BufferWarehouseAdj* because this adjustment has a longer planning horizon. It is also observed that there are no KPI associate with *ClientStorageAdj*. Although it is permissible to have goal independent adjustments, this observation suggests that not all of the KPIs have been identified during the workshop.

Thus, representation of the workshop finding in the form of the capability model introduces technical aspects of capability design, clarifies associations among the elements and identifies potentially missing elements of the model.

5   Conclusions

The workshop was successful in introducing the CDD methodology to the industry representatives and the dialogical approach proved more efficient than previous attempts based on presentations and discussions but without actual modeling. The usage of the capability definition template rather than a fully-fledged modeling effort was efficient time-wise because it required less time for explaining the modeling process and left more time for the actual definition of capabilities. This approach also has some limitations. There is a relatively wide gap between naming of the concepts and a reasonably complete capability model. The experiment does not provide evaluation of the overall model or the methodology as a whole. However, the experiment shows that the capability concept is considered useful and KPIs, context and adjustments are useful for analyzing the capabilities.

The workshop with industry representatives was one of several activities aimed at promoting the CDD methodology to industry representatives. In terms of the DSR, the workshop contributed to additional validation of the design artifact as well as helped to explicate additional problems related to the adoption of the CDD methodology in practice. In response to the latter, a lightweight version [23] of CDD was proposed, particularly to advance its usage among start-ups and small and medium size enterprises.

Currently, it is too early to judge about the potential for take-up of the methodology in industry. However, two applied research and technology transfer projects were initiated as the result of the workshop. In these projects, the CDD methodology is not used as a whole; rather its selected method components are used. This is in accordance of what was envisioned during elaboration of the methodology by making it a component-based methodology [24, 25].

References

1. Teece, D.J.: Explicating dynamic capabilities: the nature and microfoundations of (sustainable) enterprise performance. Strateg. Manag. J. **28**, 1319–1350 (2007)
2. Open Group. TOGAF-enterprise architecture methodology, version 9.1 (2012). http://www.opengroup.org/togaf/
3. Open Group. ArchiMate 2.1 Specification. The Open Group, December 2013 (2013)
4. Zdravkovic, J., Stirna, J., Grabis, J.: A comparative analysis of using the capability notion for congruent business- and information systems engineering. CSIMQ **10**, 1–20 (2017)
5. Grabis, J., Henkel, M., Kampars, J., Koç, H., Sandkuhl, K., Stamer, D., Stirna, J., Valverde, F., Zdravkovic, J.: D5.3 The final version of Capability driven development methodology, FP7 proj. 611351 CaaS. https://doi.org/10.13140/rg.2.2.35862.34889
6. Bravos, G., Grabis, J., Henkel, M., Jokste, L., Kampars, J.: Supporting evolving organizations: IS development methodology goals. In: Johansson, B., Andersson, B., Holmberg, N. (eds.) BIR 2014. LNBIP, vol. 194, pp. 158–171. Springer, Cham (2014). https://doi.org/10.1007/978-3-319-11370-8_12
7. Mårtensson, P., Lee, A.S.: Dialogical action research at Omega Corporation. MIS Q. Manag. Inf. Syst. **28**, 507–536 (2004)
8. Bērziša, S., Bravos, G., González, T., Czubayko, U., España, S., Grabis, J., Henkel, M., Jokste, L., Kampars, J., Koç, H., Kuhr, J., Llorca, C., Loucopoulos, P., Pascual, R.J., Pastor, O., Sandkuhl, K., Simic, H., Stirna, J., Giromé, F.V., Zdravkovic, J.: Capability Driven Development: An Approach to Designing Digital Enterprises. Bus. Inf. Syst. Eng. **57**, 15–25 (2015)
9. Grabis, J., Kampars, J.: Design of capability delivery adjustments. In: Krogstie, J., Mouratidis, H., Su, J. (eds.) CAiSE 2016. LNBIP, vol. 249, pp. 52–62. Springer, Cham (2016). https://doi.org/10.1007/978-3-319-39564-7_5
10. Wissotzki, M.: An exploration of capability research. In: Proceedings-IEEE International Enterprise Distributed Object Computing Workshop, EDOCW, pp. 179–184 (2015)
11. Offerman, T., Stettina, C.J., Plaat, A.: Business Capabilities: A Systematic Literature Review and a Research Agenda (2017)

12. Mohd Salleh, N.A., Rohde, F., Green, P.: Information systems enacted capabilities and their effects on SMEs' information systems adoption behavior. J. Small Bus. Manag. **55**, 332–364 (2017)
13. Aldea, A., Iacob, M.E., Van Hillegersberg, J., Quartel, D., Franken, H.: Capability-based planning with ArchiMate: Linking motivation to implementation. In: ICEIS 2015-17th International Conference on Enterprise Information Systems, Proceedings, pp. 352–359 (2015)
14. Blomqvist, S., Halén, M., Helenius, M.: Connecting enterprise architecture with strategic planning processes: case study of a large Nordic finance organization. In: Proceedings-17th IEEE Conference on Business Informatics, CBI 2015, pp. 43–50 (2015)
15. Mohan, K., Ahlemann, F.: Understanding acceptance of information system development and management methodologies by actual users: a review and assessment of existing literature. Int. J. Inf. Manage. **33**, 831–839 (2013)
16. Yilmaz, N., Stirna, J.: Factors influencing productization of enterprise modeling: a qualitative inquiry into the scandinavian strand of methods and tools. In: Ralyté, J., España, S., Pastor, Ó. (eds.) PoEM 2015. LNBIP, vol. 235, pp. 193–208. Springer, Cham (2015). https://doi.org/10.1007/978-3-319-25897-3_13
17. Persson, A., Stirna, J.: Organizational adoption of enterprise modeling methods – experience based recommendations. In: Frank, U., Loucopoulos, P., Pastor, Ó., Petrounias, I. (eds.) PoEM 2014. LNBIP, vol. 197, pp. 179–192. Springer, Heidelberg (2014). https://doi.org/10.1007/978-3-662-45501-2_13
18. McBride, T., Henderson-Sellers, B.: A method assessment framework. In: Ralyté, J., Mirbel, I., Deneckère, R. (eds.) ME 2011. IAICT, vol. 351, pp. 64–76. Springer, Heidelberg (2011). https://doi.org/10.1007/978-3-642-19997-4_7
19. Kacmar, C.J., McManus, D.J., Duggan, E.W., Hale, J.E., Hale, D.P.: Software development methodologies in organizations: field investigation of use, acceptance, and application. Inf. Resour. Manag. J. **22**, 16–39 (2009)
20. Sandkuhl, K., Seigerroth, U.: Balanced scorecard for method improvement: approach and experiences. In: Reinhartz-Berger, I., Gulden, J., Nurcan, S., Guédria, W., Bera, P. (eds.) BPMDS/EMMSAD -2017. LNBIP, vol. 287, pp. 204–219. Springer, Cham (2017). https://doi.org/10.1007/978-3-319-59466-8_13
21. Hevner, A.R., March, S.T., Park, J., Ram, S.: Design science in information systems research. MIS Q. **28**(1), 75–105 (2004)
22. Baskerville, R.: Investigating information systems with action research. Commun. Assoc. Inf. Syst. **2**(19), 1–31 (1999)
23. Koç, H., Ruiz, M., España, S.: LightCDD: a lightweight capability-driven development method for start-ups. In: Krogstie, J., Mouratidis, H., Su, J. (eds.) CAiSE 2016. LNBIP, vol. 249, pp. 15–26. Springer, Cham (2016). https://doi.org/10.1007/978-3-319-39564-7_2
24. Sandkuhl, K., Koç, H.: Component-Based Method Development: An Experience Report. In: Frank, U., Loucopoulos, P., Pastor, Ó., Petrounias, I. (eds.) PoEM 2014. LNBIP, vol. 197, pp. 164–178. Springer, Heidelberg (2014). https://doi.org/10.1007/978-3-662-45501-2_12
25. Stirna, J., Zdravkovic, J., Grabis, J., Sandkuhl, K.: Development of capability driven development methodology: experiences and recommendations. In: Poels, G., Gailly, F., Serral Asensio, E., Snoeck, M. (eds.) PoEM 2017. LNBIP, vol. 305, pp. 251–266. Springer, Cham (2017). https://doi.org/10.1007/978-3-319-70241-4_17

Towards Improving Adaptability of Capability Driven Development Methodology in Complex Environment

Renata Petrevska Nechkoska[1,2(✉)], Geert Poels[1], and Gjorgji Manceski[2]

[1] Faculty of Economics and Business Administration,
Ghent University, Ghent, Belgium
{renata.petrevskanechkoska,geert.poels}@ugent.be
[2] Faculty of Economics, University St. Kliment Ohridski, Bitola, Macedonia
gmanceski@t-home.mk

Abstract. We are triggered to incorporate adaptability in information system designs and methodologies corresponding to complex and unpredictable environment of today and tomorrow and to complex adaptive systems they are aimed for. Adaptability as non-functional requirement is being portrayed and investigated from broad multidisciplinary perspective that influences how dynamic business-IT alignment can be accomplished. Capability Driven Development methodology has supported delivering dynamic capabilities by providing context-aware self-adaptive platform in the CaaS project implementations, as our case study. Along with the already incorporated mechanisms, components that enable adaptability, there is open space for further evolutionary and deliberate change towards becoming truly appropriate methodology for dynamic reconfigurations of capabilities in organizations and business ecosystems that operate in complexity and uncertainty. The analysis and evaluation of adaptability of the CDD methodology through three dimensions (complexity of the external and internal environment, managerial profiling and artifact-integrated components) in this paper conclude with instigation of starting points towards achieving higher adaptability for complexity of the CDD methodology.

Keywords: Adaptability · Adaptiveness · Adaptation
Non-functional requirements · Capability Driven Development methodology
Complexity

1 Introduction

Adaptability is emerging as an important type of non-functional requirement (NFR) for just about any system, including information systems, embedded systems, e-business systems, and the like. It represents the system's ability to accommodate changes in its environment - in order to succeed or even to survive [1]. Especially in the service design phase, there is the additional requirement for high system adaptiveness along different technical requirements and different user expectations [2]. Complementary to the basic qualities (functionality, reliability, ease of use, economy and safety) there are

© Springer International Publishing AG, part of Springer Nature 2018
R. Matulevičius and R. Dijkman (Eds.): CAiSE 2018 Workshops, LNBIP 316, pp. 15–27, 2018.
https://doi.org/10.1007/978-3-319-92898-2_2

extra qualities, NFRs or soft-goals – flexibility, reparability, adaptability, understand-ability, documentation and enhanceability [3, 4].

The ability for system to change is essential to its continued survival and ability to provide requisite functions for its stakeholders [5] either through evolutionary [6] or goal-seeking, deliberate adaptation [7]. According the NFR (non-functional require-ments) framework [3], there are functional requirements specifying 'what' should be achieved, and non-functional requirements - specifying 'how' outcomes will be achieved. Generally, the NFRs are "informally stated, often contradictory, difficult to enforce during development and evaluate for the customer prior to delivery" evaluated subjectively and qualitatively ('satisfying' or 'not satisfying') [8]. Adaptability as NFR is defined as the ease of system/component modification, modification of behavior in response to environment changes, adjustment to changing requirements [5].

Capability Driven Development (CDD) applies enterprise models representing enterprise capabilities to create executable software with built-in contextualization. It attempts to overcome the limitations of Model Driven Development (MDD) towards more suitable capture of business requirements, modeling execution contexts, offering functionality in different business contexts, capturing dynamic behavior of both functional and non-functional requirements – all of which enabling 'plasticity' in software applications that are business context aware [10]. It situates itself in complex and dynamically changing business environments, incorporating principles of agile and iterative IS development thus enabling continuous dynamic business-IT alignment in a structured and systematic way, using the concept of business capability. CDD aims for rapid response to changes in the business context and development of new capabilities which also requires run-time configuration and adjustment of the IS [11–13].

The external environment in which we operate is complex and unpredictable, portrayed in the Cynefin framework [14–18], and the Stacey matrix [19–21] (Fig. 1). This imposes specific considerations to deliver dynamic capabilities, in terms of managerial approach, internal environment as Complex Adaptive Systems (CAS) [22].

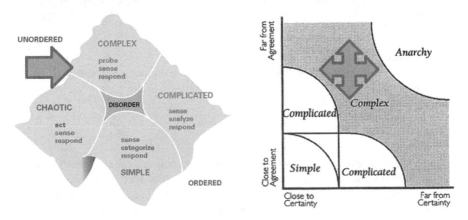

Fig. 1. The Cynefin Framework and recommended managerial approaches for complexity (left) [16, 60] and Stacey Matrix and managerial approaches for complexity (right) [20, 21]

This paper compiles a novel qualitative evaluation framework that investigates adaptability for complexity, using the case of the CDD as state of the art methodology designed for function in complex and unpredictable environment, through its incorporation in the CaaS project, as one of its most comprehensive, robust and exemplary implementations. Using this evaluation prism we detect and point out the existence of components of adaptability in CDD methodology (element and architectural) through 3 dimensions, and instigate future directions to improve CDD methodology and its effectiveness in supporting context-aware, self-adaptive platforms that model and deliver dynamic capabilities, such as CaaS.

The paper is structured as follows: In Sect. 2 we are discussing the main concepts of adaptation, adaptability and adaptiveness, meaning, names; as well as how they can be achieved and measured. In Sect. 3 we are decomposing the evaluation prism to aspects that ought to be incorporated in the adaptability components (on architectural and element level) and investigating in qualitative manner their existence, implicit incorporation or non-existence in the CDD methodology through 3 dimensions. Section 4 concludes the evaluation, assembles the recommendations for improvement, opening horizons for future multidisciplinary research.

2 Main Concepts

Adaptability and Adaptation. 'Adaptation means change in the system to accommodate change in its environment' [8, 9]. "Adaptation of a system (S) is caused by change from an old environment (E) to a new environment (E') and results in a new system (S') that ideally meets the needs of its new environment (E')" [9]. Adaptability involves three tasks: environment change detection, system change recognition and effectuating system change. The environment can be observed as inner and outer and changes can derive from it all – with regards to Complex Adaptive Systems [23–26]. Some changes entity needs to adapt to, but also changes being initiated in order to reach purpose(s), goal(s) – in the sense of evolutionary and revolutionary learning and adaptation as well as double loop learning [27–29]. The route of changes within the organization range from changes on operational level, or in resources, changes in goals, expectations, principles, KPIs [30].

Adaptability, from systems engineering perspective, as architectural property, is defined as: 'Degree to which a product or system can effectively and efficiently be adapted for different or evolving hardware, software or other operational or usage environments' [5]. "A characteristic of a system amenable to change to fit altered circumstances, where 'circumstances' include both the context of a system's use and its stakeholders' desire" is definition of adaptability by [31]. Adaptability as 'degree to which adjustments in practices, processes or structures of systems are possible to projected or actual changes of its environment' [32, 33] has the elements of what it is (degree of adjustment), to which changes it responds (projected or actual), and how it can be achieved (through adjustments in practices, processes or structures). In taxonomy of service qualities (described as a behavior), adaptability is alongside availability, assurance, usability, interoperability, scalability, portability, extensibility [34, 35].

In [5] it is in changeability, and in COBIT [36], it is into supportability. The authors [37, 40] use adaptability and flexibility as concepts. In [41] ISO/IEC 25010:2011 for Systems and software Quality Requirements and Evaluation (SQuaRE), the definition of flexibility as 'adapting a product for additional user groups, tasks, cultures, enabling products to take account of circumstances, opportunities and individual preferences that had not been anticipated in advance' fits best.

Achieving and Measuring Adaptation. Our next point of interest is to analyze various approaches achieving adaptation. Today's CAS are 'socio-technical, characterized by the interplay between social and technical components, consisted of human actors but also software, hardware; representing the environment (the context) to which systems need to be aware of and functioning in. Context is the current state of the user or system to the objects in their surrounding environment. Human and automatic components are involved in the process of identification of and response to the context. Contextualization is used as a way to allow adaptation to changes both at design time and at run-time' [42]. Adaptation is done through monitoring and actuation. A system is adaptable if it can be altered by someone, while adaptive if it can sense the need and generate the alteration from within itself.

Rule-based adaptation, as analyzed in [43, 44] recognizing 'content analysis rules, content adaptation, corrective, enhancing, fuzzy, integration, monitor, production, matching rules'. They are directed towards various entities (concerning adaptable software) such as process adaptation, workflow and service-flow adaptation, content, GUI/AUI, software configuration, features adaptation. Adaptability transformations enable implementing simple and complex transformations through composition of basic refactoring; sensors and effectors; and design patterns [45–48].

Variability in the field of requirements engineering, variability analysis focuses on 'prioritizing one or few possible solutions to be implemented in the final product, with the strive to enable users to adjust and adapt the product as needed' [37, 49].

The Tropos development methodology in information system design is based on i* organizational modeling framework, through early requirements, late requirements, architectural design and other detailed dependencies [37]. [38–40] use mapping and measurement of adaptability, turbulence and adaptability indices, focused mainly on the external environment and business dimension. Founded on CAS approach, the analysis of IS architecture complexity paralleled with IS efficiency and flexibility (as opposing characteristics that can be mediated by evolutionary and revolutionary IS change), is the approach of [50]. Research in CAS specificity incorporates top-down 'official' and bottom-up 'emergent' co-evolutionary adaptation of information systems design with changing user requirements towards effective system design [51]. PAWS as framework for executing adaptive web-service processes [2, 52] aims for 'self-configuring, self-optimizing, self-healing, self-protecting computing systems'.

Through decomposition of the NFR of interest the POMSA framework (Process-Oriented Metrics for Software Architecture [9]) investigates adaptability of system's components, connections, patterns, constraints, styles that reflect changeability (decomposability, cohesiveness, understandability, simplicity), replaceability, reusability.

Important aspects of the adaptability of any system are controls ranging from classic, advanced, knowledge-based, game/queuing theory controls, feedback and feed-forward controls [51, 53, 54]. Authors [55–57], distinguish: semantic, syntactic, contextual and quality adaptation; [1, 8, 9] recognize: element and architecture adaptability incorporating effectors and adaptors and signature level (level of the entity), protocol level, service level and semantic level of adaptation.

3 Evaluating Adaptability of Capability Driven Development (CDD) for Complex Environment

The main challenges designers of CDD methodology have in front of themselves [10, 11, 13] in the CaaS implementations, are what CDD methodology should achieve: *to model the desired capabilities – using dynamic capabilities that contain variability; to model the impact of context; towards context-aware self-adaptive platform.*

The primary purpose [58] of the CDD methodology is directed towards increasing the value of business services by providing efficient development methodology and capability management lifecycle to continuously design and deliver capabilities that are adjusted for the context of use. We will be examining the adaptability components both through element and architectural prism, in an attempt to perceive how CDD methodology can achieve semantic, syntactic, contextual and quality adaptation on conceptual level, as being implemented and enhanced by the CaaS project.

The three main dimensions for achieving adaptation in complexity that represent frame of analysis are: *Complexity of the environment (External and Internal), Managerial (Strategic, Tactical, Operational) profiling, Artifact-integrated components.*

These three dimensions incorporate a set of interrelated and complex aspects that need to be present on architectural and elementary level of a CDD-like methodologies to achieve higher level of adaptability as necessary NFR for addressing complexity. The qualitative assessment of the important aspects that compose the dimensions is threefold: 'Satisfying (+/+)', 'Semi-satisfying (+/–)', 'Non-satisfying (–/–)'. The evaluation results with starting points for improvement of certain aspects of the methodology towards greater adaptability for complexity (Table 1).

Dimension 1. The external environment is consisted of interrelated agents networked together (in known and unknown manner to the observer, manager, facilitator) producing emergent effect where cause and effect, only coherent in retrospect. Its complexity is perceived in the incomplete knowledge for all the external and internal relations among the entities and here *Probe-Sense-Respond strategy* fits best (Cynefin framework [14–18] (Fig. 1, left)). In the Stacey matrix [19–21] (Fig. 1, right), which considers certainty of outcome and agreement on outcome for various management approaches (relevant here through the decision logic incorporated in CDD), the zone of complexity enlists un-programmable decision making, 'outcomes' instead of 'outputs and solutions'. Organizations as socio-technical Complex Adaptive Systems (CAS) are the internal complex environment. *CAS characteristics* of nonlinearity, self-organization, emergence, co-evolution initiate a question: how do we facilitate a complex adaptive system towards purpose(s) and emergent effects? CAS need to be

Table 1. Main dimensions and their interrelated aspects for analyzing and evaluating adaptability as non-functional requirement, case of CDD methodology

Dimension 1: Complexity of the environment (external & internal)	Dimension 2: Managerial (Strategic, Tactical, Operational) Profiling	Dimension 3: Artifact-integrated components
Probe-Sense-Respond strategy (+/−) CAS characteristics (+/−) Broad business ecology (+/+) Multifaceted context capture (+/+) SIDA & PDCA loops (+/+) Top-down/bottom-up/lateral learning (+/−)	Clarification and proper addressing of strategy, tactics, operations (+/−) Purposeful/Purposive system (+/−) Outcomes/Outputs (+/−) Qualitative/Quantitative information (+/−)	Adaptability transformations (+/+) Variability support (+/+) Modularity (+/+) Positive and negative feedback (+/+) Patterns (±)

addressed with (1) simple rules, (2) moderately dense connections, (3) human rules on how to detect information, how to interpret information, how to act in response [22].

In the example of [13] 'the search for error' approach in method component for context modeling exists in definition of exception types, investigation, development, linkage with the context sets; run-time adaptation options. This supports un-programmable decision making and identification-development-selection approach in CDD. 'Probe' is missing of the Probe-Sense-Respond and is assessed as (+/−).

In the example of [61], CDD's runtime adaptation options range from fully automatic, semi-automatic, to manual − where the system discovers change needs but the change in itself is too complex to implement and human intervention is needed to handle the situation [61]. *CAS specificities* towards emergent effect, as well as loose relations and dependencies, alternative influence on other capabilities, business goals [68] are not fully incorporated in the design or exhibited in the implementations (±).

CDD in the example [69] uses the Onion framework portraying all considerations taken into account in the architectural design and clarifying that the context is not the only source of variability incorporating *broad business ecology* (+/+) through a scope of entities that describe and detect the context considering invariant characteristics such as domain, entity, problem, dynamic processes. In component 1 of the architecture of the CDD environment for context modeling, it is clearly visible that the inputs, the data providers can be internal and external, while contextual elements are captured in multifaceted manner (device, user, task, data source, document representation, time, geo-location) − ensuring *comprehensive multifaceted context capture* (+/+).

The adaptability loop *Sense-Interpret-Decide-Act (SIDA)* or OODA, is effectuated through the CDD actions of capturing context (Sense/Observe) − use patterns & predict (Interpret/Orient) − decision logic (Decide) − runtime adjust, pattern update, deploy (Act) (Fig. 2 (left). However, the loop detects changes in external context, the system continues to reason according pre-defined decision logic on how to react. If we expand the need for the system to detect the changes in expected outcomes (KPIs, goals) and reconfigure accordingly, it may have limited response within a 'given' set of alternative reactions, requiring new system instance. The *top-down approach* should be combined

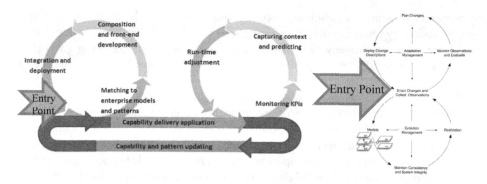

Fig. 2. Capability Driven Development Methodology (left) [10], and Processes involved in runtime adaptation (right) [59]

with *bottom-up and lateral learning* (Fig. 4). *Plan-Do-Check-Act* loop is the one necessary to initiate deliberate changes or model planned responses (evolution and adaptation management). For complex environment, it may have been better situated on secondary level, immediately after the execution, in the process of learning (Fig. 4). Its existence is sufficient mechanism for deliberate change (Fig. 2 (right)) assessed as (+/+). Adaptation and evolution management are in perfect constellation for context-aware CDD. Applicability in various contexts is directly handled by method extension for evolutionary development of capabilities delivered as software service bundles where the system allows the client switch from one configuration to another to adapt to changes.

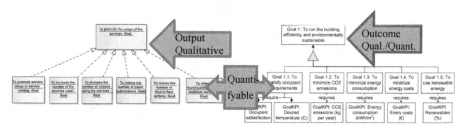

Fig. 3. To promote usage of the municipality services (left) [10], and Generic goal model for building operator (right) [59]

Dimension 2. Clarification and proper *addressing of the managerial functions – strategy, tactics, operations* is especially important for complexity. CDD binds with strategic management and operationalizes directly. For tactical and strategic management, it needs better focus (±). '*Purposive system* is multi-goal- seeking system whose goals result with the system's purpose. This type of system can pursue different goals but it does not select the goal to be pursued. It does choose the means by which to pursue its goals. *Purposeful system* is one which can change its goals, it selects ends as well as means, and thus displays will.' [64] CDD methodology supports development of purposive systems – dynamically reconfiguring towards goals, primarily changing own behavior, by choosing means to pursue goals. It doesn't, aim to offer purposeful search for goals and strategy (±). CDD expects stable strategy [59], given goals [66] and KPIs providing dynamic capabilities. To avoid the mismatch between systems and their models [27, 64] we need not to rely not just on simple/complicated (but deterministic) mechanistic relations among entities and among outputs (±). CDD follows top-down the business model, enterprise architecture, context and capabilities - which are consisted of *qualitative and quantitative values*. Goals and KPIs are values and ranges, with 'hard-coded' decision logic and measurable properties [67], but there is a lot of space for adding qualitative inputs to relate to reality. Goals and KPIs are *mixture of outputs and outcomes*, in *qualitative and quantitative terms* (evaluated with (±)). A goal model in example [10] declares 'to promote the usage of the services' (Fig. 3, left) as qualitative output (put all efforts into promoting usage of the services) decomposed as: promote service usage in service catalog, increase the number of services used, number of citizens, reduce number of paper submissions. Outcome would be 'achieve increased usage of services by X% by customer Y' portraying mixture of outcomes/outputs with mostly quantitative KPIs. In reality, these issues cannot and should not be quantifiable, but combine with qualitative information towards adaptive management on 'how' to make choices.

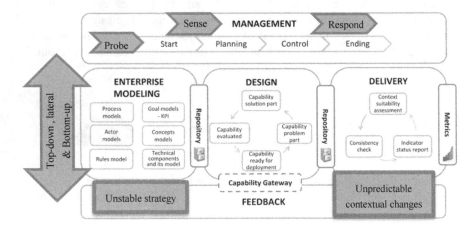

Fig. 4. CDD Methodology [59] and adaptability needs for complex environment

Dimension 3. CDD has numerous important components integrated in its core providing adaptability. *Adaptability transformations,* evaluated with (+/+) help adaptability at most granular level, like refactorings, creational transformations required by sensors and effectors complementing *variability* which requires existing variables receiving various parameters in introducing new blocks to be composed dynamically at run-time striving to enable users adjust and adapt the product as needed [37]. Adaptation as adjustment on baseline level (case study [13]) incorporates scheduled and event-based adjustment coordinated through integrated procedure, use/re-use the constant multiple instances [13]. *Positive and negative feedback* in capability delivery adaptation can be triggered by search based adaptation allowing deliberate adaptation as structural adjustment [65], with context modelling in alternative method pathways and in the capability pattern lifecycle. Here predictive analysis runs adjustment algorithm that adapts capability delivery in response to changes in context to meet capability delivery goals (evaluated with (+/+)). CDD method extension with strategies: Global-as-local, assuming overall optimization changing behavior of local system which requires information about global one; Local-as-Global, assuming local systems adapting behavior using only their local context information makes bridge human intervention and re-alignment of strategies across the ecosystem. *Patterns* in CDD are reusable solutions for reaching business under different situational context [13]. In the example [62] they filter contexts and perspectives relating with complex environment where the probe-sense-respond approach is recommended. Patterns are recommended initially according the capability structure, currently applied patterns and contextual conditions, but CDD can also provide run-time recommendations of other patterns to perform better in given context and situation. However, patterns in CDD are mostly perceived for efficiency, while in complexity, patterns also help orient, gain knowledge about the context, how to make proper moves in the solution space [63] ($\pm$).

4 Conclusion

CDD methodology incorporates many necessary components and traits on element and architectural level to support development of context-aware self-adaptive platforms delivering dynamic capabilities (Fig. 4). Dimensions of adaptability as NFR for complex environment reflect complexity of the environment (external, internal), managerial profiling and artifact components influencing semantic, syntactic, contextual and quality adaptation. CDD has SIDA & PDCA loops necessary for evolutionary and goal-seeking adaptation to crawl through the problem/solution space; multifaceted context capture, open information flows from broad business ecology to detect changes, effectors to address them; diverse range of adaptability transformations to provide extensive variability; modularity. Envisioned improvement points suggested here are in direction of CDD methodology configuration to face unstable strategy in dynamic reconfiguration of capabilities, design to learn bottom-up, laterally and top-down. The Interpret-Decide stages (of the SIDA loop) can be enhanced – detection and configuration of patterns should transcend the notion of using them for efficiency but also effective situation awareness about the context and the solution space. CDD needs to combine qualitative and quantitative information in unprogrammable decision making, through clarification of outcomes (customer-back defined and accomplishment of purpose) or outputs (company-forward definition and judgement of accomplishment of goals), especially on strategic and tactical level where the decision logic, purposefulness or purposiveness of the managerial function play role. And last, but not least, adaptive and adaptable denote different abilities – and different systems' behavior. In this paper we investigated adaptability of CDD methodology, while the true adaptiveness of socio-technical artifacts, is predominantly unaccomplished mission.

References

1. Chung, L., Subramanian, N.: Adaptable system/software architectures. J. Syst. Archit. **50**(7), 365–366 (2004)
2. Cappiello, C., Comuzzi, M., Mussi, E., Pernici, B.: Context management for adaptive information systems. Electron. Notes Theor. Comput. Sci. **146**(1), 69–84 (2006). SPEC. ISS.
3. Chung, L., Nixon, B.A., Yu, E., Mylopoulos, J.: Non-Functional Requirements in Software Engineering. Springer, Boston (2000). https://doi.org/10.1007/978-1-4615-5269-7
4. Borgida, A.T., Chaudhri, V.K., Giorgini, P., Yu, Eric S. (eds.): Conceptual Modeling: Foundations and Applications. LNCS, vol. 5600. Springer, Heidelberg (2009). https://doi.org/10.1007/978-3-642-02463-4
5. Adams, K.M.: Adaptability, flexibility, modifiability and scalability, and robustness. Nonfunctional Requirements in Systems Analysis and Design. TSRRQ, vol. 28, pp. 169–182. Springer, Cham (2015). https://doi.org/10.1007/978-3-319-18344-2_9
6. National Geographic Society, "National Geographic Encyclopedia - Adaptation," Encyclopedia of Evolution (2018). https://www.nationalgeographic.org/encyclopedia/adaptation/
7. New England Complexity Science Institute, Concepts: Adaptive, NECSI (2018)
8. Subramanian, N., Chung, L.: Metrics for software adaptability. Softw. Qual. Manag. SQM **2001**, 95–108 (2001)
9. Chung, L., Subramanian, N.: Process-oriented metrics for software architecture adaptability. In: Proceedings of IEEE International Conference Requirements Engineering, pp. 310–311 (2001)
10. Bērziša, S., Bravos, G., Gonzalez, T.C., Czubayko, U., España, S., Grabis, J., Henkel, M., Jokste, L., Kampars, J., Koç, H., Kuhr, J.-C., Llorca, C., Loucopoulos, P., Pascual, R.J., Pastor, O., Sandkuhl, K., Simic, H., Stirna, J., Valverde, F.G., Zdravkovic, J.: Capability driven development: an approach to designing digital enterprises. Bus. Inf. Syst. Eng. **57**(1), 15–25 (2015)
11. Zdravkovic, J., Stirna, J., Grabis, J.: A comparative analysis of using the capability notion for congruent business and information systems engineering. Complex Syst. Inf. Model. Q. **10**, 1–20 (2017)
12. Bērziša, S., España, S., Grabis, J., Henkel, M., Jokste, L., Kampars, J., Koç, H., Sandkuhl, K., Stirna, J., Valverde, F., Zdravkovic, J.: Capability as a Service in digital enterprises Task 5. 1 Result Report : State-of-the-Art in relevant methodology areas, no. 611351 (2014)
13. Bērziša, S., España, S., Grabis, J., Henkel, M., Jokste, L.: Deliverable 5.3: The Final Version of Capability Driven Development Methodology-Capability as a Service in digital enterprises (2016)
14. Snowden, D.J.: Complex acts of knowing: paradox and descriptive self- awareness. J. Knowl. Manag. **6**(2), 100–111 (2002)
15. Snowden, D.J.: Multi-ontology sense making: a new simplicity in decision making. Inform. Prim. Care **13**(1), 45–53 (2005)
16. Kurtz, C.F., Snowden, D.J.: The new dynamics of strategy: sense-making in a complex-complicated world. IBM Syst. J. **42**(3), 483 (2003)
17. Snowden, D.J., Boone, M.E.: A leader's framework for decision making. Harvard Bus. Rev. **85**(11), 68–76 (2007)
18. Dettmer, B.H.W.: Systems thinking and the Cynefin Framework: a strategic approach to managing complex system. Goal Syst. Int., 1–13 (2007)
19. Stacey, R.: Strategic Management and Organisational Dynamics. Pearson Education, London (1996)

20. Stacey, R.: Complexity and management papers. Gr. Anal. Complex. Manag. Pap. **35**, 1–16 (2001)
21. Stacey, R.D.: Strategic Management and Organisational Dynamics: The challenge of complexity to ways of thinking about organisations. Pearson, London (2011)
22. Waldrop, M.M.: Complexity: the emerging science at the edge of order and chaos. J. Chem. Inf. Model. **53**(9), 1689–1699 (2013)
23. Gell-Mann, M.: Complexity and complex adaptive systems. In: The Evolution of Human Languages. (Santa Fe Institute Studies in the Sciences of Complexity. Proceedings vol. 10), pp. 3–18 (1992)
24. Holland, J.H.: Complex Adaptive Systems. In: Daedalus, vol. 121, no. 1 (2010)
25. Lichtenstein, B., Uhl-Bien, M., Marion, R., Seers, A., Orton, J.D., Schreiber, C.: Complexity leadership theory. ECO Emerg. Complex. Organ. **8**, 2–12 (2006)
26. Mitchell, M., Newman, M.: Complex systems theory and evolution. In: Encyclopedia of Evolution. Oxford University Press, Oxford (2002
27. Ackoff, R.L.: Towards a system of systems concepts. Manage. Sci. **17**(11), 661–671 (1971)
28. Argyris, C.: Double loop learning in organizations. Harv. Bus. Rev. **55**, 115–125 (1977)
29. Anon, Smith, M.: Chris Argyris: Theories of Action, Double-Loop Learning and Organizational Learning, no. Elkjaer 2000, pp. 1–16 (2000). http://www.Infed.Org/Thinkers/Argyris.Htm
30. Petrevska Nechkoska, R.: Tactical management Sense-and-Respond framework enhancement using ICT. Ghent University Belgium, Ghent (2017)
31. Engel, A., Browning, T.R., Reich, Y.: Designing products for adaptability: insights from four industrial cases. Decis. Sci. **48**(5), 875–917 (2017)
32. Andrzejak, A., Reinefeld, A., Schintke, F., Schütt, T.: On adaptability in grid systems BT. In: Getov, V., Laforenza, D., Reinefeld, A. (eds.) Future Generation Grids, pp. 29–46. Springer, Boston (2006). https://doi.org/10.1007/978-0-387-29445-2_2
33. Fricke, E., Schulz, A.P.: Design for changeability (DfC): principles to enable changes in systems throughout their lifecycle. Syst. Eng. **8**(4), 342–359 (2005)
34. The Open Group, Application Platform Service Qualities (2018)
35. Radhakrishnan, R.: Non-Functional Requirements (NFR) Framework: A Subset of the Enterprise Architecture Framework (2009)
36. Oluwaseyi, O.: Developing business capabilities with COBIT 5. In: ISACA (2017)
37. Castro, J., Kolp, M., Mylopoulos, J.: Towards requirements-driven information systems engineering: the Tropos project. Inf. Syst. **27**(6), 365–389 (2002)
38. Andresen, K., Gronau, N.: An approach to increase adaptability in ERP systems. In: Managing Modern Organizations with IT, pp. 15–18 (2005)
39. Andresen, K., Gronau, N.: Managing change–determining the adaptability of information systems. In: European and Mediterranean Conference on Information Systems 2006, pp. 1–9 (2006)
40. Gronau, N., Rohloff, M.: Managing change: Business/IT alignment and adaptability of information systems. In: ECIS, no. 2007, pp. 1741–1753 (2007)
41. International Standardization Organization, ISO/IEC 25010:2011(en): Systems and software engineering—Systems and software Quality Requirements and Evaluation (SQuaRE)—System and software quality models (2017)
42. Santos, E., Pimentel, J., Dermeval, D., Castro, J., Pastor, O.: Using NFR and context to deal with adaptability in business process models. In: Proceedings of 2011 2nd International Workshops on Requirements RE@RunTime, no. May 2014, pp. 43–50 (2011)
43. Jokste, L., Grabis, J.: Rule based adaptation : literature review. In: Proceedings of 11th International Science Practice Conference, vol. 2, pp. 42–46 (2017)
44. Kalareh, M.A.: Evolving Software Systems for Self-Adaptation (2012)

45. Opdyke, W.F.: Refactoring Object-oriented Frameworks. University of Illinois at Urbana-Champaign, Champaign, IL, USA (1992)
46. J. Kerievsky, "Refactoring to Patterns (Google eBook)," p. 400, 2004
47. Mens, T., Tourwé, T.: A survey of software refactoring. IEEE Trans. Softw. Eng. **30**, 126–139 (2004)
48. Tokuda, L., Batory, D.: Evolving object-oriented designs with refactorings. Autom. Softw. Eng. **8**(1), 89–120 (2001)
49. Mackrell, D., Mcdonald, C.: Evaluation into Action Design Research (2014)
50. Schilling, R.D., Beese, J., Haki, K.M., Aier, S., Winter, R.: Revisiting the impact of information systems architecture complexity: a complex adaptive systems perspective. In: Thirty Eighth International Conference on Information System, no. December (2017)
51. Benbya, H., McKelvey, B.: Toward a complexity theory of information systems development. Inf. Technol. People **19**, 12–34 (2006)
52. Ardagna, D., Comuzzi, M., Mussi, E., Pernici, B., Plebani, P.: PAWS: a framework for executing adaptive web-service processes. IEEE Softw. **24**(6), 39–46 (2007)
53. Onix, M.F.A., Fielt, E., Gable, G.G.: Complex adaptive systems theory in information systems research - a systematic literature review. In: Twenty-Fourth European Conference on Information System, pp. 1–18 (2016)
54. Shevtsov, S., Berekmeri, M., Weyns, D., Maggio, M.: Control-theoretical software adaptation: a systematic literature review. IEEE Trans. Softw. Eng. **43**, 1–28 (2017). https://ieeexplore.ieee.org/document/7929422/
55. Cechich, A., Piattini, M.: Managing COTS components using a six sigma-based process. In: LN Product Focused Software Process Improvement 5th International Conference PROFES Proceedings 2004, Japan, 5–8 April 2004 (2004)
56. Cechich, A., Piattini, M.: Quantifying COTS component functional adaptation. In: Bosch, J., Krueger, C. (eds.) ICSR 2004. LNCS, vol. 3107, pp. 195–204. Springer, Heidelberg (2004). https://doi.org/10.1007/978-3-540-27799-6_16
57. Brogi, A., Cámara, J., Canal, C., Cubo, J., Pimentel, E.: Dynamic contextual adaptation. Electron. Notes Theor. Comput. Sci. **175**(2), 81–95 (2007)
58. Haeckel, S.H.: Adaptive Enterprise: Creating and Leading Sense-And-Respond Organizations, vol. 33, no. 2. Harvard Business School Press, Boston (1999)
59. Stirna, J., Grabis, J., Henkel, M., Zdravkovic, J.: Capability driven development – an approach to support evolving organizations. In: Sandkuhl, K., Seigerroth, U., Stirna, J. (eds.) PoEM 2012. LNBIP, vol. 134, pp. 117–131. Springer, Heidelberg (2012). https://doi.org/10.1007/978-3-642-34549-4_9
60. Snowden, D.: Cynefin: A Sense of Time and Place, pp. 1–35 (1999)
61. Henkel, M., Stratigaki, C., Stirna, J., Loucopoulos, P., Zorgios, Y., Migiakis, A.: Extending capabilities with context awareness. In: Krogstie, J., Mouratidis, H., Su, J. (eds.) CAiSE 2016. LNBIP, vol. 249, pp. 40–51. Springer, Cham (2016). https://doi.org/10.1007/978-3-319-39564-7_4
62. Kampars, J., Stirna, J.: A repository for pattern governance supporting capability driven development. In: Business Informatics Research (2017)
63. Andrews, M., Pritchett, L., Woolcock, M.: Building State Capability - Evidence, Analysis, Action. Oxford University Press, Oxford (2017)
64. Ackoff, R.L., Gharajedaghi, J.: On the mismatch between systems and their models. Syst. Res. **13**(1), 13–23 (1996)
65. Walker, B., Holling, C.S., Carpenter, S.R., Kinzig, A.: Resilience, adaptability and transformability in social – ecological systems. Ecol. Soc. **9** (2004). https://www.ecologyandsociety.org/vol9/iss2/art5/manuscript.html

66. Alter, S., Sherer, S.A.: A general but readily adaptable model of information system risk. Commun. ACM **14**, 1–28 (2004)
67. Liu, J., Xue, C., Dong, L.: The Adaptability Evaluation of Enterprise Information Systems BT (2011)
68. Danesh, M.H., Yu, E.: Modeling enterprise capabilities with i*: reasoning on alternatives. In: Iliadis, L., Papazoglou, M., Pohl, K. (eds.) CAiSE 2014. LNBIP, vol. 178, pp. 112–123. Springer, Cham (2014). https://doi.org/10.1007/978-3-319-07869-4_10
69. Rosemann, M., Recker, J., Flender, C.: Contextualisation of business processes. Int. J. Bus. Process Integr. Manag. **3**(1), 47 (2008)

Using Open Data to Support Organizational Capabilities in Dynamic Business Contexts

Jelena Zdravkovic[1], Janis Kampars[2], and Janis Stirna[1(✉)]

[1] Department of Computer and Systems Sciences, Stockholm University,
Postbox 7003, 164 07 Kista, Sweden
`{jelenaz,js}@dsv.su.se`
[2] Information Technology Institute, Riga Technical University, Kalku iela 1,
Riga, Latvia
`Janis.Kampars@rtu.lv`

Abstract. In essence, Open Data (OD) is the information available in a machine-readable format and without restrictions on the permissions for using or distributing it. Open Data may include textual artifacts, or non-textual, such as images, maps, scientific formulas, and other. The data can be publicized and maintained by different entities, both public and private. The data are often federated, meaning that various data sources are aggregated in data sets at a single "online" location. Despite its power to distribute free knowledge, OD initiatives face some important challenges related to its growth. In this paper, we consider one of them, namely, the business and technical concerns of OD clients that would make them able to utilize Open Data in their enterprise information systems and thus benefit in terms of improvements of their service and products in continuous and sustainable ways. Formally, we describe these concerns by means of high-level requirements and guidelines for development and run-time monitoring of IT-supported business capabilities, which should be able to consume Open Data, as well as able to adjust when the data updates based on a situational change. We illustrated our theoretical proposal by applying it on the service concerning regional roads maintenance in Latvia.

Keywords: Open Data · Capability · Context · Requirements
CDD

1   Introduction

Deriving from diverse sources and immensely growing, digital data is emerging as the essential resource to organizations, enabling them to by enlarging their body of knowledge advance in highly demanding business situations and markets.

Unfortunately, not many of existing digital data are available to organizations to use them. A large proportion belongs to *proprietary data* owned by specific entities and thus permitted only for their use. Some examples are internally generated documents by the means of data mining and analytics that contain company's private business information or the information related to its competitive position. *Public data* is available to the public, but typically, it is not machine-readable, and sometimes obtainable only through explicit requests they may take days to weeks to get responses.

R. Matulevičius and R. Dijkman (Eds.): CAiSE 2018 Workshops, LNBIP 316, pp. 28–39, 2018.
https://doi.org/10.1007/978-3-319-92898-2_3

Some examples are health-related data, housing data, Wikipedia, labor statistics, and other.

Open Data (OD) is the data available in a machine-readable format, without restrictions on the permissions for using or distributing the information that it contains [1]. Open Data initiatives can be differently organized, starting from providing data at the national (country) level, and further below, to the regional and city levels. Data are often federated, meaning that various sources of data are aggregated to data sets at a single location. Individual sectors may also have their own data with a specific thematic focus, such as transport, utilities, geospatial data and other. Even public and open data may thematically overlap, the main difference is that the latter are provided through well-defined application program interface (API). Around 100 sources of open datasets are available from US states, cities and counties, and over 200 sources are registered from other countries and regions in the world [2].

To have value and impact, Open Data needs to be used. Therefore, the main requirement is making the data available by creating and maintaining OD sources. As with any initiative, this is a remarkable effort requiring resources and technical skills. However, Open Data has a huge potential to, by being refined, transformed and aggregated, provide significant benefits in terms of: transparency of information; public service improvement; innovation and economic value by using the data to improve current, or build new products and services; efficiency by reducing acquisition costs, redundancy and overhead; and interoperability of systems and intermix of data sets.

For successful OD initiatives, it is therefore an essential aspect to make them needed to organizations to facilitate for these entities to, using the data, improve their products and services, and which will in turn lead to even higher demand to Open Data, creating thus a self-sustained growing-need cycle.

Today's organizations operate in highly competitive and dynamically changing situational environments. Having a continuous access to relevant, accurate and usable data is therefore highly important for organizations, but in turn, it leads also to the requirements to improve their business capabilities to be able to benefit from new and often changed and updated data [3].

One methodological approach for dealing with dynamic business capabilities implemented by the means of information systems is Capability Driven Development, CDD [4]. It is a methodology developed to support continuous delivery of business capabilities by being able to capture and take advantage of changes in business context. The success of a business and IS infrastructure following CDD, is therefore highly tight to the ability for continuously and entirely fetching the relevant surrounding business context and where Open Data plays a highly significant role as a transparent, structured, accurate, and machine-readable information source.

The goal of this paper is to, taking the OD client perspective, discuss and exemplify overall design and run-time requirements for provisioning and using Open Data by means of dynamic business capabilities.

The rest of the paper is organized as follows. Section 2 outlines a background to the Open Data initiative and to the Capability Driven Development approach. Section 3 presents the requirements for use of Open Data by IT-supported business capabilities and their application specifically in a CDD-enabled client environment. Section 4 illustrates the proposal on a real business case concerning regional roads maintenance. A discussion and concluding remarks are given in Sect. 5.

2 Background

2.1 About Open Data

Open Data is data that can be freely used, re-used and redistributed by anyone. In this way, knowledge is becoming open and free to access, use, modify, and share it. According to [5], there are two dimensions of data openness:

– The data must be legally open, meaning they must be placed in the public domain or under liberal terms of use with minimal restrictions.
– The data must be technically open, meaning they must be published in electronic formats that are machine readable and non-proprietary, so that anyone can access and use the data using common, freely available software tools. Data must also be publicly available and accessible on a server, without password or firewall restrictions.

To make Open Data easier to find, most initiatives create and manage Open Data catalogs. The core technology model of the data catalog is shown in Fig. 1:

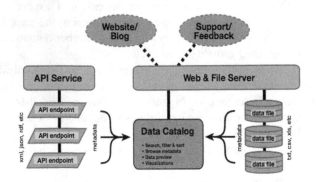

Fig. 1. A technology model of an Open Data catalog [6]

The data catalog is a list of datasets available in an Open Data initiative. Its essential services include searching, metadata, visualization, and access to the datasets themselves through well-defined API services. An online platform is used to provide a front-end for users to access all resources available under an Open Data initiative. Aside from the data catalog, the platform includes the description of API services, online forum for questions, technical support and feedback, background materials and other. Some more advanced alternatives of the model presented in Fig. 1 comprise: (a) separation of the File Server to use a Cloud infrastructure and (b) decentralization of the data catalog to the contributing data participants (such as ministries, for example).

2.2   Capability-Driven Approach

From the business perspective, *a capability describes what the business does that creates value for customers* [8]. It represents a design from a result-based perspective including various dimensions including organization's values, goals, processes, people, and resources. In brief, the emergence of the use of the capability notion seems having the following motivations:

- In the context of business planning, capability is becoming recognized as a fundamental component to describe what a core business does and, in particular, as an ability for delivering value, beneath the business strategy [7];
- Capability supports configurability of operations on a higher level than services and process, and according to changes in operational business context [4, 8].

The Capability Driven Development (CDD) approach [4] has developed an integrated methodology for context-aware business and IT solutions. It consists of a meta-model and guidelines for the way of working. The areas of modeling as part of CDD are Enterprise Modeling (EM), context modeling, variability modeling, adjustment algorithms and patterns for capturing best practices. The meta-model is implemented in a technical environment to enable the support for the methodology by consisting of the following key components presented in Fig. 2:

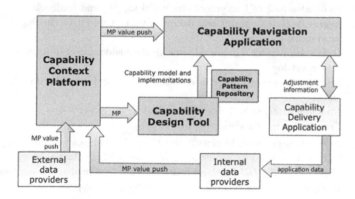

Fig. 2. Components of the CDD environment.

Capability Design Tool (CDT) is a graphical modeling tool for supporting the design of capability elements. Capability Navigation Application (CNA) is an application that makes use of the models (capability designs) created in the CDT to monitor the capability context by receiving the values of measurable property (MP in Fig. 2) and handle run-time capability adjustments. Capability Context Platform (CCP) is a component for distributing context data to the CNA. Capability Delivery Application (CDA) represents the business applications that are used to support the capability delivery. This can be a custom-made system, or a configured standard system such as SAP ERP. The CNA communicates, or configures the CDA to adjust for changing data contexts during capability design and delivery. Monitoring of defined KPIs facilitate capability refinement and pattern updating.

3   Results

Many organizations are still reluctant to use Open Data due to a lack of information on how to find the data, as well as because some data are not available in a fully machine-readable form, not up-to-date, or not offering rich or efficient API [11]. On the other side, organizations should know which data they need for fulfilling their business goals, as well as they should have IS capable to connect to Open Data and download it whenever the data is changed. In Table 1 below, we have summarized the requirements for managing Open Data from the provider and the client perspectives:

Table 1. Main requirements for provisioning and using Open Data

Role	Requirement for Open Data
Provider	– *Create a data catalog* as a list of rich datasets available in an Open Data initiative, including also supporting services (search, etc.) and the metadata – *Provide a portal (platform)* as an online front-end for users to access all resources available under a data initiative, including the data catalog, a knowledge base of background, technical support and feedback – *Aggregate data* from different data files using a suite of technologies and store them in the catalog – *Define API Service*, i.e. provide machine-readable access in form of API to the data in catalog – *Provide permanent storage* using a centralized or decentralized (federated) data model – *Update the data* in real time or near real time – *Create ontology* for reuse
Client	– *Define business goals* to identify the external data types needed by capabilities – *Classify data types* as the elements of a capability context – *Find a matching OD catalog* for desired data, and finalize the definition of the capability context according to available open data types – *Connect to the API service* to enable machine-to-machine interoperability with the data provider – *Fetch and use data* in the pace needed, and as the data changes – *Evaluate the quality of the data,* such as completeness, and provide feedback

As a brief illustration of the outlined requirements, we consider the Swedish OD catalog containing real estate data "Booli bostads" [9]. Booli provides the data on the apartments for sale, in a given area, such as: all apartments/houses for sale in a particular city, all real estates for sale near a geographic coordinate, including prices. Using the RESTful service technology, the API gives an opportunity to access real estates data and thus integrate with third-party applications. The data provided include the number of offered real estates, the number of offered real estates in an area, prices, and other.

Depending on their goals, different clients can use the Booli OD differently. For real-estate brokers, one important use needs accurate data on the number of offered estates on a location of interest (context), and whenever that number drops below a certain value, the broker may activate activities (capability) to increase again that number. As another example, if the prices on the market are too high, the broker may activate "advertising" capability to increase the number of apartments for sale. Finally, the Booli OD may be used by the broker to easy create periodical company analytics/reports to make future business plans/strategy.

Application in CDD Design and Run-Time

First capabilities need to be designed. This can be carried out according to the capability design method component presented in [10] consisting of steps such as goal and KPI modeling, context modeling, capability adjustment modeling, as well as, if needed pattern modeling. This process is primarily supported by the capability design tool (CDT, see Fig. 2), but also the context platform is involved in terms of providing available context elements that are related to the capability. With respect to the use of Open Data a particular task that needs to be supported is finding relevant open data that can be linked as measurable properties on the basis of which context element calculations can be defined to specify context elements. Table 2 summarizes the main activities of capability design based on Open Data.   At the run-time, the status of business context and related KPIs are continuously monitored. When a KPI decreases below a desired value, utilization of capabilities is adjusted by invocation of other capabilities from the repository. Table 3 summarizes open-data related capability run-time activities:

Table 2. Capability design with Open Data sources

Capability design steps	Description
Define goals	Goals and KPIs are defined in order to define capabilities. This can be done on the basis of the existing business models as well as the service level agreements with customers and suppliers
Design context elements	Design context elements according to the envisioned capability. Consider processes and process variants as well as what situational properties influence variations
Find open data	Analyze the available open data sources with respect to the KPIs and context elements. At this stage the data available needs to be analyzed in the format they are offered by the data providers. In some cases, this also requires creating a model for example for aggregating atomic data into measurable properties
Implement context data broker	If no data APIs exist or they are incompatible with Capability Context Platform, a specialized context data broker needs to be implemented. The goal of the context data broker is ensuring near real-time data flow from the data provider to the Capability Context Platform

(continued)

Table 2. (*continued*)

Capability design steps	Description
Update context elements and measurable properties	Specify how context elements are calculated from measurable properties based on open data sources
Update adjustment algorithms with new data types	The capability adjustment algorithms are updated with respect to the context calculations and expected data availability
Design access to open data API (technical)	Develop adapters to the context platform for integration with the open data using the APIs or other means provided by the data providers

Table 3. Capability run-time with open data

Capability delivery at run-time	Description
Data retrieval	Data is retrieved from the data provider and sent to the CCP
Passing data to CNA	Data is integrated by the CCP and sent to the CNA
Calculating context element values	CNA performs calculation of Context element values
Triggering adjustments	Event-based adjustments are triggered when matching contextual situation occurred
Interaction with CDA	Execution of an adjustment usually results in interacting with the CDA via its API
Review of KPIs and run-time improvements	User reviews the KPIs available in CNA and modifies the value of adjustment constant if necessary. Adjustment constants are used for altering context element calculations or adjustments during run-time

4   Example Case - Regional Road Maintenance Company

To illustrate the principles of Open Data use in capability management we have developed a demo case for a regional Road Maintenance Company (RMC) company operating in Latvia. The main capability of RMC is that of providing proactive road maintenance. The capability is delivered in winter season and it primarily consists of deicing services such as snow plowing as well as removal of ice and frost. These services are to be carried out in varying weather conditions, which, for the purpose of this case, are considered as the business context. The top goal for the RMC business service provided is refined into three sub-goals, namely (1.1) to prevent road icing, (1.2) to minimize road maintenance costs, and (1.3) minimize times for transporting maintenance vehicles (Fig. 3).

Road conditions as well as the actual weather data and forecasts are seen as the context elements relevant to the adjustments of the proactive road maintenance capability. In this respect, the following open data providers have been identified:

- Latvian State Roads (LSR) – a Latvian government agency which owns weather stations that have been installed along the major Latvian roads,

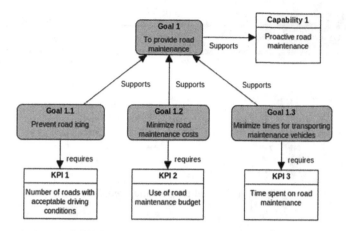

Fig. 3. A fragment of Goals Model of RMC showing goals related to the proactive road maintenance capability

- Estonian Road Administration (ERA) – an Estonian government agency that owns weather stations in Estonia,
- Twitter – a social network containing user feedback that is relevant for the use case .

Both the LSR and the ERA provides access to their open data upon contacting them via email. In order to access a live feed of tweets a developer needs to register an application on dev.twitter.com. The data in LSR and ERA information systems is provided as HTML content. In order to extract the required information, the developer has to implement a bot that opens the web site and extracts the needed information from the Document Object Model (e.g. using a website tasting framework like CasperJS).

Twitter provides a structured tweet object that contains the potentially useful information about the author of the tweet, its content and location properties. The LSR and the ERA provide current road conditions and prediction for the next hours. It has been discovered that the prediction is slightly different in both data sources; also, there are some road or weather-related data that are made available only by one data provider (see LSR data in Fig. 4 and ERA prediction in Fig. 5).

Twitter API can be searched for the tweets containing geolocation information and keywords indicating hazardous driving conditions. The model containing context and adjustment is given in Fig. 6.

A total of 8 measurable properties are used in a Driving conditions calculation (Context: Calculation 1) for calculating the value of the Driving conditions (Context: Element 1). Factor weights, which are formalized as an Adjustment constant, are used to specify the importance of each measurable property. Factor weights can be altered during run-time by change the corresponding Adjustment constant in the CNA. The value of the Driving conditions context element is used for triggering the Perform road maintenance Adjustment that notifies the operator that road maintenance operations should be performed.

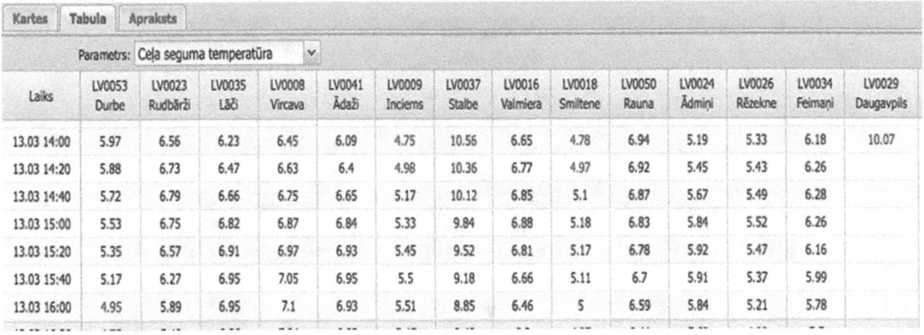

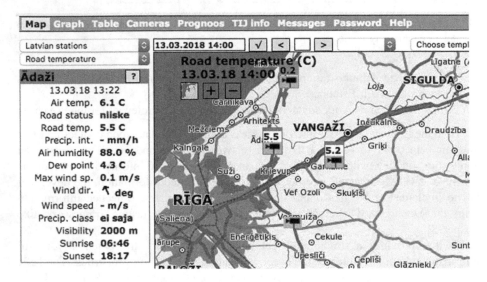

Fig. 4. LSR road temperature prediction.

Fig. 5. ERA road temperature prediction.

Demo case of the RMC is summarized in Fig. 7. Driving conditions related data from ERA and LSR is retrieved by custom data broker and is then sent to the CCP. The data from Twitter is retrieved by the CCP itself since Twitter has well defined API and data models. All data is integrated by the CCP and then sent to the CNA. Upon receiving new measurable property values from CCP, CNA recalculates the value of the corresponding context element, which triggers execution of the Perform road maintenance Adjustment. The CDA of the RMC has an API that Adjustment utilizes to notify the operator that a road maintenance operation must be performed on a certain road due to a high risk of icing.

If during the run-time it has been discovered that a certain data provider or road-condition factor has greater impact on the actual road conditions, factor weights

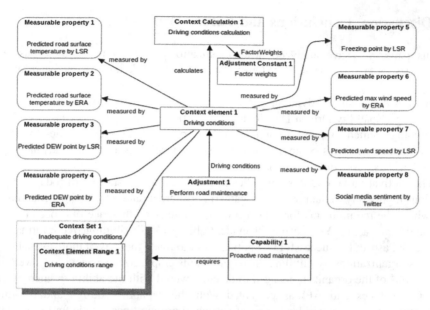

Fig. 6. Adjustment and context model

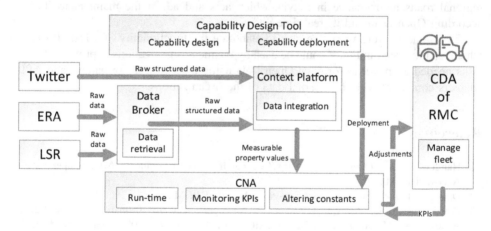

Fig. 7. Summary of the demo case

can be altered without re-deploying or restarting the capability in CNA. KPI values received from the CDA can also indicate a necessity to adjust a value of the Adjustment constant. If new Measurable properties or new data providers are identified design level changes in CDT and re-deployment of the capability are required. Adding new measurable properties still wouldn't require any changes in the Adjustment itself since context is interpreted using the Context Calculation – Driving conditions calculation.

5   Discussion, Conclusions and Future Work

In this paper we have analyzed how organizations could improve their business capabilities by taking advantage of Open Data initiatives. We have defined and further exemplified design and run-time requirements and guidelines for provisioning using Open Data by means of dynamic business capabilities. The proposal is specifically concerning Capability Driven Development (CDD) enabled clients, because the CDD methodology aimed to support continuous delivery of business capabilities by being able to capture business context – in this case data, as well as to take advantage of changes in business context, i.e. data.

The motivation behind this study lies in the fact that the success of today's organizations highly rely to their ability for gathering different data from their surroundings, and where the requirements for data accuracy, amount and the pace of processing are constantly increasing. Yet, despite its evident ability for distributing free information, an essential aspect for successful OD initiatives is to make them even more available to business organizations by fulfilling the requirements emphasized in Sect. 3. As well the IS solutions of the organizations need to be empowered with the ability to interoperate with OD sources and API as presented with the capability design and run-time guidelines. This in-turn will lead to a self-sustained growing-need cycle for Open Data. We illustrated our theoretical proposal by applying it on the service concerning regional roads maintenance in Latvia, which acts and adjust the maintenance tasks according Open Data and its real-time updates.

For the near future work, we plan to elaborate the functionality of a Data Broker, which, as illustrated in Fig. 7 could be used by business organizations to provide all the tasks needed to make raw/original Open Data using a set of transformations and API adapters compliant with the internal data of the organizations.

References

1. Handbook on Open Data. http://opendatahandbook.org/guide/en/what-is-open-data/. Accessed 12 Mar 2018
2. Data.gov. https://www.data.gov/open-gov/. Accessed 12 Mar 2018
3. Zeleti, F.A., Ojo, A.: Capability matrix for open data. In: Camarinha-Matos, L.M., Afsarmanesh, H. (eds.) PRO-VE 2014. IAICT, vol. 434, pp. 498–509. Springer, Heidelberg (2014). https://doi.org/10.1007/978-3-662-44745-1_50
4. Bērziša, S., et al.: Capability driven development: an approach to designing digital enterprises. Bus. Inf. Syst. Eng. (BISE) 57(1) (2015). https://doi.org/10.1007/s12599-014-0362-0
5. The World Bank. Data, Open Data Essentials. http://opendatatoolkit.worldbank.org/en/essentials.html. Accessed 12 Mar 2018
6. The World Bank. Data, Technology Options. http://opendatatoolkit.worldbank.org/en/technology.html. Accessed 03 Mar 2018
7. Ulrich, W., Rosen, M.: The business capability map: building a foundation for business/IT Alignment. Cutter Consortium for Business and Enterprise Architecture. http://www.cutter.com/content-and-analysis/resource-centers/enterprise-architecture/sample-our-research/ea110504.html. Accessed 28 Feb 2017

8. Zdravkovic, J., Stirna, J., Grabis, J.: A comparative analysis of using the capability notion for congruent business- and information systems engineering. Complex Syst. Inf. Model. Q. CSIMQ (10), 1–20 (2017). https://doi.org/10.7250/csimq.2017-10.01

9. OPENDATA.se. http://www.opendata.se/2010/05/booli-api.html. Accessed 12 Mar 2018

10. Grabis, J., Henkel, M., Jokste, L., Kampars, J., Koç, H., Sandkuhl, K., Stamer, D., Stirna, J., Valverde F., Zdravkovic, J.: Deliverable 5.3: the final version of capability driven development methodology. FP7 Project 611351 CaaS – Capability as a Service in digital enterprises, Stockholm University, p. 266 (2016) https://doi.org/10.13140/RG.2.2.35862.34889

11. Open Data Barometer. Global Report. https://opendatabarometer.org/4thedition/report/. Accessed 13 Mar 2018

Capability Management in the Cloud: Model and Environment

Jānis Grabis[✉] and Jānis Kampars

Institute of Information Technology,
Faculty of Computer Science and Information Technology,
Riga Technical University, Kalku street 1, Riga 1658, Latvia
{grabis,janis.kampars}@rtu.lv

Abstract. Capabilities represent key abilities of an enterprise and they encompass knowledge and resources needed to realize these abilities. They are developed and delivered in various modes including in-house and as a service delivery. The as a service delivery mode is provided in the cloud environment. The cloud-based approach allows offering capabilities possessed by the service provider to a large number of potential consumers, supports quick deployment of the capability delivery environment and enables information sharing among the users. The paper describes a cloud-based capability management model, which support multi-tenant and private modes. The architecture and technology of the cloud-based capability development and delivery environment is elaborated. The pattern repository shared among capability users is a key component enabling information sharing. Additionally, this paper also shows usage of the cloud-based capability and delivery environment to build cloud native capability delivery applications.

Keywords: Capability management · Capability as a service · PaaS
Scalability

1   Introduction

Capabilities represent key abilities of an enterprise and they encompass knowledge and resources needed to realize these abilities. These capabilities can be used internally or provided to external companies as a service. Capability as a service implies that the capability bearer delivers abilities and resources to other companies on a contractual basis. For instance, a consulting company has IT management capabilities and these capabilities are delivered to its contractors as well as internally in the company itself.

Providing capability as a service stipulates specific requirements towards capability development and delivery:

- Rapid deployment to onboard new consumers quickly without forcing them to alter existing IT landscape;
- Scalability to support many consumers and to deal with computationally demanding context processing and adaption needs;

© Springer International Publishing AG, part of Springer Nature 2018
R. Matulevičius and R. Dijkman (Eds.): CAiSE 2018 Workshops, LNBIP 316, pp. 40–50, 2018.
https://doi.org/10.1007/978-3-319-92898-2_4

- Collaboration to enable participative capability design and evaluation of capability delivery results;
- Knowledge sharing to benefit from exchange of capability usage experiences by different consumers.

These requirements can be met by using cloud technologies. Capability development and delivery over the cloud combines features of Platform as a Service (PaaS), Software as a Service (SaaS) and Business Process as a Service (BPaaS). PaaS enables quicker and better software development and deployment by using on-demand development and execution tools catering to specific needs [1, 2]. SaaS provides on-demand access to various software packages and reduces efforts associated with software maintenance. In order to improve business and IT alignment in the cloud environment, a next level of abstraction is introduced – BPaaS [3, 4] Domaschka et al. [5] define that the key part of BPaaS is an ability to specify and executed distributed multi-tenant workflows and BPaaS should be naturally integrated with other layers of cloud computing. Customization is an important concern of BPaaS. Taher et al. [6] show that business processes can be customized on the basis of the meta-solution. A multi-layered approach to customization where different customization aspects are separated in dedicated layers contributes to tailoring business services to individual consumers [7]. Capability management in the cloud can be perceived as yet a higher level abstraction relative to BPaaS focusing on development of enterprise core competencies as a service offering.

The Capability Driven Development (CDD) methodology [8] can be used for capability development and it is supported by an Eclipse based capability design tool. This paper describes conversion of this tool for the cloud environment. However, the cloud-based CDD environment is not only a technological change, it also enables capability delivery as a service. A company possessing specific knowledge and resources of providing services in varying circumstances is able to specify those abilities in terms of the capability model and to provide the cloud-based CDD environment to offer them to potential consumers. Additionally, the cloud-based capability management both enables and benefits from capability delivery information sharing. The pattern repository [9] is the key component for information and knowledge sharing.

The paper describes the Capability as a Service (CaaS) capability management model and cloud-based CDD environment as a key enabler of this model. Additionally, this paper also shows usage of the CDD methodology to build cloud native capability delivery applications combining the cloud-based CDD environment and cloud ready CDA. These applications concern development and delivery of the scalability capability. Scalability, which is one of the requirements for cloud-based capability development and delivery, itself is context dependent [10], and the CDD approach can be used to develop the scalability capability. The scalability capability ensures that computational resources used by CDA are adjusted in response to the context situation.

The rest of the paper is structured as follows. Section 2 describes a cloud-based capability management model, which is supported by the cloud-based CDD environment presented in Sect. 3. Application of the cloud-based CDD environment is demonstrated in Sect. 4. Section 5 concludes.

2 Management Model

The CDD methodology supports capability delivery in various modes including internal capability development as well as provisioning capability as a service to external consumer. The cloud-based delivery is essential in the latter case. Two main delivery modes (Fig. 1) can be distinguished in the case of capability delivery as a service (CaaS). The service provider owns some of the knowledge and resources needed to deliver the capability and the service consumer uses this knowledge and resources to serve its customers or support her internal processes. The service consumer also contributes some of the knowledge and resources to capability delivery, chiefly in the form of knowledge and resources committed to running information systems involved in capability delivery referred as to Capability Delivery Applications (CDA). The first CaaS mode implies usage of the shared multi-tenant CDD environment. The second CaaS mode is deployment of the private CDD environment for every consumer (be it private or public cloud and operated by capability provider, service consumer or third party).

In the case of the shared multi-tenant mode, the capability owner has developed the capability design, which describes capability delivery goals, context, processes and context-dependent adaptions. The capability is deployed in a shared CDD environment. Multiple instances of the capability can be setup within this deployment and configured according to the needs of individual capability consumers. However, this setup is limited to providing individualized data binding for context data and consumer specific treatment of context and performance indicators.

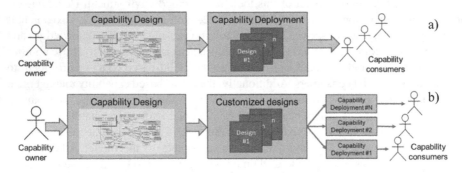

Fig. 1. CaaS design and delivery modes: (a) shared multi-tenant mode; and (b) private mode.

In the case of the private mode, the capability design is used as a reference model for creating customized designs for individual consumers. These customized designs are used to configure private capability deployment for each capability consumers. This way every consumer gets an individualized capability design, which supports unique requirements while also requires separate maintenance. From the cloud base capability management standpoint, it is important to emphasize that the customized designs still retain clearly identifiable elements from the reference design (Fig. 2) to enable information sharing among the capability consumers. The customized design consists of

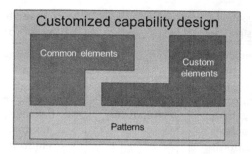

Fig. 2. Composition of the customized capability design

common elements inherited from the reference design, custom elements added to a design tailored for specific consumers and capability delivery patterns. The patterns are reusable chunks of capability design what are used to design and customize capabilities [9].

The CDD environment consists of the Capability Design Tool (CDT), the Capability Navigation Application (CAN), which is responsible for configuration of individual deployments, monitoring of capability delivery and context-dependent run-time adaption of capability delivery, the Capability Context Platform (CCP), which captures capability delivery context, and CDA (see [11] for more details). The CDD environment can be deployed on the cloud-based infrastructure for both CaaS delivery modes. Using the cloud-based infrastructure enables horizontal scalability of the CDD environment (see Sect. 3). Thus, the capability service provider is able to serve a large number of potential capability consumers.

3 Cloud-Based Deployment

All components of the CDD environment are deployed in the cloud environment (Fig. 3). The deployment backbone is the Infrastructure as a Service (IaaS) layer. In this case, open source Apache CloudStack[1] software is used to create and manage the IaaS layer. It allows managing large networks of virtual machines what is necessary for quick deployment of all components of the CDD environment. CDT and CCP form the Platform as a Service (PaaS) layer of the cloud-based CDD environment while CNA forms the Software as a Service (SaaS) layer. In the case of the private deployment mode, every capability consumer is provisioned with a set of virtual machines hosting CDT, CCP and CNA. Kernel-based Virtual Machine (KVM)[2], which is a full virtualization solution for Linux on x86 hardware, was chosen as a hypervisor for the cloud-based CDD due its open-source nature. While KVM was used to provision fully pledged virtual machines, Docker[3] allowed to host applications inside lightweight,

---

[1] https://cloudstack.apache.org/.

[2] https://www.linux-kvm.org/.

[3] http://docker.com/.

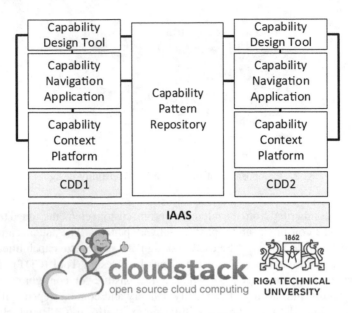

Fig. 3. Overview of cloud-based CDD environment

customized software containers. Experiments show that containerization results in equal or better performance than traditional virtual machines in almost all cases [12]. Docker was especially useful for CCP as it required Apache Camel, Apache ActiveMQ, PostgreSQL and Redhat Wildfly, which were deployed in a form of software containers on a single KVM virtual machine. This approach allows to run multiple isolated instances of CCP on a single virtual machine thus minimizing usage of cloud resources. CDA also could be deployed in the same cloud if requested by the consumer.

The capability pattern repository is managed by the capability service provider as a single instance. It is accessed by all capability service consumers and ensures information and knowledge sharing among all involved parties.

CDT is natively developed as an Eclipse based application. It is made available over the cloud using desktop virtualization technologies (Fig. 4). A single CDT virtual machine instance can be used by multiple users having either dedicated or shared workspaces. The cloud-based CDT supports all functionality of the desktop CDT, does not require installation of any specific software and is available on multiple devices and platforms.

The cloud-based CDD environment is vertical scalability. The components also can be made to support horizontal scalability. Both CNA and CCP of the single deployment can be replicated across multiple virtual machines though dynamic resource allocation is not supported out-of-the-box. A fully horizontally scalable context data integration, processing and adjustment solution is described in [13].

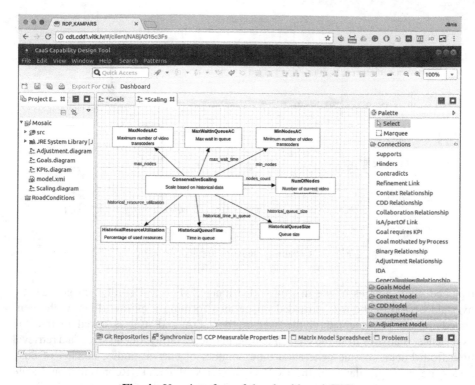

Fig. 4. User interface of the cloud-based CDT

4 Scalability Capability

The CDD methodology in combination with cloud-enabled capability management allows to develop highly scalable applications. That is demonstrated by development of a simplified auto-scaling capability using the cloud-based CDD environment and supported by cloud native CDA. It serves as a demo project that is shipped together with the cloud-based CDT. The CDA of the demo capability is a NodeJS[4] and AngularJS[5] based web application that can be used to generate a mosaic from image and keyword provided by a user. The logic of the CDA is shown in Fig. 5.

Once the user has submitted the mosaic generation form, the data about the mosaic generation job is added to a RabbitMQ[6] message queue. One of the worker nodes, implemented as Docker containers, picks up this job and starts the mosaic generation process. In order to find the small tiles that correspond to the user provided keyword it queries the Flickr API[7]. The list of relevant images is downloaded, they are resized and

---

[4] https://nodejs.org/.

[5] https://angularjs.org/.

[6] https://www.rabbitmq.com/.

[7] https://www.flickr.com/services/api/.

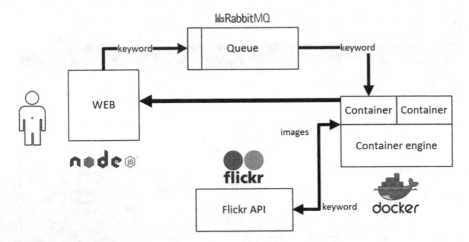

Fig. 5. Capability delivery application logic

matched with sections of the user provided image. The most similar image tiles are overlaid on top of the user provided image thus forming a mosaic. Finally, the generated mosaic is presented to the user of the CDA and user is asked to rate the experience. Statistics from the CDA like time in queue, rating, queue size, data retrieval time from Flickr, mosaic generation time, number of current nodes, number of busy nodes are made available to the CCP via a series of REST (Representational state transfer) web services. The corresponding configuration of the CCP is shown in Fig. 6.

The CDT model containing goals, KPIs, context set, context ranges, context elements and measurable properties is presented in Fig. 7.

Reactive										
# ▾	Name ⇕	Protocol ⇕	Measurable Property ⇕	Frequency ⇕	URI	Encryption Type ⇕	Created by ⇕			
1675368	Queue size	REST	queue_size	10000ms	http://mosaic.vitk.lv/api/mp/queue_length	None	industry			
1666381	Rating	REST	rating	10000ms	http://mosaic.vitk.lv/api/mp/rating	None	industry			
1666395	Queue	MQTT	queue_time	10000ms	http://mosaic.vitk.lv/api/mp/queue	None	industry			
1666401	Flickr	MQTT	flickr_time	10000ms	http://mosaic.vitk.lv/api/mp/flickr	None	industry			
1666397	Mosaic	MQTT	mosaic_time	10000ms	http://mosaic.vitk.lv/api/mp/mosaic	None	industry			
1666436	Nodes	REST	nodes	10000ms	http://mosaic.vitk.lv/api/mp/nodes	None	industry			
1680892	Busy nodes	REST	busy_nodes	10000ms	http://mosaic.vitk.lv/api/mp/busy	None	industry			

Fig. 6. CCP configuration for the scalability capability

The main goal of the capability is to ensure scalability of the mosaic generation application through minimizing cloud resource consumption and maximizing the Quality of Service. The number of busy nodes (Docker containers currently performing mosaic generation), queue size (unprocessed mosaic generation jobs stored in the

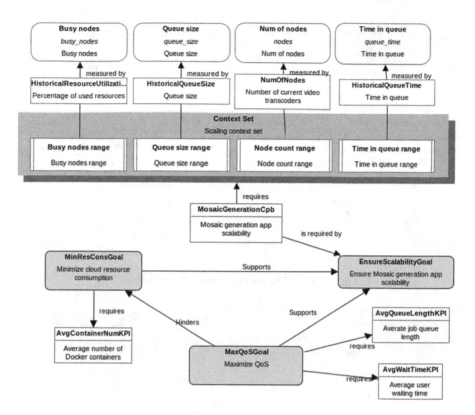

Fig. 7. Scalability capability

message queue), number of nodes (running Docker containers) and average time in queue serve as the context for the scalability capability. A scheduled adjustment is created to monitor the values of the context elements and to scale the mosaic generation application accordingly (see Fig. 8). Besides previously documented context elements it uses three adjustment coefficients that can be altered during run-time to change the scaling algorithm behavior (see Fig. 9). The scheduled adjustment is implemented as a Java class which makes a decision whether the mosaic generation application should be scaled down, up or left intact. The names on the arrows in Fig. 8 are equal to the names of variables that are made available in the adjustment for retrieving values of context elements and adjustment constants.

The source-code of the scheduled adjustment is given in Fig. 10. The method `this.scale()` is used for calling a REST scaling web-service that changes the number of running Docker containers during run-time.

The end results from the demo CDA and list of running containers retrieved from the Docker engine are shown in Fig. 11.

The results from command `docker ps` show that there are four running Docker containers. This information is also visible in the user interface of the CNA together with other context indicators like average waiting time and current queue length.

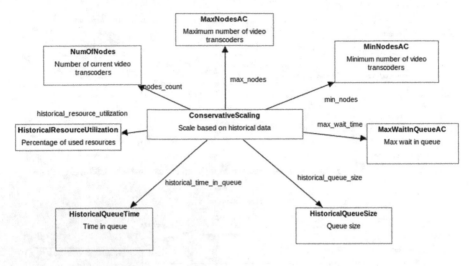

Fig. 8. Input data for the scheduled adjustment

Fig. 9. Changing adjustment coefficients during run-time

Fig. 10. Implementation of a scheduled adjustment

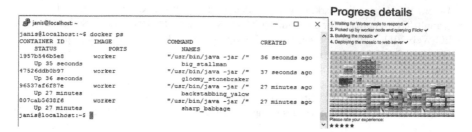

Fig. 11. Results from CDA and Docker engine status

5 Conclusion

This paper has described cloud-based capability management as an enabler of the CaaS approach. In comparison with typical service-oriented approaches, CaaS still requires a relatively high degree of collaboration between the capability provider and the capability consumer. Both parties are required to commit their abilities and resources to capability delivery. Additionally, one can argue that capabilities are traditionally viewed as a company's internal asset. Some of competencies and resources can be procured from providers, however, capability consumers are still expected to evolve the capabilities by themselves at least partially. Therefore, the private capability delivery mode involving capability design customization is suitable for the CaaS approach. The capability design customization leads to challenges associated with model management and handling of different versions of the capability design in a distributed environment. The service consumers also must have sufficient incentives for information sharing and a greater degree of customization potentially leads to lower returns on information sharing. This challenge relates to the overall issue of valuing and trading data what becomes more and more relevant in the area.

References

1. Cohen, B.: PaaS: new opportunities for cloud application development. Computer **46**(9), 97–100 (2013)
2. Gass, O., Meth, H., Maedche, A.: PaaS characteristics for productive software development: an evaluation framework. IEEE Internet Comput. **18**(1), 56–64 (2014)
3. Papazoglou, M.P., van den Heuvel, W.-J.: Blueprinting the cloud. IEEE Internet Comput. **15**(6), 74–79 (2011)
4. Barton, T., Seel, C.: Business process as a service - status and architecture. In: Proceedings - Series of the Gesellschaft fur Informatik (GI). Lecture Notes in Informatics (LNI), p. 145 (2014)
5. Domaschka, J., Griesinger, F., Seybold, D., Wesner, S.: A cloud-driven view on business process as a service. In: Proceedings of the 7th International Conference on Cloud Computing and Services Science, CLOSER 2017, p. 739 (2017)
6. Taher, Y., Haque, R., Van Den Heuvel, W.-J., Finance, B.: α BPaaS - a customizable BPaaS on the cloud. In: Proceedings of the 3rd International Conference on Cloud Computing and Services Science, CLOSER 2013, pp. 290–296 (2013)

7. Taher, Y., Haque, R., Parkin, M., van den Heuvel, W.-J., Richardson, I., Whelan, E.: A multi-layer approach for customizing business services. In: Huemer, C., Setzer, T. (eds.) EC-Web 2011. LNBIP, vol. 85, pp. 64–76. Springer, Heidelberg (2011). https://doi.org/10. 1007/978-3-642-23014-1_6

8. Berzisa, S., Bravos, G., Gonzalez, T., Czubayko, U., España, S., Grabis, J., Henkel, M., Jokste, L., Kampars, J., Koç, H., Kuhr, J., Llorca, C., Loucopoulos, P., Juanes, R., Pastor, O., Sandkuhl, K., Simic, H., Stirna, J., Valverde, F., Zdravkovic, J.: Capability driven development: an approach to designing digital enterprises. Bus. Inf. Syst. Eng. 57(1), 15–25 (2015)

9. Kampars, J., Stirna, J.: A repository for pattern governance supporting capability driven development. In: Johansson, B. (ed.) Joint Proceedings of the BIR 2017 pre-BIR Forum, Workshops and Doctoral Consortium co-located with 16th International Conference on Perspectives in Business Informatics Research (BIR 2017). CEUR-WS.org (2017)

10. Kampars, J., Pinka, K.: Auto-scaling and adjustment platform for cloud-based systems. In: Environment. Technology. Resources: Proceedings of the 11th International Scientific and Practical Conference, 15–17 June, vol. 2, pp. 52–57 (2017)

11. Henkel, M., Kampars, J., Hrvoje, S.: The CDD environment architecture. In: Sandkuhl, K., Stirna, J. (eds.) Capability Management for Digital Enterprises. Springer, Cham (2018)

12. Felter, W., Ferreira, A., Rajamony, R., Rubio, J.: An updated performance comparison of virtual machines and Linux containers. Technology 25482, 171–172 (2014)

13. Kampars, J., Grabis, J.: Near real-time big-data processing for data driven applications. In: Proceedings of the 3rd International Conference on Big Data Innovations and Applications, Innovate-Data 2017, Czech Republic, Prague, 21–23 August 2017, pp. 35–42. IEEE, Piscataway (2017)

BDA – Business Data Analytics:
Techniques and Applications

International Workshop on Business Data Analytics: Techniques and Applications (BDA 2018)

Preface

Data analytics currently represents a revolution that cannot be missed. It is significantly transforming and changing various aspects of our modern life including the way we live, socialize, think, work, and do business. There is increasing interest in the application of data analytics in many industries (e.g., retail, manufacturing, finance) and business functions (e.g., marketing, customer relationship management, and supply chain management). In fact, data are becoming a key ingredient for informing every step and element of modern business.

The aim of the Workshop on Business Data Analytics (BDA) is to discuss opportunities and challenges of applying data analytics in business. As such, it targets researchers interested in all aspects of developing effective data analytics solutions and evaluating applications in different business domains.

The first edition of this workshop, held in Tallinn on June 11, 2018, was organized in conjunction with the 30th International Conference on Advanced Information Systems Engineering (CAiSE 2018). The workshop received seven submissions. After careful assessment by the members of the Program Committee, three submissions were accepted for inclusion in the proceedings (43%). The paper by Ahmad et al. shows how feedback by customers on the performance of a process provides an angle for analysis in the absence of more traditional business data. Schneider et al., in turn, focus on the question of how to establish trust in BDA results and provide metrics to assess their robustness against noisy data. Finally, Mateush et al. present a BDA case study on payment classification at a financial institution.

We owe special thanks to the workshop chairs of CAiSE 2018, Remco Dijkman and Raimundas Matulevičius, for supporting us in the organization of the workshop. We would also like to thank the members of the Program Committee for providing timely and insightful reviews of the submitted papers.

April 2018

Oliver Müller
Sherif Sakr
Matthias Weidlich

BDA Organization

Organizing Committee

Oliver Müller   IT University of Copenhagen, Denmark
Sherif Sakr   University of Tartu, Estonia
Matthias Weidlich   Humboldt-Universität zu Berlin, Germany

Program Committee

Ahmed Awad   Cairo University, Egypt
Amin Beheshti   Macquarie University, Australia
Florian Daniel   Politecnico di Milano, Italy
Claudio Di Ciccio   Vienna University of Economics and Business, Austria
Boudewijn Van Dongen   Eindhoven University of Technology, The Netherlands
Marcelo Fantinato   University of São Paulo, Brasil
Daniela Grigori   Laboratoire LAMSADE, Paris-Dauphine University,
                          France
Christian Janiesch   University of Würzburg, Germany
Henrik Leopold   Vrije Universiteit Amsterdam, The Netherlands
Fabrizio Maria Maggi   University of Tartu, Estonia
Raghava Rao Mukkamala   Copenhagen Business School, Denmark
Manfred Reichert   University of Ulm, Germany
Johannes Schneider   University of Liechtenstein, Liechtenstein
Michael Sheng   Macquarie University, Australia

Using BPM Frameworks for Identifying Customer Feedback About Process Performance

Sanam Ahmad, Syed Irtaza Muzaffar, Khurram Shahzad[✉],
and Kamran Malik

Punjab University College of Information Technology,
University of the Punjab, Lahore, Pakistan
{sanam.ahmad,irtaza,khurram,
kamran.malik}@pucit.edu.pk

Abstract. Every organization has business processes, however, there are numerous organizations in which execution logs of processes are not available. Consequently, these organizations do not have the opportunity to exploit the potential of execution logs for analyzing the performance of their processes. As a first step towards facilitating these organizations, in this paper, we argue that customer feedback is a valuable source of information that can provide important insights about process performance. However, a key challenge to this approach is that the feedback includes a significant amount of comments that are not related to process performance. Therefore, utilizing the complete feedback without omitting the irrelevant comments may generate misleading results. To that end, firstly, we have generated a customer feedback corpus of 3356 comments. Secondly, we have used two well-established BPM frameworks, Devil's Quadrangle and Business Process Redesign Implementation framework, to manually classify the comments as relevant and irrelevant to process performance. Finally, we have used five supervised learning techniques to evaluate the effectiveness of the two frameworks for their ability to automatically identify performance relevant comments. The results show that Devil's Quadrangle is more suitable framework than Business Process Redesign Implementation framework.

Keywords: Business data analytics · Customer reviews
Process performance analysis · Text analytics · Supervised learning techniques

1 Introduction

Business processes are everywhere [1] and they are widely pronounced as the basic unit of work for every organization [2, 3]. Recognizing the pivotal role of processes, growing number of organizations are automating their processes [4] and utilizing their execution logs for the performance analysis [5]. However, presently, there are numerous organizations that are yet to automate their processes. Consequently, these organizations cannot exploit the potential of execution logs for analysing processes' performance.

© Springer International Publishing AG, part of Springer Nature 2018
R. Matulevičius and R. Dijkman (Eds.): CAiSE 2018 Workshops, LNBIP 316, pp. 55–69, 2018.
https://doi.org/10.1007/978-3-319-92898-2_5

To facilitate these organizations, a possible alternate is to collect the customer feedback about the business process under consideration, and use the collected feedback to gain insights about the process performance. Such an approach is particularly useful for service-oriented companies, such as insurance companies and restaurants, where customer satisfaction is of higher significance [6]. In addition to service-oriented companies, the effective utilization of customer feedback has the potential to offer manifold benefits to every organization [7]. These benefits include, but not limited to, introducing new products or services, evaluating customer satisfaction, identifying customer preferences, sustaining existing features and introducing new features [8, 9]. However, customer feedback includes the comments that are not related to process performance. Hence, any insights obtained by processing the entire collection of comments, that is, without segregating irrelevant comments, may be misleading. This arises the question how to distinguish between performance relevant and irrelevant comments? The answer to this question essentially requires a clear understanding of the notion of performance in the context of business processes. To this end, in this paper we have used two well-established BPM frameworks to evaluate the effectiveness of the two frameworks for their ability to distinguish between relevant and irrelevant comments. Specifically, we have made the following three main contributions:

- *Feedback Corpus:* We have generated a corpus of over 3356 comments by collecting feedback from two sources, social media and survey.
- *Benchmark Annotations:* We have generated two datasets by manually annotating each comment as relevant or irrelevant, using two different criteria. The criteria stem from the constituents of two well-established conceptual frameworks: Devil's Quadrangle framework [10] and Business Process Redesign [11] framework.
- *Suitability Evaluation:* We have thoroughly evaluated the effectiveness of the two frameworks, using the generated datasets as their proxies, for their abilities to distinguish between relevant and irrelevant comments. For the evaluation, we have performed experiments using five established supervised learning techniques to automatically classify the comments in both datasets.

1.1 Problem Illustration

To illustrate the problem that all the comments in the customer feedback are not related to process performance which may mislead process analysts; consider an excerpt version of admission process of an institute. The process starts when an applicant collects an application form. Each form has a unique ID that is used to track an application throughout the admission cycle. The application form comprises of several subsections including biography, academic background, experience and an entry test slip. Each candidate is required to fill the form and deposit entry test fee. There are two modes of fee payment, online payment and payment through bank. If a candidate desires to pay through bank, he/she must use a part of the admission form as an invoice. Once the payment is deposited, the completed form along with all the documents is submitted to the institute.

Presently, neither any part of the admission process is automated nor the specification of the process is documented in the form of a process model. However, for a better comprehension of the example, we have presented an excerpt of the admission process model in Fig. 1.

Fig. 1. An excerpt version of the admission process model.

Table 1 contains six example comments about the admission process to illustrate the classification problem. From the table it can be observed that some of the comments are about process performance whereas others are irrelevant to process performance. In the rest of the paper, the former is referred to as relevant comments and the latter are referred to as irrelevant comments. For instance, the comment 'the application form was so lengthy that it took me one hour to complete it' is clearly about the time consumed in completing the application form. Therefore, it is declared as a relevant comment. Similarly, the comments about the ease of use, delays and longer queues are also related to process performance. In contrast, the two comments, 'the campus is very far from my place' and 'my friend helped me to prepare for the test' are not relevant to process performance. Therefore, these comments are declared as irrelevant comments.

Table 1. Example of relevant and irrelevant comments.

Example comments	Relevance
1. The application form was so lengthy that it took me one hour to complete it	Yes
2. The application portal was easy to use	Yes
3. I had to wait for one hour to get access to computer when I went to campus for applying	Yes
4. There were longer queues at the bank	Yes
5. I am happy that my friend helped me in test preparation	No
6. The campus is very far from my place	No

Consider that the institute's administration is interested in knowing, how often applicants talk negatively about admission process? Generating the answer to this question requires classifying comments as positive or negative and then counting the number of negative comments. However, if the complete set of comments are used, without excluding irrelevant comments, misleading results may be generated. For instance, the comment 'I am happy that my friend helped me in test preparation' is a positive comment. However, from the process analysis perspective it is an irrelevant comment that should not be counted in generating the answer to the posed question. Similarly, 'the campus is very far from my place' is a negative comment but the institute may not like to consider this comment due to its irrelevance with process performance. Therefore, this comment should not be used in generating the answer of the posed question. However, if the two comments are used in answering the question, it may mislead the administration.

Based on the illustration it can be concluded that it is necessary to first identify the comments that are related to process performance, before they can be used to gain insights about process performance. Else, if the complete set of feedback is used, the irrelevant comments may skew the results and mislead analysts. To address this problem, in this paper, we aim to use two well established BPM frameworks for identification of performance relevant comments.

2   The BPM Frameworks

Development of a comprehensive and adequately crisp criteria for the classification of customer feedback is a challenging task, due to the involved intricacies. Our initial attempt to invent classification criteria from scratch, resulted in a long list of heuristics and their prolonged descriptions, which hindered the development of a common understanding of the criteria. Therefore, we rely on two well-established and widely used conceptual frameworks for the development of relevance criteria. The frameworks are, Devil's Quadrangle framework and Business Process Redesign Implementation framework. The key reason for choosing these frameworks is their strong association with business processes. That is, DQ framework describes the performance dimensions that must be taken into consideration for analyzing process performance, whereas, BPRI framework describes the elements that must be considered in improving the design of a process. A brief overview of each frameworks is as follows:

Devil's Quadrangle (DQ) Framework. The DQ framework is composed of four dimensions that were introduced to evaluate the impact of each best practice on business process [10]. The framework is widely pronounced as an *ideal* framework for the performance analysis of a process [10, 11]. The four performance dimensions are, time, cost, quality and flexibility. In the framework, time dimension refers to the amount of time consumed or delayed in executing a process P. Cost refers to the effort, resources or revenue consumed during the execution of P. Quality refers to the satisfaction with the specification and execution of P, and flexibility refers to the ability of process to respond to a change.

Business Process Redesign Implementation (BPRI) Framework. The framework was developed with the intent to help process designers in delivering a design that is superior than the existing design, by identifying the elements that should be considered and relationships between these elements [11, 12]. Furthermore, the framework has also been used to think and reason about the most important manifestations of redesign [13]. It consists of seven elements, customers, products, business process (operation and behavior view), participants, information, technology, and environment. Customer, the first element of the framework, refers to the internal or external customers of the process that benefit from the process. Product refers to the items or services generated or consumed by the process. Business process refers to the set of activities as well as dependencies between activities. The element, participants in the framework, refers to the individuals or roles that execute the activities. Information refers to the data produced or generated by the process. Technology refers to the methods or techniques used in the process, and environment refers to the external conditions or surroundings in which the process executes.

3 Customer Feedback Corpus

In this section, we outline the corpus generation procedure and the classification criteria corresponding to each framework. Subsequently, the procedure for generating the two datasets is presented.

3.1 Corpus Generation

For the study, we collected student feedback about the admission process of an academic institute. Every year, the institute receives several thousand applications for admission to its various programs. The admission process starts with announcement of the admissions schedule and ends with the announcement of admissions decisions. Due to the space limitations, we only present key activities of the admission process. These are, announce admissions, collect application form, complete application form, choose preferred program, choose campus, submit application form, collect fee voucher, pay fee through bank, verify academic record, generate entry test slip, appear in the admission test, rank students, and announce admission decisions.

For this study, we collected student feedback from two sources, social media and a survey. To collect student feedback from social media, we scrapped the Facebook page of the institute to extract over 1000 student posts and comments on these posts. To further extend the corpus, we conducted an unstructured survey with applicants. The survey was composed of a brief introduction to the study, few open-ended questions and a few example answers. We opted to use open-ended questions due to two reasons, (a) to give respondents the complete freedom to share their feelings or experiences, and (b) to avoid emphasizing any fragment of the process for feedback. The participants were given three weeks to fill the survey with the freedom to save and updated their comments.

At first, we compiled a corpus of 3510 comments from the two sources. However, after omitting the incomplete comments, non-English, and trivial comments, the corpus size was reduced to 3356. Subsequently, the corpus was pre-processed by correcting the spellings and replacing the abbreviations with complete words. For spelling correction, we used a two-step semi-automated approach. In the first step, a python script tokenized each comment and searched each token in WordNet (an online English dictionary), to identify the tokens that were not available in the dictionary. In the second step, a researcher reviewed each unverified token and corrected it. The corpus generation procedure is presented below in Fig. 2.

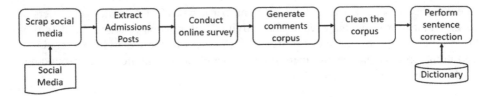

Fig. 2. Corpus generation procedure.

3.2   Generating Relevance Criteria

Once the feedback corpus was generated, the next step was to generate the benchmark datasets by manually classifying the comments as relevant or irrelevant. However, as discussed earlier, declaring a comment relevant or irrelevant is a challenging task due to the involved intricacies. Hence, it is essential to develop a common understanding about which type of comment should be declared as relevant and which type of comment should be declared as irrelevant. To that end, we rely on two well-established and widely used frameworks, as discussed in the preceding section. While both the frameworks are widely pronounced as precious artifacts in their respective context [10–14], the mere description of performance dimensions (in DQ framework) or key constituents of process redesign (in BPRI framework) are not adequate for the classification of feedback. An accurate classification rather requires a scale, rule, or principle for evaluating whether a given comment is relevant or irrelevant. For this study we generated two separate criteria based on the two frameworks. An excerpt version of each criteria is presented below in Tables 2 and 3.

Table 2. An excerpt of the DQ criteria.

Relevance criteria	Remarks
Is the comment related to robustness of the process?	A comment related to delay, queue or waiting time is relevant
Is the comment related to cost incurred by the candidate for the process?	A comment about the characteristic of the product is irrelevant
Is the comment related to quality of the process?	Any feeling or suggestion about the execution of the process is relevant
Is the comment related to flexibility of the process?	Any suggestion about the changes in process is relevant

For generating the first criteria, hereafter DQ criteria, we defined at least one question corresponding to each performance dimensions of the DQ framework. Similarly, for generating the second criteria, hereafter BPRI criteria, we included at least one question corresponding to each element of the BPRI framework. While the development of DQ criteria was a straightforward task the development of BPRI criteria was found to be challenging. This was due to the peculiar nature of some elements of the framework. For each such element, we defined a candidate question and iteratively tweaked the question by improving its formulation and adding remarks

Table 3. An excerpt of the BPRI criteria.

Relevance criteria	Irrelevance/Remarks
Is the comment or suggestion related to the use of an object in an activity?	A comment on the object used in the activity. For instance, the prospective quality was good
Is the comment or feeling related to the technology used for performing an activity?	A comment on the technology used in an activity is irrelevant
Is the comment related to the manual use of the data generated/produced by an activity?	A comment related to the data/information used/generated/produced during the activity
Is the comment related to the response or behaviors of the participant?	A comment on the participant that has no effect on the perform an activity
Is the related to the quality of service delivered by third party or environment?	A comment related to the third part or the environment

against the question. Each iteration was performed by two researchers and each tweak was performed based on the assessment of the question on 10 relevant and 10 irrelevant comments. Accordingly, we finalized a question corresponding to each element of the framework. For instance, *information* is an element of the BPRI framework that cannot be easily used for developing relevance criteria for process performance. As an outcome of the two iterations, we developed the following question regarding this element. Is the comment related to the manual use of the data generated or produced by an activity? In addition to the question, an example comment was also added i.e. 'So, disappointing that the spellings of my name in the list were incorrect'.

3.3 Generating Datasets for Each Framework

Once the two criteria are defined, the next step in generating the benchmark datasets for each framework is to use the criteria for manually classifying the 3356 comments in the feedback corpus. For that, at first, we randomly collected 1000 comments from the corpus and asked two researchers, R_1 and R_2, to independently classify all the collected comments using the DQ criteria. Both the researchers are PhD candidates and they had taken at least two courses on natural language processing and business process management. Furthermore, both the researchers are familiar with the concept of annotation procedures, annotation guidelines and inter-annotator agreement. The results generated by the two researchers were compared and their inter-annotator agreement was computed. From the comparison it was observed that out of the 1000 comments, there were 895 agreements, 105 disagreements and a Kappa statistic of 0.762. The detailed specifications are presented in the Table 4.

After three weeks, two researchers were asked to classify the same collection of 1000 comments using the BPRI criteria. The time gap between the two cycles was maintained to ensure that the researchers cannot reuse the knowledge of applying the DQ criteria [15]. Similar to the DQ criteria based classification, the two researchers classified comments using the BPRI criteria, and their inter-annotator agreement was computed. From the comparison of two annotated datasets it was observed that the use of the BPRI criteria resulted in 778 agreements, 222 disagreements, and a Kappa statistic of 0.49.

Table 4. Specification of the annotations.

	DQ Framework	BPR Framework
Total number of comments	3356	3356
Size of random sample size	1000	1000
Identical markings	895	778
Different markings	105	222
Kappa statistics	0.762	0.49
Remaining annotations	1	2

We have the following observations from the application of BPRI and DQ criteria:

- Both the researchers expressed that the task of classifying comments using BPRI criteria was harder than that of DQ criteria. It is because, the BPRI criteria involves several intricacies which increases the cognitive effort required to apply the BPRI criteria. For instance, the researchers found it hard to distinguish between the comments *about* the technology from the comments related to the *use* of the technology.
- The impact of the preceding observation can also be noted in the results. That is, the number of agreements for DQ criteria are greater than BPRI criteria (895 > 778). Similarly, the inter annotator agreement for DQ criteria is higher than BPRI criteria (0.762 > 0.49).

Due to the higher inter-annotator agreement in the first cycle of using DQ criteria, the remaining 2356 comments were classified by a single researcher. However, prior to that, each disagreement was discussed by the two annotators and a common under-standing of the criteria was developed. The dataset generated by this approach is referred to as DQ dataset in the rest of the paper. In contrast to the DQ criteria, the inter annotator agreement was low when BPRI criteria was used. Therefore, the remaining 2356 comments were classified by both researchers, and subsequently conflicts were resolved by discussion and mutual consent. The dataset generated by this approach, is referred to as BPRI dataset. Table 5 shows a confusion matrix of the two frameworks.

Table 5. Confusion matrix of two frameworks.

		DQ framework		
		Relevant	Irrelevant	Total
BPRI Framework	Relevant	998	35	1033
	Irrelevant	1618	705	2323
	Total	2616	740	3356

To gain further insights about the classified comments, we compared the classified comments to reveal the following:

- The 2616 comments classified as relevant by using the DQ criteria includes a significant share of the comments (998 out of 1033) that are declared relevant by the BPRI criteria.

- The 2323 comments classified as irrelevant by using the BPRI criteria includes a significant share of the comments (705 out of 740) that are declared irrelevant by the DQ criteria.

The two results represent that the relevant comments in the DQ dataset subsumes the relevant comments in the BPRI dataset. Similarly, the irrelevant comments in the BPRI dataset subsumes a significant percentage of the irrelevant comments in the DQ dataset. More specifically, the first observation represents that the use of DQ criteria enables identification of a large share of comments that are also declared as relevant by BPRI framework. Furthermore, the DQ criteria enables identification of 1618 additional relevant comments that were declared as irrelevant by the BPRI framework. This number is so large that it can skew the answer of virtually every question and may also generate entirely different perception about the performance of the process.

4 Automatic Classification of Customer Feedback

We have performed experiments using two datasets and five supervised learning techniques to evaluate the effectiveness of the two frameworks for distinguishing between relevant and irrelevant comments. In case all the supervised techniques achieve higher accuracy for one dataset, it conclusively represents that the framework used for generating the dataset is more effective for classifying comments. It is because, all five techniques rely on a set of feature values for learning and predicting the relevance of a comment, and the presence of similar and non-conflicting feature values results in boosting the effectiveness of supervised learning techniques and vice versa. These similar or non-conflicting feature values represent that majority of the comments in the dataset, that are placed in one class, have identical or similar feature values.

The following subsections provide an overview of the five supervised learning techniques and our evaluation setup. Subsequently, we present a detailed analysis of the results.

4.1 Supervised Learning Techniques

We have used five widely used supervised learning techniques for experimentation, Logistic Regression (LR) [16], Support Vector Machine (SVM) [17], Decision Tree (DT) [18], Random Forest (RF) [19] and K Nearest Neighbors (KNN) [20].

Support Vector Machines (SVM). The basic idea behind the training process in SVM is to find the hyperplane which optimally separates data points of different classes. The optimal hyperplane is the one which yields maximum margin. Margin is the distance between hyperplane and closest data point of other classes. In our domain two possible classes of comments to be classified are relevant and irrelevant. Each comment to be classified is denoted by document d. The SVM model is defined as

$$h_w(d) = \{1 \quad if \quad w^T d \geq 1 \qquad 0 \quad if \quad w^T d \leq -1\}$$

Logistic Regression (LR). Logistic regression is one of the most widely used and powerful algorithms for classification problems. In logistic regression, the selected hypothesis function always predicts output values between 0 and 1.

$$0 \leq h_w\left(w^T d\right) \leq 1$$

The hypothesis function is represented by the sigmoid function as follows:

$$h_w\left(w^T d\right) = \frac{1}{\left(1 + e^{-w^T d}\right)}$$

Where $h_w(w^T d)$ is the hypothesis function for logistic regression, parameterized by w, and d is the input variable or feature which is in our case comment.

K Nearest Neighbor (KNN). KNN is an instance based classification technique where comment is classified either relevant or irrelevant by comparing its similarity to the comments in training data that are already labelled.

Each comment is treated as document. Let U is set of unlabeled documents and L is set of labelled documents. A given document $d \in U$, Let NN_K^L (d) is set of top K documents in L that are most similar to the input document d using some similarity function. We label the document d as the label of K most similar documents to the document d.

Decision Tree (DT). Decision tree is non-parametric classification methodology. Decision tree model predicts the value of class for a given data point by learning the decision rules inferred from labelled data set.

Random Forest (RF). Random Forest technique is used to overcome the problem of being over fitted to the training data set in decision trees. Random Forest uses random feature selection for individual decision tree development. Random forest also uses bagging method. The trees in random forest are tested using out-of-bag sample and predictions of these trees is either averaged or voted for final prediction calculation.

4.2   Experimentation

For the experimentation, we have used DQ and BPRI datasets. Recall, the DQ dataset includes 2616 relevant comments and 740 irrelevant comments. In contrast to that, BPRI dataset includes 740 relevant comments and 2323 irrelevant comments. Evaluation is carried out using three widely used measures Precision, Recall and F_1 score [21]. Precision is the fraction of correctly classified comments among the classified comments. Recall is the fraction of correctly classified comments among the comments that should have been classified correctly. F_1 score is the harmonic mean of Precision and Recall.

As discussed above, we have performed experiments using five supervised learning techniques. For the experiments we have used Scikit-learn library in Jupyter notebook. The input to each technique is a set of numeric values called feature values. In our case, for both the datasets, we have performed separate experiments using unigram, bigram and trigram feature matrices. Generating each feature matrix involves the following steps (i) tokenize the dataset, (ii) preprocessing dataset by omitting stop words and stemming each token using Stanford parser [22], (iii) generating a set (unique) of word tokens of length N, called N grams (unigrams, bigrams or trigrams), and (iv) generating feature matrix. In a matrix, columns represent the set of N grams generated from the third step of the above procedure and rows represent the comments. A cell in the matrix corresponding to Row J (say, R_J) and column K (say, C_K) contains a binary score of 1 or 0. The value 1 in (R_J, C_K) represents that the comment in R_J contains the word token C_K, whereas, the value 0 in (R_J, C_K) represents that the comment in R_J does not contain the word token C_K.

For each experiment, we have used a training and testing ratio of 65:35. The results are calculated by using 10-fold cross validation to rationalize the bias that may be induced due to the choice of training and testing samples. The results presented in the subsequent section are the average scores of the 10-fold cross validation. Additionally, experiments are also performed by using all possible combinations of preprocessing, removing punctuations, removing stop words and stemming, to choose the most appropriate combination.

4.3   Results and Analysis

Table 6 summarizes the results of 10-fold cross validation for both datasets. From the table it can be observed that for DQ dataset, LR technique achieved very high F_1 score (F_1 = 0.95) using unigram feature matrix. Also, the precision and recall scores are comparable with the F_1 score (P = 0.93 and R = 0.96). From the table, it can also be observed that RF achieved a very low F_1 score using trigram feature matrix (F_1 = 0.56). In this case, the precision score is still higher (P = 0.96), however, the Recall is very low (R = 0.39). These results represent that most of the comments declared relevant by RF techniques are also relevant in the benchmark dataset. However, majority of the relevant comments in the gold standard are declared irrelevant by RF technique.

For the BPRI dataset, overall LR and DT achieved a high F1 score (F_1 = 0.77) using unigram feature matrix. Also, both Precision and Recall scores are comparable, i.e. for LR and DT techniques, P = 0.83 and 0.78, respectively; and R = 0.73 and 0.77, respectively. Below, we present some key observations about the results.

Most Appropriate Feature. Figures 3 and 4 shows a comparison of N-gram feature matrices (Unigram, Bigram and Trigram) in supervised learning techniques. From the figures it can be observed that the unigram is the most appropriate feature for both datasets. Furthermore, it can be observed from Fig. 3, all supervised learning techniques are equally effective for Unigram (i.e. N = 1). However, as the value of N increases the difference in performance becomes more visible. From Fig. 4 it can be observed that all the techniques are not equally effectively for BPRI dataset. These observations represent that the feature values in DQ dataset are similar and non-conflicts, hence, more suitable for learning. In contrast, the feature values in BPRI dataset are diverse and conflicting, hence, not suitable for learning.

Table 6. Summary results of the experiments.

Feature	Algorithm	DQ dataset			BPRI dataset		
		P	R	F1	P	R	F1
Unigram	KNN	0.94	0.88	0.91	0.73	0.44	0.54
	SVM	0.95	0.94	0.94	0.78	0.74	0.76
	LR	0.94	0.96	0.95	0.83	0.73	0.77
	RF	0.93	0.96	0.94	0.84	0.64	0.71
	DT	0.94	0.93	0.93	0.78	0.77	0.77
Bigram	KNN	0.79	0.97	0.87	0.75	0.15	0.24
	SVM	0.95	0.74	0.83	0.8	0.62	0.69
	LR	0.93	0.9	0.92	0.87	0.53	0.66
	RF	0.94	0.77	0.84	0.87	0.51	0.65
	DT	0.94	0.76	0.84	0.74	0.65	0.69
Trigram	KNN	0.78	0.99	0.87	0.72	0.08	0.14
	SVM	0.96	0.57	0.71	0.86	0.29	0.43
	LR	0.78	0.99	0.87	0.91	0.21	0.34
	RF	0.96	0.39	0.56	0.88	0.22	0.37
	DT	0.96	0.43	0.59	0.78	0.37	0.49

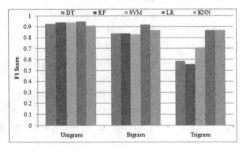   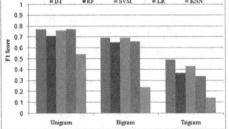

Fig. 3. Feature selection for DQ dataset   **Fig. 4.** Feature selection for BPRI dataset

Performance Variation Across Datasets. Figures 5, 6 and 7 shows a comparison of five techniques for the two datasets. From the figures it can be observed that using unigram feature matrix (i.e. the most discriminating feature), the performance scores of all the techniques for the DQ dataset are higher than BPRI datasets. Similar trends can be observed for the bigram and trigram features. These higher performance scores of all techniques and across all features represent that, the DQ dataset contains similar and non-conflicting feature values. These results represent that the comments having identical or similar feature values belong to the same class. In contrast, the BPRI dataset contains diverse and conflicting feature values, representing that the dataset includes several comments having similar feature values but they are placed in different classes. These results, together with the expression of the researchers (that the use of BPRI criteria for classifying comments is harder than DQ criteria), are abundantly conclusive to declare that DQ framework is more effective than BPRI framework.

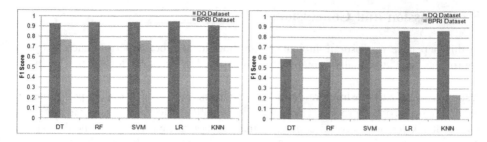

Fig. 5. Comparison of both frameworks using unigram feature

Fig. 6. Comparison of both frameworks using bigram feature

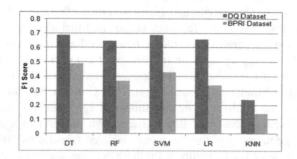

Fig. 7. Comparison of frameworks using trigram feature

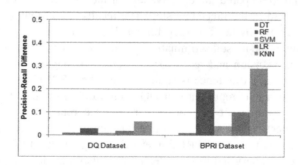

Fig. 8. Difference between Precision and Recall.

Variation Between Precision and Recall Across Dataset. Figure 8 shows the absolute difference between Precision and Recall scores across the two datasets using unigram feature matrix. The plotted values are computed by taking modulus of the difference between Precision and Recall scores. From the figure it can be observed that for DQ dataset the difference between Precision and Recall is very small compared to that of BPRI dataset. These results further affirm the suitable of the DQ framework.

5 Discussion and Conclusions

In this paper we propose an alternate to the traditional process performance analysis approaches that essentially requires the execution log or event log of the business process, whose performance analysis is desired. Our proposed alternate involves collecting and utilizing unstructured customer feedback and using it for the performance analysis of a business process. However, a key challenge to such an approach is that, the feedback includes several comments that are not related to process performance. Therefore, utilizing the complete feedback may generate misleading results. This arises the question, how to identify the comments that are related to process performance? To answer this question, in this paper we have used two well-established BPM frameworks to evaluate their suitable for identifying process performance related comments. The frameworks are, Devils Quadrangle and Business Process Redesign Implementation. For that, we have first generated a feedback corpus that includes 3356 comments.

Secondly, we have generated two criteria, based on the two frameworks, and used them for manually classifying relevant and irrelevant comments. During the classification it was observed the use of BPRI framework based criteria (BPRI criteria) is harder than that of DQ framework based criteria (DQ Criteria). The impact of that can also be observed in the results, that is, the number of agreements in applying the DQ criteria are significantly more than BPRI criteria. An analysis of the two datasets revealed that a large majority of the comments declared relevant by BPRI criteria are also declared relevant by the DQ criteria. Furthermore, the use of DQ criteria leads to identification of additional relevant comments, in addition to the relevant compared identified by the BPRI criteria.

Thirdly, we have compared the effectiveness of the two frameworks by using the two datasets generated in the preceding step. The results reveal that, (a) all five techniques generate achieve higher accuracy for the DQ dataset as compared the BPRI dataset, (b) unigram is the most discriminating feature for classification, (c) the absolute difference between precision and recall for DQ dataset is negligible for all the techniques, whereas the same difference is significant for the BPRI datasets.

The summarized results represent that DQ framework is more suitable because, it not only identifies a large set of process performance related comments, but also classifies the comments in the same class that has similar feature set. In contrast, the cognitive effort required to use BPRI framework is higher due to intricacies in the criteria and its use in supervised learning techniques also impedes the performance of supervised learning techniques.

Given that all organizations have business processes, in this study we argue that there is a need to engage the organizations that are yet to embrace BPM. For that, we have taken an initial step towards proposing an innovative solution in which such organizations can get a sense of their business process performance without going through the complete BPM lifecycle. The solution involves, application of data analytics on the customer feedback to gain insights about the process performance. In the future we plan to utilize the classified comments for business process redesign.

References

1. van der Aalst, W.M.P., Pesic, M., Song, M.: Beyond process mining: from the past to present and future. In: Pernici, B. (ed.) CAiSE 2010. LNCS, vol. 6051, pp. 38–52. Springer, Heidelberg (2010). https://doi.org/10.1007/978-3-642-13094-6_5
2. Zhang, Y., Liang, R., Shi, Z., Ma, H.: The design and implementation of a process-driven higher education administrative system. IERI Procedia **2**(5), 176–182 (2012)
3. Krajewski, L., Ritzman, L., Malhotra, M.: Operations Management: Processes and Value Chains, 8th edn. Prentice Hall, Upper Saddle River (2006)
4. Jorge, M.: Conformance Checking and Diagnosis in Process Mining: Comparing Observed and Modeled Processes. LNBIP. Springer, Heidelberg (2016). https://doi.org/10.1007/978-3-319-49451-7
5. van der Aalst, W.M.P., Ardiansyah, A., Dongen, B.: Replay history on process model for conformance checking and performance analysis. WIREs Data Min. Knowl. Discov. **2**(2), 182–192 (2012)
6. Danaher, P.J., Mattsson, J.: Customer satisfaction during the service delivery process. Eur. J. Mark. **28**(5), 5–16 (1994)
7. Thomke, S., von Hippel, E.: Customers as innovators: a new way to create value. Harvard Bus. Rev. **80**(4), 74–85 (2002)
8. Hauser, J.R.: How Puritan-Bennett used the house of quality. Sloan Manag. Rev. **34**(3), 61–71 (1993)
9. Kujala, S.: User involvement: a review of the benefits and challenges. Behav. Inf. Technol. **1**(22), 1–16 (2003)
10. Reijers, H.A., Mansar, S.L.: Best practices in business process redesign: an overview and qualitative evaluation of successful redesign heuristics. Omega **33**(4), 283–306 (2005)
11. Mansar, S.L., Reijers, H.A.: Best practices in business process redesign: validation of a redesign framework. Comput. Ind. **56**(5), 457–471 (2005)
12. Dumas, M., Rosa, M.L., Mendling, J., Reijers, H.A.: Fundamentals of Business Process Management. Springer, Heidelberg (2013). https://doi.org/10.1007/978-3-642-33143-5
13. Dumas, F., Aalst, W., Hofstede, A.H.M.: Process Aware Information Systems. Wiley, Hoboken (2005)
14. Jansen-Vullers, M.H., Kleingeld, P.A.M., Netjes, M.: Quantifying the performance of workflows. Inf. Syst. Manag. **25**(4), 332–343 (2008)
15. Cornal, K., Schuff, D., Louis, R.D.S.: The impact of alternative diagrams on the accuracy of recall: a comparison of star schema and entity relationship diagrams. Decis. Support Syst. **42**(1), 450–468 (2006)
16. Kutner, M.H., Nachtsheim, C., Neter, J.: Applied Linear Regression Models. McGraw-Hill/Irwin, New York (2004)
17. Scholkopf, B., Smola, A.J.: Learning with Kernels: Support Vector Machines, Regularization, Optimization and Beyond. MIT Press, Cambridge (2001)
18. Rokach, L., Maimon, O.: Data Mining with Decision Trees. Theory and Applications, 2nd edn. World Scientific, River Edge (2014)
19. Zhang, C., Mai, Y.: Ensemble Machine Learning Methods and Application. Springer, New York (2012). https://doi.org/10.1007/978-1-4419-9326-7. p. 157
20. Kirk, M.: Thoughtful Machine Learning a Test-Driven Approach. O'REILLY, Sebastopol (2015)
21. Yates, R.B., Neto, B.R.: Modern Information Retrieval. ACM Press, New York (1999)
22. Version S.P.1.6: SPSS Inc., ChicagoIII (2008). https://nlp.stanford.edu/software/lex-parser.shtml

Increasing Trust in (Big) Data Analytics

Johannes Schneider, Joshua Peter Handali[(✉)], and Jan vom Brocke

University of Liechtenstein, 9490 Vaduz, Liechtenstein
{johannes.schneider, joshua.handali,
jan.vom.brocke}@uni.li

Abstract. Trust is a key concern in big data analytics (BDA). Explaining "black-box" models, demonstrating transferability of models and robustness to data changes with respect to quality or content can help in improving confidence in BDA. To this end, we propose metrics for measuring robustness with respect to input noise. We also provide empirical evidence by showcasing how to compute and interpret these metrics using multiple datasets and classifiers. Additionally, we discuss the state-of-the-art of various areas in machine learning such as explaining "black box" models and transfer learning with respect to model validation. We show how methods from these areas can be adjusted to support classical validity measures in science such as content validity.

Keywords: Big data · Trust · Validation metrics · Concept drift
Noise robustness · Transferability · Model interpretability

1 Introduction

Lack of trust in big data (analytics) is an important issue in industry according to studies from companies such as KPMG [20]. In fact, a study [21] found that just one-third of CEOs trust data analytics. Trust has also been recognized by academia as an important concern for the success of analytics [1].

Trust is the willingness to rely on another [8]. Multiple factors ranging from more subjective reasons such as an individual's predisposition to more objective reasons underlie the formation of trust [34]. Here we focus more on providing objective reasons for increasing trust namely knowledge-based reasons and reasons based on interaction, e.g. the possibility for verification.

Trust in the field of big data is often related to data quality [13] that can be increased by means of data quality assurance processes. There has been less emphasis on the relation of trust and models or computation [29], e.g. the impact of data changes on deployed models. In this work, we elaborate on trust in the outcomes of big data analytics. Outcomes are of course impacted by the nature of the data but also by the model chosen during the analysis process. Big data is often characterized using 4Vs [7]: (i) volume relating to the large amount of data; (ii) velocity expressing the speed of data processing (often in the form of streams), (iii) variety highlighting the diversity of data types covering both unstructured and structured data; and (iv) veracity emphasizing data uncertainty and imprecision. In particular, veracity is associated with credibility, truthfulness and objectivity as well as trust [25]. Uncertainty can stem from data

R. Matulevičius and R. Dijkman (Eds.): CAiSE 2018 Workshops, LNBIP 316, pp. 70–84, 2018.
https://doi.org/10.1007/978-3-319-92898-2_6

inconsistencies and incompleteness, ambiguities, latency, deception and model approximations [7]. Uncertainty also has a time dimension, meaning that data distributions are not necessary stable over time. Concepts found in big data might change over time. For example, text from social media might show a strong variation of topics across time. Even the meaning of individual words might change over time or by region. Data might also be impacted by various sources of noise. For example, sensor data might vary due to environmental factors such as weather that are not recorded in the data. Furthermore, data might be created intentionally with the goal of deception. For instance, credit loan applications might contain forged data to obtain a loan. Veracity embraces the idea that despite poor data quality one might obtain valuable insights. Therefore, to account for variation of data (and its quality), model assessment should include an analysis of sensitivity of the proposed models with respect to veracity. How much will the model deteriorate if the data distribution changes? Is the model robust to random noise or carefully crafted deception attempts? To this end, we propose to compute metrics covering various aspects of veracity, such as expected deviation of performance metrics of models due to noise. We also propose to adjust methods intended to handle deception and concept drifts to compute validation metrics that allow to address a model's robustness to attacks and changes in concepts. Empirical evaluation using eight classifiers and four datasets helps in deepening the understanding of the metrics and provides valuable detailed guidelines for practitioners. Whereas our noise metrics enhance those by Garcia et al. [14], our other metrics are novel to the best of our knowledge.

To counteract mistrust, opening up the black-box of analytics such as machine learning techniques is one way [20]. Many models such as deep learning have a reputation of being uninterpretable. These models are often very complex, encoding knowledge using millions of parameters and are only poorly understood conceptually [15]. Despite being seemingly uninterpretable deep learning, for instance, has been regarded as breakthrough technology [18]. Deep neural nets do not just outperform other more interpretable techniques by large margins but sometimes even humans [15]. Therefore, relying on simpler but more intuitive models might come with a significant degradation in desired performance. Fortunately, the boom of big data, analytics and the surge in performance has also led to an increased effort in providing better intuition on how such models work [19, 22, 24, 28, 36]. Though some ideas for classifier explanation date back almost 20 years, the field is currently undergoing rapid evolution with many potential approaches for interpretation emerging. In this paper, we provide a brief overview of existing work on model interpretation. Model interpretation might be a suitable means to assess whether decision making is corresponding to policies or laws such as being fair and ethical [16]. For example, European legislation has granted the right to explanation for individuals with respect to algorithmic decisions. Thus, interpretability might not just increase trust but might even be a legal requirement.

Trust in a model might also be improved, if the model can be used to solve other related tasks. For example, one might expect that a tennis player might also play table-tennis better than the average person, since both sports require hitting balls with a racket. In a machine learning context, an image classifier that is being able to distinguish between bicycles and cats, should also be able to classify between motorbikes and dogs. The idea of transferability of outcomes is well-known to establish trust in qualitative research [31]. It might refer to the idea that the finding of a small population under study can be transferred to a wider population. The idea of transferability of results encoded in models (and its parameters) is captured by transfer learning [27]. Roughly, transfer learning for a classifier might also relate to the scientific concept of external validity, i.e. content validity, which assesses to what extend a measure represents all meanings of a given construct [3]. Some classifiers might be seen as learning features (measures). Transfer learning assesses the usefulness of these features (measures) in other contexts. Though the idea of transfer learning has been around for a long time, to the best of our knowledge using it as an operationalization for assessing validity in the context of analytics is novel.

The paper is structured as follows: First, we discuss general aspects of input sensitivity in Sect. 2 outlining key ideas for metrics for different changes of inputs (and outputs). The state-of-the-art in blackbox model interpretability and transfer learning as well as their relevance to model validation is discussed in Sects. 3 and 4. Section 5 shows detailed implementation and evaluation of some measures.

2 Validation Measure: Input Sensitivity

Robustness refers to the ability of tolerating perturbations that might affect a system's performance. Sensitivity analysis is a common tool to assess robustness with respect to input changes. The main goal is often to assess how the change of certain (input) parameters impacts the (stability) of outcomes. In control theory, if minor changes in the input lead to large changes in the output a feedback system is deemed to be unstable [2]. In the context of machine learning robustness is often related to over- and underfitting. Overfitting resorts to the situation, where a machine learning algorithm mimics too closely the input data and fails to abstract from unnecessary details in the data. Underfitting covers the opposite effect, where a model is too general and does not cover important characteristic of the given input data [10]. Measuring robustness is typically done by partitioning the entire data set into a training and validation set using techniques such as cross-validation. The former data set is used to learn a model, i.e. infer model parameters. The latter is used to assess model performance on novel unseen data, e.g. by computing metrics such as classification accuracy. This split of the dataset supports the choice of a model that balances between over- and underfitting. However, model assessments based on the standard splitting procedure into training and validation sets, do not answer the question how the model behaves given changes to the input data. In the context of BDA and supervised learning, one can distinguish between robustness with respect to label perturbations and attribute perturbations. The source of the perturbation can be classified as:

– Malicious, deceptive: Data might be crafted by an attacker as an attempt to trick the system into making wrong decisions. The current data set used to create the model might not contain any form of such deceptive data. Therefore, the exact nature of the deceptive data might be unknown. This is analogous to conventional cyber security risks on computer systems, i.e. zero-day attacks [6] where a system is confronted with an unexpected attack that exploits a previously unknown security hole, i.e. vulnerability. However, even if the general nature of attacks or data manipulation are known, preventing such attacks might be difficult. Deep learning applied to image recognition has shown to be susceptible to such attacks as illustrated in Fig. 1. Such data might sometimes be outliers, since they are often distinct from the majority of input data.

Fig. 1. Left shows the original, correctly classified image. The center shows perturbations that are added to the original image to yield the right image that is visually identical for a human. Still it is classified as ostrich [32].

– Concept drift: It refers to a change (over time) of the relationship between input and output values in unforeseen ways. This might lead to a deterioration of predictive performance. Reasons of concept drift might be unknown hidden contexts or unpredicted events. For example, a user's interest in online news might change, while the distribution of incoming news documents remains the same [12].
– Noise: There are a variety of noise sources that might impact data samples. Noise might also change over time. For example, classification labels might be noisy, i.e. due to human errors. Sensor values could exhibit random fluctuations visible as white noise in the data. Neither of these sources might have an impact on the relationship between input and output.

2.1 Measuring Robustness Against Concept Drift

Concept drift refers to the phenomenon that the relation between input and output changes over time. Changes can occur sudden or gradual. A simple strategy to cope with concept drift is to periodically retrain the model on new training data. This corresponds to forgetting all prior data. However, it could be that forgetting old data is either not feasible or non-desirable, e.g. since novel data is only unlabeled and relatively sparse.

While some models can adapt to drastic concept drifts, others might only handle minor changes in concept drift well and some models might behave a lot worse due to small changes in the relationship between input and output. Therefore, it is important to assess the robustness with respect to such changes. One can distinguish three types of drifts [12]. Two of them are illustrated in Fig. 2. The (real) concept drift refers to the changes of the conditional distribution of the output given the input, while the input distribution might remain the same. Population drift refers to change of the population from which samples are drawn. Virtual drift corresponds to a change of the distribution

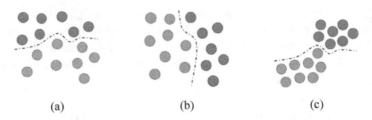

Fig. 2. Illustration of concept drift: (a) shows the original data, (b) real concept drift due to changes of the conditional distribution, and (c) virtual drift where the input distribution changes but not the conditional distribution of the output given the input

from which samples are drawn but not of the conditional distribution of the output given the input.

Our goal is to assess robustness of a model against concept drift. To this end, we propose to derive multiple data sets from the original data sets based on the assumed changes over time, e.g. sudden, incremental and gradual. These data sets can be used to measure the difference in performance between the original data and data where concepts have altered. A detailed case study will be given in Sect. 5.

2.2 Measuring Robustness Against Noise

Noise in the data can also cause a deterioration of model performance. Noise can be handled during the preprocessing phase, e.g. using filtering algorithms. Noisy data can also directly be used for training [14]. Noise might impact labels and attributes. It has been shown [37] that (in general) attribute noise is more harmful than label noise and that noise on attributes strongly correlating with labels has more impact than noise on weakly correlating attributes.

Frénay and Verleysen [11] provide the following taxonomy of (label) noise:

- Noisy completely at random model (NCAR): In a setting with binary labels an error occurs uniformly at random, independent of all data, i.e. class labels and/or attributes are altered with constant error probability.
- Noisy at random model (NAR): This model includes error dependencies on the class label but does not account for dependency of input data. In the case of binary labels NAR equals NCAR.
- Noisy not at random model (NNAR) is the most general noise model. It enables to capture the dependency of the error based on the inputs. For example, one can account for the frequently observed phenomenon that label error rates are larger near the decision boundary.

To assess the robustness against noise the first step is to create multiple data sets from the original data through perturbation according to the above noise models. As suggested in [14] one can compute a measure for the expected deterioration of the classifier. We also suggest to compute the standard deviation. This provides a coarse estimate of the risk that for a noisy dataset the deviation is significantly higher than the expectation. A detailed case study will be given in Sect. 5.

2.3 Measuring Robustness Against Malicious Data

Big data is often associated with large economic value. Systems based on big data might make decisions that can have a profound impact on individuals. For that reason, these individuals have an interest of manipulating the big data system. For example, credit loan applications decide whether a customer is supposed to get a loan. Face recognition such as Facebook's DeepFace using deep learning [33] might not only tag users but also be used to identify criminals. Thus, a party might conduct attacks by injecting tampered data. Such attacks can be categorized along three dimensions [4]:

- The influence dimension characterizes the degree of control of the malicious party. Causative attacks assume some control of the attacker over the training data. An attacker attempts to manipulate learning itself. Exploratory attacks only exploit misclassifications but do not alter training.
- Security violations can occur in the form of reduced availability of the system. For example, denial of service attacks often rely on forging false positive data. Integrity attacks target assets using false negatives, e.g. by obfuscating spam messages.
- Specificity describes the scope of the attack ranging from a single instance to a wide class of instances.

For example, an exploratory attack might seek to trick a spam filter by crafting a message that appears benign for a static spam filter that does not evolve over time. If an attacker successfully poisons a mail inbox with millions of messages he might render the system temporary unusable (denial of service). An attacker might send a single message that is being classified as false positive multiple times.

Perfect security might be impossible to achieve, e.g. due to the possibility of unforeseen attacks. Thus, quantifying the exact level of security on a finite scale might be very difficult. Still, metrics can support the assessment of the resilience towards (some) attacks. Our proposed metrics are rooted on two existing strategies to handle and identify malicious data [4]:

i) General robustness measures from statistics might limit the impact that a small fraction of training data can have. The idea underlies the assumption that the majority of training data is correct and only a small amount of training data stems from adversaries. Furthermore, these data are distinguishable from benign data. In scenarios where most labels are incorrect, training is generally very difficult. Two common concepts used in safeguarding algorithms against attacks are breakdown point and influence function [26]. They could both be used to assess the robustness of the trained model to attacks. Loosely speaking the breakdown point (BP) measures the amount of contamination (proportion of atypical points) that the data may contain up to which the learned parameters still contain information about the distribution of benign data. The influence function describes the asymptotic behavior of the sensitivity curve when the data contains a small fraction of outliers. The idea is to create (artificial) malicious data and compute the breakdown point and the influence function. A large breakdown point and a small sensitivity to outliers expressed by the influence function indicate robustness.

ii) The Reject on Negative Impact (RONI) defense disregards single training examples if they profoundly increase the number of misclassifications. To this end, two classifiers are trained. One classifier is trained on a base training set and another one on the same base training set enhanced with the training example under consideration. If the accuracy of the classifier including the examined sample is lower, the sample is removed from the training data.

To compute a metric the idea is to identify the samples that are supposed to be rejected first. Then a metric for a classifier can be calculated where the training data contains all samples that are supposed to be rejected and the training data without those samples. The deterioration of the classification accuracy serves as a measure for resilience to malicious data. A detailed case study will be given in Sect. 5.

3 Validation: Model Interpretability

Interpretability is seen as a prerequisite for trust [28]. In research, internal validity serves as a source of trust in a scientific study. Internal validation is a vital part in verifying that a research study was done right. It highlights the extent to which the ideas about cause and effect are supported by the study [3]. However, supervised learning is optimized towards making associations between the target and input variable and not towards causality. For instance, the common fallacy of neglecting a hidden factor explaining input and output is possible to happen in supervised learning. Still, associations might at least provide some indication whether certain assumptions upon causality might hold. Associations could also be deemed as unintuitive or unlikely, discrediting the learnt model. Models might not only be used to make decisions (e.g. decide to which class a data sample belongs), but they might also provide information to humans for their own decision making. This information might be based on an interpretation of a model's decision. If this interpretation matches the intuition of a human decision maker, it might increase trust.

Interpretable models can be characterized by the following properties [23]:

- Post-hoc interpretability refers to interpreting decisions based on natural language explanations, visualizations or by examples. Using a separate process for decision making and explaining is similar to humans where the two processes might also be distinct. Post-hoc interpretations are also most suitable to provide intuition on complex models such as deep learning that (at the current stage of research) are deemed non-transparent.
- Transparency: A transparent model allows to understand the inner workings of the model in contrast to a black box model. It might be looked at in three different ways: (i) in terms of simulatability suggesting that the model should be simple so that a person can contemplate the entire model at once; (ii) in terms of decomposability referring to the idea that each aspect of the model has an intuitive explanation; (iii) with respect to algorithmic transparency relating to the learning mechanism covering aspects such as being able to prove convergence of the algorithm.

There exist multiple strategies for explaining models [17]. Examples of transparent models that are deemed relatively easy to interpret include decision trees, rules and linear models. One strategy to explain black-box models involves approximating the complex model by one of these three simpler and more transparent models. For example, neural networks can be explained using decision trees [19, 22]. Rules might also be extracted from neural networks [36]. There are also methods that are agnostic to the classification method such as Generalized Additive Models (GAM) estimating the contribution of individual features to a decision [24].

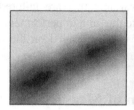

Fig. 3. Learnt saliency mask (left) for an image of the class "flute" shown on the right [9]

Rather than explaining the entire model, the focus can be on explaining individual outcomes, i.e. predictions. For example, for deep learning algorithms saliency masks show area of attention. Figure 3 provides a saliency mask for images [9].

Multiple agnostic methods exist to explain predictions. An example is LIME [28] which uses local approximations based on generated random samples near the sample which outcome is supposed to be explained.

Black box inspection dealing with the goal of understanding of how the black box works or why it prefers certain decisions to others. For instance, one might measure the impact of features on the outcomes using sensitivity analysis.

All these approaches might be used to improve model interpretability and, therefore, trust. Since the field witnesses very rapid progress, better tool support can be expected in the near future.

4 Validation: Model Transferability

The idea of model transferability is to assess a model designed for one problem based on its ability to solve other but related tasks. This relates to the idea of external validity in research, e.g. in social sciences. External validity describes whether results of the study can be used for related populations. One would expect that this is the case, thus, transferability while not being a requirement for trust, demonstrating transferability can increase trust.

Conventional machine learning is characterized by solving a single task where training and test data have the same distribution. In transfer learning, one might consider one or several domains where the two distributions might vary called source and a target domain (distribution). In homogeneous transfer learning the two domains have the same input space but different labels. In heterogeneous transfer learning the input space of the source and target domain are different. For illustration, a strategy for transfer learning for deep learning networks is to train a network on the source dataset (potentially even in an unsupervised manner). Then one might only keep lower layers that capture general features and remove higher layers that might be too specific to the source dataset. Finally, the model is trained (additionally) using the target dataset [5]. This is referred to parameter sharing. However, there is a multitude of transfer learning strategies [27, 35]. These are often specific to certain machine learning techniques.

To assess transferability quantitatively, a first step is to identify suitable tasks and datasets to which a model can be transferred to. Then the method of transfer has to be defined. For many classifiers there exist variants that are tailored towards transfer learning [27, 35]. The final step is to compute the gain in performance of a model using transfer learning compared to a model that is only trained on the target domain data without any form of transfer.

5   Implementation and Evaluation of Measures

In this section we show how robustness against noise (Sect. 2.2) can be specified in detail, implemented and interpreted. Detailed assessments of other measures are deferred to future work. We use several datasets and classifiers. Our performance metric that should be maximized is accuracy. Other metrics such as F1-Score might be used in the same manner.

5.1   Datasets and Classifiers

We conducted the experimental evaluation involving four datasets (MNIST, Artificial, Spambase, Phoneme) and seven classifiers (KNN, SVM, logistic regression, random forests, neural networks, decision trees, Naïve Bayes). The four considered datasets are frequently used within the data mining community. We used 5000 samples of the MNIST database of handwritten digits each consisting of 16×16 pixels. The Spambase collection of about 4000 spam e-mails with 57 attributes. The artificial dataset of 20000 samples was generated using the make_classification function from the scikit-learn package. The phoneme dataset consists of 5 real-valued features and 5404 samples. SVM was implemented based on [30]. All other algorithms stem from the scikit-learn package version 0.19.1 implemented in Python 2.7.12. We relied largely on default parameters and did not perform any parameter tuning. Thus, there was no need for a validation set. We used 5-KNN, a neural network with two hidden layers of 30 neurons each, a random forest with 50 trees and multinomial Naïve Bayes using 100 bins for discretizing continuous values.

5.2   Implementation of Robustness Against Noise

The detailed steps to compute the metrics capturing robustness against noise outlined which were briefly described in Sect. 2.2 are as follows:

(1) Choose a noise model: An analyst should choose an adequate noise model with the right amount of detail, i.e. an analyst might incorporate detailed anticipation of how noise might impact individual attributes or he might rely on general models. The latter requires substantially less effort, but probably leads to less accurate estimates.

We use the NCAR noise model described in Sect. 2.2. We consider two scenarios, one for label noise and one for attribute noise. To cover label noise, we exchange a label of a data point with another label of a randomly chosen sample with a probability of 0.25. Thus, an exchange does not necessarily imply the label is altered, i.e. if the chosen sample for exchange has the same label. Therefore, it is unclear, how many samples will obtain incorrect labels. This is a disadvantage of the method that could of course be addressed. However, requiring that every sample obtains a different label than it originally had might lead to pathologies, i.e. for a binary classification task samples from class A would become class B and samples from class A would become class B, i.e. the dataset would not change from the point of view of the classification algorithm. Compared to choosing a random class uniformly at random of all classes, our permutation approach has the advantage that the overall number of labels of each class stays the same. In turn, imbalanced datasets remain imbalanced and the other way around. This allows for easier comparison of certain performance metrics such as accuracy. The choice of the probability is arbitrary to a certain degree. The probability should be larger than the standard deviation of the performance metric (using cross-validation) on the unmodified data. Otherwise it might be difficult to reliably judge the sensitivity to noise for individual classifiers as well as to conduct a meaningful comparison among different classifiers. A large probability indicating very dramatic changes, essentially saying that (new) data will have almost no relation to the past, might be unrealistic. Attribute noise for a continuous attribute was computed by adding Gaussian noise with half the standard deviation of all instances of the attribute. Again, the choice of half the standard deviation is somewhat arbitrary. The same reasoning as for label noise applies with respect to avoiding extreme values, i.e. close to 0 or 1. Gaussian noise is a common model occurring frequently in engineering. But depending on the scenario, other models might be more appropriate.

(2) Create multiple datasets with noise:
Based on the original dataset multiple noisy datasets are computed. In our case we computed 10. The more datasets the more reliable are the estimates.

(3) The performance metric is computed on all datasets:
We computed the accuracy on seven different classifiers and four datasets using all 10 noisy datasets and the original datasets. We employed cross-validation with 10 folds.

(4) Computation of the robustness metrics:
We computed the mean and standard deviation of the accuracy of all folds of all datasets, i.e. the original dataset (DO), the datasets with label noise (DL) and with attribute noise (DA). Denote the average values for the accuracy computed using cross validation for each dataset and each classifier separately as E[DO], E[DL]

and E[DA] and the standard deviations as std[DO], std[DL] and std[DA]. We computed the sensitivity SE as the relative change of each noise model compared to original dataset: $SE(X) = (O - X)/X$. For example, the sensitivity with respect to attribute noise becomes:

$$SE(E[DA]) = (E[DO] - E[DA])/E[DA]$$
$$SE(std[DA]) = (std[DO] - std[DA])/std[DA]$$

Garcia et al. [14] computed the sensitivity SE for noise for averages as well but did not include a study on the standard deviations and used a different model for creating noisy data. Furthermore, their noise model was different. The work also did not discuss other aspects such as concept drift or transferability.

The sensitivity of the average values indicates how much the accuracy is impacted by the noise on average. One expects this value to be in [0,1]. Zero indicates absolute resilience against noise. One indicates a very strong impact of noise. Generally, the value will be less than one, since random guessing achieves a non-zero accuracy, e.g. E[DA] will generally not be zero. Negative values are possible. They indicate that noise improved the classifier. An improvement could stem from a very unlikely coincidence (the noise simplified the problem by chance) or it might hint that the classifier is far from optimal, so that noise improves its performance. The sensitivity of the standard deviation indicates how much the accuracy fluctuates for noisy data relative to the original data. A value close to zero means that we can expect the same absolute deviation of the classification accuracy as for the original dataset. A positive value means that the deviation is smaller for the noisy dataset than for the original dataset and a negative value indicates that it is larger.

5.3   Results

Overall our findings suggest that no algorithm outperforms all others on all metrics with respect to sensitivity. Given the no free lunch theorem saying that no classifier dominates all others, this is expected. Good performance in traditional measures such as accuracy do often not imply good performance with respect to sensitivity. For instance, we have identified scenarios, where classifiers show similar outcomes with respect to accuracy but show a quite different behaviour with respect to noise sensitivity. Thus, sensitivity metrics should be taken into account in addition to other metrics when choosing a classifier.

Table 1 shows all metrics using the setup discussed in Sect. 5.2. The first column E [DO] shows that classifiers perform differently with respect to the accuracy metric on the original datasets. Some models such as neural networks also show extremely poor behaviour in some cases (e.g. the MNIST dataset). The suggested architecture of the neural network might not contain sufficient parameters to learn the task and thus underfit or learning rates might not be set optimally. It is known that more complex neural network architectures behave better on this dataset. No single classifier dominates on all benchmarks though overall random forests perform best. The standard

Table 1. Validation metrics for attribute and label noise

Dataset	Classifier	Unmodified		LabelNoise		AttributeNoise	
		E[DO]	std[DO]	SE(E[DL])	SE(std[DL])	SE(E[DA])	SE(std[DA])
Artificial	LogisticRe	0.83	0.04	0.12	0.25	0.09	0.05
	RandomFore	0.95	0.02	0.15	0.17	0.18	−0.42
	KNN	0.92	0.03	0.15	0.2	0.18	−0.36
	SVM	0.81	0.1	0.11	0.41	0.1	0.41
	NeuralNetw	0.95	0.02	0.15	0.27	0.16	−0.38
	DecisionTr	0.9	0.04	0.26	0.65	0.23	−0.52
	MultiNaive	0.82	0.1	0.11	0.31	0.07	0.25
Phoneme	LogisticRe	0.75	0.01	0.06	0.41	0.02	0.0
	RandomFore	0.9	0.01	0.12	−0.1	0.21	−0.3
	KNN	0.88	0.01	0.11	−0.3	0.19	−0.33
	SVM	0.75	0.01	0.06	0.03	0.03	−0.02
	NeuralNetw	0.81	0.01	0.08	−0.44	0.06	−0.25
	DecisionTr	0.87	0.01	0.18	−0.16	0.24	0.19
	MultiNaive	0.73	0.01	0.07	0.0	0.03	−0.19
Spambase	LogisticRe	0.91	0.01	0.15	−0.43	0.07	−0.35
	RandomFore	0.95	0.01	0.16	−0.38	0.13	−0.31
	KNN	0.91	0.01	0.15	−0.27	0.08	−0.17
	SVM	0.92	0.01	0.16	−0.32	0.08	−0.27
	NeuralNetw	0.93	0.01	0.13	−0.36	0.08	−0.38
	DecisionTr	0.91	0.01	0.23	−0.39	0.22	−0.41
	MultiNaive	0.89	0.01	0.11	−0.25	0.06	−0.02
MNIST	LogisticRe	0.86	0.02	0.9	−0.38	0.18	−0.08
	RandomFore	0.87	0.02	0.37	−0.29	0.31	−0.32
	KNM	0.9	0.01	0.34	−0.19	0.14	−0.22
	SVM	0.81	0.02	0.88	0.04	0.21	0.31
	NeuralNetw	0.12	0.05	0.19	2.7	0.24	1.1
	DecisionTr	0.7	0.03	0.69	0.44	0.73	0.19
	MultiNaive	0.81	0.02	0.32	−0.43	0.1	−0.25

deviation std[DO] in column 2 of the accuracy for some classifiers on some datasets is rather large (e.g. 10% for SVMs and the artificial dataset) but generally below 3%.

Label Noise Sensitivity: The label noise sensitivity SE(E[DL]) is also quite different among classifiers and datasets. For example, for the first two datasets Logistic Regression, SVMs and Multinomial Naïve Bayes are quite robust. On the third dataset SVM does not show good robustness against noise. Decision trees are most impacted by label noise on all datasets. Label noise on the MNIST dataset has drastic impact on model performance, in particular on Logistic Regression and SVMs. A practical finding is that while Random Forests perform best on the Spambase data, they deteriorate more quickly with label noise than neural networks, which achieve comparable performance on the unmodified data. Thus, neural networks might be preferable under the assumption that label noise is likely to be a concern. Even more extremely the same reasoning applies to logistic regression and SVMs on the MNIST dataset compared to random forests. Although all datasets are heavily impacted by label noise for this dataset, the extreme degradation of the former two classifiers is surprising. It might hint convergence problems or unsuitable parameter setting of the algorithms (in the presence of noise). The variation in outcomes in the presence of label noise (SE(std[DL])) is, for example, much larger for neural networks than for random forests for the artificial dataset. Otherwise the methods behave almost identical (E[DO], std[DO]) and SE(E [DL]). This suggests that random forests are a safer bet to ensure a certain level of model performance.

Attribute Noise Sensitivity: For attribute noise there seems to be a correlation with label noise but there are several cases where attribute noise and label noise show different behaviour for the same classifier. For example, for Random Forests on the Spambase dataset the attribute noise sensitivity is among the highest, whereas the label noise is comparable to most other methods. For the Phoneme dataset Decision Trees and Random Forests behave comparably with respect to attribute noise except for the variation in the attribute noise sensitivity SE(std[DA]). It decreases for random forests but increases for decision trees. Though the relative difference in SE(std[DA]) is considerable, overall it is not a key concern since the standard deviation of the accuracy on the original dataset std[DO] is low.

6 Discussion and Conclusions

We have elaborated on the issue of trust in big data analytics. Based on various existing techniques from machine learning we have derived a set of validation metrics that might yield more transparency to how models react to changes of data. They also show how models could be validated using transferability and explanation. Some of our proposals require significant effort to use, since they might be different for each classifier and dataset, e.g. transferability. Our current evaluation is also limited to noise robustness on a limited number of datasets. To provide more general conclusions on the behavior of classifiers across different datasets, more empirical evidence is needed. Furthermore, in general, it is very difficult to anticipate the exact behavior of concept drift or noise. Still, it is possible to use general assumptions on various future scenarios as an approximation. Those general assumptions lead to instantiations of the metrics that are easy to use as our evaluations for noise sensitivity has shown. Thus, we believe that the validation metrics are not only of conceptual interest but also of practical value to increase trust in big data analytics.

References

1. Abbasi, A., et al.: Big data research in information systems: toward an inclusive research agenda. J. Assoc. Inf. Syst. **17**(2), 1–32 (2016)
2. Åström, K.J., Hägglund, T.: PID Controllers: Theory, Design, and Tuning. Instrument society of America, Research Triangle Park (1995)
3. Babbie, E.R.: The Basics of Social Research. Cengage Learning, Boston (2013)

4. Barreno, M., et al.: The security of machine learning. Mach. Learn. **81**(2), 121–148 (2010)
5. Bengio, Y.: Deep learning of representations for unsupervised and transfer learning. In: Proceedings of ICML Workshop on Unsupervised and Transfer Learning, pp. 17–36 (2012)
6. Bilge, L., Dumitras, T.: Before we knew it: an empirical study of zero-day attacks in the real world. In: Proceedings of the 2012 ACM Conference on Computer and Communications Security, pp. 833–844 (2012)
7. Claverie-Berge, I.: Solutions Big Data IBM. http://www-05.ibm.com/fr/events/netezzaDM_2012/Solutions_Big_Data.pdf. Accessed 16 Mar 2018
8. Doney, P.M., Cannon, J.P.: An examination of the nature of trust in buyer-seller relationships. J. Mark. **61**, 35–51 (1997)
9. Fong, R.C., Vedaldi, A.: Interpretable explanations of black boxes by meaningful perturbation. In: IEEE International Conference on Computer Vision (2017)
10. Franklin, J.: The elements of statistical learning: data mining, inference and prediction. Math. Intell. **27**(2), 83–85 (2005)
11. Frénay, B., Verleysen, M.: Classification in the presence of label noise: a survey. IEEE Trans. Neural Netw. Learn. Syst. **25**(5), 845–869 (2014)
12. Gama, J., et al.: A survey on concept drift adaptation. ACM Comput. Surv. (CSUR) **46**(4), 44 (2014)
13. Gao, J., Xie, C., Tao, C.: Big data validation and quality assurance–issues, challenges, and needs. In: 2016 IEEE Symposium on Service-Oriented System Engineering (SOSE), pp. 433–441. IEEE, March 2016
14. García, S., et al.: Data Preprocessing in Data Mining. ISRL, vol. 72. Springer, Cham (2015). https://doi.org/10.1007/978-3-319-10247-4
15. Goodfellow, I., et al.: Deep Learning. MIT Press, Cambridge (2016)
16. Goodman, B., Flaxman, S.: European Union regulations on algorithmic decision-making and a "right to explanation". AI Mag. **38**(3), 50–57 (2016)
17. Guidotti, R., et al.: A survey of methods for explaining black box models. arXiv preprint arXiv:1802.01933 (2018)
18. Hof, R.D.: Deep learning with massive amounts of computational power. https://www.technologyreview.com/s/513696/deep-learning/. Accessed 16 Mar 2018
19. Johansson, U., Niklasson, L.: Evolving decision trees using oracle guides. In: IEEE Symposium on Computational Intelligence and Data Mining, CIDM 2009, pp. 238–244 (2009)
20. KPMG: Building trust in analytics: breaking the cycle of mistrust in D&A. https://assets.kpmg.com/content/dam/kpmg/xx/pdf/2016/10/building-trust-in-analytics.pdf. Accessed 16 Mar 2018
21. KPMG: Now or never: CEOs mobilize for the fourth industrial revolution. https://assets.kpmg.com/content/dam/kpmg/pdf/2016/07/2016-ceo-survey.pdf. Accessed 16 Mar 2018
22. Krishnan, R., et al.: Extracting decision trees from trained neural networks. Pattern Recogn. **32**(12), 1999–2009 (1999)
23. Lipton, Z.C.: The mythos of model interpretability. In: Proceedings of ICML Workshop on Human Interpretability in Machine Learning (2016)
24. Lou, Y., et al.: Accurate intelligible models with pairwise interactions. In: Proceedings of the 19th ACM SIGKDD International Conference on Knowledge Discovery and Data Mining, pp. 623–631 (2013)
25. Lukoianova, T., Rubin, V.L.: Veracity roadmap: Is big data objective, truthful and credible? Adv. Classif. Res. Online **24**(1), 4–15 (2013)
26. Maronna, R.A., Martin, R.D., Yohai, V.: Robust Statistics. Wiley, Chichester (2006)
27. Pan, S.J., Yang, Q.: A survey on transfer learning. IEEE Trans. Knowl. Data Eng. **22**(10), 1345–1359 (2010)

28. Ribeiro, M.T., et al.: Why should i trust you?: explaining the predictions of any classifier. In: Proceedings of the 22nd ACM SIGKDD International Conference on Knowledge Discovery and Data Mining, pp. 1135–1144 (2016)

29. Saenger, J., Richthammer, C., Hassan, S., Pernul, G.: Trust and big data: a roadmap for research. In: 2014 25th International Workshop on Database and Expert Systems Applications (DEXA), pp. 278–282, September 2014

30. Schneider, J., Bogojeska, J., Vlachos, M.: Solving Linear SVMs with multiple 1D projections. In: Proceedings of the 23rd ACM International Conference on Conference on Information and Knowledge Management, pp. 221–230. ACM, November 2014

31. Shenton, A.K.: Strategies for ensuring trustworthiness in qualitative research projects. Educ. Inf. **22**(2), 63–75 (2004)

32. Szegedy, C., et al.: Intriguing properties of neural networks. In: International Conference on Learning Representations (2014)

33. Taigman, Y., et al.: Deepface: closing the gap to human-level performance in face verification. In: Proceedings of the IEEE Conference on Computer Vision and Pattern Recognition, pp. 1701–1708 (2014)

34. Wang, W., Benbasat, I.: Attributions of trust in decision support technologies: a study of recommendation agents for e-commerce. J. Manag. Inf. Syst. **24**(4), 249–273 (2008)

35. Weiss, K., et al.: A survey of transfer learning. J. Big Data **3**(1), 9 (2016)

36. Zhou, Z.-H., et al.: Extracting symbolic rules from trained neural network ensembles. AI Commun. **16**(1), 3–15 (2003)

37. Zhu, X., Wu, X.: Class noise vs. attribute noise: a quantitative study. Artif. Intell. Rev. **22**(3), 177–210 (2004)

Building Payment Classification Models from Rules and Crowdsourced Labels: A Case Study

Artem Mateush, Rajesh Sharma, Marlon Dumas[(✉)], Veronika Plotnikova,
Ivan Slobozhan, and Jaan Übi

University of Tartu, Tartu, Estonia
{artem.mateush,rajesh.sharma,marlon.dumas,veronika.plotnikova,
ivan.slobozhan,jaan.ubi}@ut.ee

Abstract. The ability to classify customer-to-business payments
enables retail financial institutions to better understand their customers'
expenditure patterns and to customize their offerings accordingly. However, payment classification is a difficult problem because of the large and
evolving set of businesses and the fact that each business may offer multiple types of products, e.g. a business may sell both food and electronics.
Two major approaches to payment classification are rule-based classification and machine learning-based classification on transactions labeled
by the customers themselves (a form of crowdsourcing). The rules-based
approach is not scalable as it requires rules to be maintained for every
business and type of transaction. The crowdsourcing approach leads to
inconsistencies and is difficult to bootstrap since it requires a large number of customers to manually label their transactions for an extended
period of time. This paper presents a case study at a financial institution in which a hybrid approach is employed. A set of rules is used
to bootstrap a financial planner that allowed customers to view their
transactions classified with respect to 66 categories, and to add labels to
unclassified transactions or to re-label transactions. The crowdsourced
labels, together with the initial rule set, are then used to train a machine
learning model. We evaluated our model on real anonymised dataset,
provided by the financial institution which consists of wire transfers and
card payments. In particular, for the wire transfer dataset, the hybrid
approach increased the coverage of the rule-based system from 76.4% to
87.4% while replicating the crowdsourced labels with a mean AUC of
0.92, despite inconsistencies between crowdsourced labels.

1 Introduction

Understanding the expenditure patterns of private customers at a fine level of
detail allows financial institutions to customize their offerings in order to address
the diverse requirements of their customer base. A basic ingredient to build a
deep understanding of expenditure patterns is to be able to classify Consumer-to-
Business (C2B) payments across product categories (e.g. utilities, food, clothing,

© Springer International Publishing AG, part of Springer Nature 2018
R. Matulevičius and R. Dijkman (Eds.): CAiSE 2018 Workshops, LNBIP 316, pp. 85–97, 2018.
https://doi.org/10.1007/978-3-319-92898-2_7

electronics). However, C2B payment classification is a difficult problem because of the large and evolving set of businesses and the fact that each business may offer multiple types of products, e.g. a business may sell both food and clothing.

As in any other automated classification problem, there are broadly two approaches available: rule-based and machine learning-based. In rule-based payment classification, a set of rules is maintained (typically bootstrapped by domain experts) in order to map each payment record to a category. For example, a rule might state that all payments made to a given account (belonging to a telco) should be classified as "Utilities & Telecommunications". This rules-based approach is simple, but it requires rules to be maintained for every possible business, especially when the data is continuously gets updated with newer cases [15].

The alternative approach is to construct a machine learning model from a set of labeled payments. In order to have enough samples, a typical approach is to crowdsource the acquisition of the labeled data from the customers themselves. This crowdsourcing approach is hard to bootstrap as it requires a large number of customers to manually label their transactions for an extended period of time. Furthermore, indistinguishably similar transactions by different customers may have different labels, a phenomenon known as the noisy data problem [10].

In this study, we partnered with a financial institution which has an existing rule-based system in place for classifying transactions. A set of rules is defined to bootstrap a financial planning tools that allows customers to view their transactions. Specifically, transactions are classified using a two-level hierarchy of categories. At the bottom level, there are labels such as *grocery, restaurants & cafeteria* and *footwear*, for example. These bottom-level labels are called categories (66 categories in total) and are grouped into 14 *category groups*, such as *food, utilities & telecommunication, clothing*. Naturally, the defined rules are not able to classify every transaction. Accordingly, users of the financial planner are able to assign labels to the transactions that are left unclassified by the rule-based system. Additionally, users are able to re-label already classified transactions if they perceive that the assigned category is not correct.

After a few years of operations of the rule-based financial planning tool, the question arose of how to exploit the labeled data collected via this tool in order to build a more complete and accurate payment classification system to replace the existing rule-based one. This paper reports on the ensuing effort to construct an improved payment classification system, which combines the existing rule-based system with the crowdsourced labels collected via the financial planning tool.

Specifically, the paper describes the development of a payment classification model that integrates the following three sources:

1. **User-independent rules:** rules that map transactions to labels based on the beneficiary and (for card payments) the Merchant Category Classification (MCC) Code (cf. Sect. 3.2 for further details).
2. **User-defined rules:** These are rules defined by users, which assign labels to a transaction based on the payment's comment text or the beneficiary name. For example, a customer may define a rule that assigns a label *food* to every

transaction where the keyword "supermarket" appears in the transaction's comment.

3. **Manual user labels:** These are labels that are manually assigned by a user to a transaction. Manual labeling typically happens when the user disagrees with the rule-based labelling or when the rule-based labelling is not able to categorise the transaction in question. For example, if a customer visits a food shop to buy cooking utensils, the rule-based system will automatically assign the label *food* to this transaction. The user might then manually re-label this transaction to *household accessories*. In this case, the user does a one-off manual re-labelling rather than defining a general user rule.

To integrate the above three sources of labels, we trained a multiclass machine learning classifier from a dataset that combines samples labeled manually, samples labeled by user rules, samples labeled by user-independent rules, and samples that could not be labeled by any rule. As the resulting system combines knowledge originating from the crowdsourced labels as well as knowledge from the user-defined and user-independent rules, we call it a *hybrid classifier*. The paper presents an empirical evaluation of this hybrid classification approach in terms of coverage and accuracy over wire transfers and credit card transactions.

The rest of the paper is organized as follows. Section 2 presents related work. In the Sect. 3 we discuss the dataset used in this study, while in Sect. 4 we present the model training approach. In Sect. 5, we evaluate our approach, and in Sect. 6 we draw conclusions and outline future directions.

2 Related Work

In this section, we describe works from three different perspectives, namely (i) classification in crowdsourced data, (ii) classification in the noisy labels and (iii) payment classifications, at the intersection of which this work lies.

Classification from Crowdsourced Data. Various classification algorithms have been proposed for crowdsourced data [2] in applications such as twitter data for the traffic congestions [7], eateries [13] and medical data [4,12]. In particular, in the medical domain crowdsourced approaches have been used for validating machine-learning classifications [4,12]. Readers can refer to [8] for a comparative study of classification algorithms for crowdsourced data.

Noisy Labels. Noisy label problem has recently attracted a lot of attention from researchers [9,10,16]. In a theoretical study performed using synthetic dataset [10], authors presented a probability based solution to overcome noisy data problem. In another work [9], a framework based on distillation techniques has been presented. To handle the missing labels, a mixed graph framework is presented for multi-label classification in [16]. Most of these techniques have been applied and tested using image based datasets.

Payment Classification. Recently, there has been research related to the comparison of various classification algorithms such as SVM, neural networks, logistic regression for automatically classifying banking transactions [1,5,6,14]. Whereas the amount of the data being used for evaluation is not mentioned in [1,14] however, in comparison, the dataset used in the present study is much larger than [6]. In addition, these datasets did not suffer from the noisy data problem unlike that of ours.

Other related work includes existing approaches to use rule-based approaches for classification in Big Data settings, such as [15], which reports on the development of a system for classifying product items into product types at Wallmart-Labs. The authors note that in real-world classification problems, it is necessary to combine rule-based classification (handcrafted rules) with machine learning so as to maintain high precision (and improve recall) as the system evolves over time. The case study we report in this paper follows a similar approach, with the additional complexity that it relies on labels crowdsourced from customers, whereas the system in [15] relies on labels coming from crowdsourcing marketplaces, where workers can be prescribed with specific instructions on how to perform their manual classification task.

3   Datasets

This section describes the datasets of payments, payment classification rules, and manually assigned labels used for automated payment classification.

3.1   Payments Datasets

This dataset contains anonymized customers' transactions collected by the financial institution over the period of 10.5 months. The transactions are from three different Northern-European countries. For anonymity, we call the three countries as C1, C2, and C3. The dataset has two types of transactions. The first type which we call *account payments*, consists of transactions made via wire transfer, that is, transactions from one bank account to another. The second type, which we term as *card payments*, contains transactions between a bank customer and a business entity through the use of payment cards. Both of these payment types transactions can further be categorised into two dimensions. The first dimension consists of incoming and outgoing payments. The second dimension describes the type of counterparty, that is the party dealing with the customer of the financial institution. Table 1 provides the exact number of transactions in each of the cases in our dataset.

Account Payments. The *account payments* (AP) dataset describes transactions made between accounts, that is, wire transfers. It can be differentiated based on the type of the counterparty. The AP includes (i) person-to-person transactions within the financial institution (AP-P2P), (ii) person-to-business transactions within the financial institution (AP-P2B), (iii) person-to-financial institution transactions (AP-P2F), and (iv) transactions outside the financial institution (AP-P2O), for which the financial institution does not have the information about one of the transacting parties. Table 1, columns P2P, P2B, P2F, P2O provide information about the number of transactions in each of the above cases. The nomenclature is based on the state of outgoing payments, but incoming payments are also present in each category. In P2P they are duplicates of the corresponding outgoing payments, and in P2B and P2F they represent cases such as salary payments, refunds and other forms of income.

Table 1. Dataset description (in millions)

Dataset	Country	Total Transactions			P2P			P2B			P2F			P2O		
Direction		I	O	Tot.	I	O	Tot.	I	O	Tot.	I	O	Tot.	I	O	Tot.
AP	C1	27.2	92.4	119.6	8.4	8.3	16.7	11.4	37.0	48.4	1.6	9.9	11.5	5.8	37.2	43.0
	C2	27.8	83.1	110.9	8.4	8.3	16.7	7.1	30.3	37.4	2.6	9.3	11.9	9.7	35.2	44.9
	C3	29.9	95.6	125.5	5.4	5.3	10.7	17.0	31.9	48.9	1.6	12.6	14.2	5.9	45.8	51.7
	Total	84.9	271.1	356.0	22.2	21.9	44.1	35.5	99.2	134.7	5.8	31.7	37.5	21.4	118.2	139.6
Dataset	Country	Total			-			CPPA			-			CPNA		
CP	C1	0.2	167.9	168.1				0.001	97.0	97.0				0.2	70.9	71.1
	C2	0.3	124.3	124.6				0.0005	35.1	35.1				0.3	89.2	89.5
	C3	0.4	116.0	116.3				0.1	46.9	47.0				0.3	69.1	69.4
	Total	0.9	408.2	409.1				0.1	179.0	179.1				0.8	229.2	230.0

Card Payments. Card payments (CP) represent the transactions made through a payment card (debit or credit). Based on the merchant that processes a transaction, we differentiate the *card payments* (CP) dataset into (i) card payments to merchants who have signed cards processing agreement (CPPA) with the financial institution with which we partnered for this study and (ii) card payments to the merchants that do not have the agreement with the financial institution of our study (CPNA)[1]. The internal information structure of the financial institution has a greater level of sophistication when it comes to transactions related to CPPA, which is the basis for our differentiation - as an example we are using CPPA transactions for augmenting our understanding about the focal businesses, when analyzing account payments. Like AP, the CP dataset also contains both incoming and outgoing payments.

3.2 User-Independent Rules

The pre-existing rule-based approach used in the financial planning tool of the financial institution is based on an ordered set of so-called user-independent rules. Each rule assigns a given label to a transaction if it fulfills certain conditions defined on the transaction's fields (e.g. account number of beneficiary, payment comment, etc.). Table 2 lists the user-independent rule types for each payment dataset in the order of priority, and the acronyms used to refer to them.

---

[1] AP-P2O contains transactions both to people and businesses outside but CPNA contains transactions only to businesses.

Table 2. Types of user-independent rules

Type	Dataset	Column
A	AP	Account number
C	AP, CP	Payment comment
R	AP, CP	Payment comment (regex)
I	AP	Internal type code associated
M	CP	Merchant Category Classification (MCC) code mapping

It is worth mentioning that the rule-based approach has a higher accuracy measure of the CP dataset compared to the AP dataset because of the external Merchant Category Classification (MCC) code field associated with the transactions. These codes categorize the payment under a different categorical hierarchy[2]. However, the rule-based mapping from the MCC to the two-level categorical hierarchy used in the financial institution leads to inherent mapping problems, as two different points of view on the consumption are considered. Additionally, MCC-based mappings introduce the problem of products heterogeneity, as a single card payment processing agreement only covers one MCC code, whereas multiple types of products are sold thereby.

3.3 User-Defined Rules and Manually Labeled Transactions

The reported payment classification case study had a scope limited to classifying consumer-to-business transactions, since these are most relevant when determining expenditure patterns. Given this scope, the dataset of transactions we took as input excluded the following categories:

1. All incoming transactions (categorised as *income*)
2. P2P transactions (categorised as *private person payments*)
3. P2F transactions (categorisation already exists inside the financial institution in another context)
4. P2O transactions in AP (we have no way to separate person-to-person transactions)

In other words, the study reported here is limited to classifying outgoing P2B transactions in AP and outgoing CPPA and CPNA transactions in CP.

Originally, in our dataset there were 266 K manually labeled transaction records in AP and 71 K in CP. However, after limiting our scope to exclude the transaction categories mentioned above, the filtered dataset has only 50 K manual labels in the AP dataset and 40 K for the CP dataset. Figure 1 provides

---

[2] The description of the MCC hierarchy is available at https://usa.visa.com/dam/VCOM/download/merchants/visa-merchant-data-standards-manual.pdf.

the initial label distribution for the AP (Fig. 1(a)) and CP (Fig. 1(b)) datasets (refer to Table 5 for the acronyms being used in the Fig. 1.). It can be inferred that the customers tend to use wire transactions for *savings* and leisure & travel payment categories, while payment cards are most often used for the *food*.

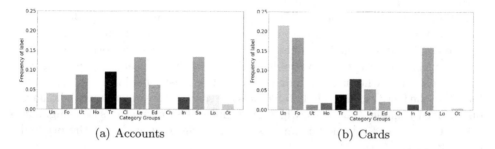

(a) Accounts   (b) Cards

Fig. 1. Label distribution of crowdsourced data

In addition to the manually labeled payments, we took as input 510 K user-defined rules created by 50 K customers. These rules work over the beneficiary field (account number of beneficiary) and/or over the payment comment. A typical user-defined rule might state example that payments made to a given company, and containing the keyword "catering" should be classified as *food*.

We applied these 510 K user-defined rules to the AP and CP dataset as an additional source of labels (to complement the user-independent rules and the manually assigned labels). We note that the user-defined rules have higher priority than the user-independent rules, meaning that if a given payment transaction matched both a user-defined rule (defined by the user who performed that transactions) as well as a user-independent rule, then the label given by the user-defined rule takes precedence (overrides) the label given by the user-independent rule. Similarly, the manually assigned labels have higher priority than the user-defined rules.

4   Model Training

We approach the problem of payment classification as a multiclass classification task, where each transaction has to be labeled with one out of 66 possible labels. For both AP and CP we exploit the following features: (1) identifier of the party, (2) transaction sum amount (log-transformed and normalized), (3) country, (4) id of counterparty bank, (5) vectorized payment comment text, (6) vectorized counterparty name text. Additionally, for AP dataset we use two more features (1) internal codes determining some transaction types and (2) labels transferred from card payments for this party, and in the CP dataset an additional feature of code is used.

If we rely only on the manually assigned labels as true labels for the purpose of training the classifier then, two problems arise which make these labels insufficient. Firstly, the number of manually assigned labels (50 K) is too small (by three orders of magnitude) compared to the size of the total dataset. Secondly, the set of manually assigned labels is non-representative by definition (not all transactions are labeled, only ones where customers are unsatisfied with automatic labeling). To prevent these issues from affecting our model's performance, we **enrich** the dataset used for training the model by adding transactions where we are confident that the labels being assigned by the rules are correct. In order to select these transactions, we limit ourselves to the transactions that belong to the customers who use the online system. The reason behind this decision is based on the fact that the rule-based labels are seen by those customers who have opted not to change the labels, which guarantees their correctness. We augment the dataset with 3 additional samples of size equal to the size of the original dataset, which consist of:

1. transactions with labels produced by user-independent rules.
2. transactions with labels produced by user-defined rules;
3. transactions without labels.

We trained the classifier over a dataset consisting of equal shares of labels from each of these sources. Since the smallest source is the first one (manually assigned labels), we took all transactions from this source (50 K for AP, 40 K for CP) and we randomly extracted equally sized samples from the other three sources.

We used the XGBoost classifier for training the model. The selection of this particular classifier has been motivated by its performance in previous evaluations such as [11], where it outperformed other classifiers such as random forest [3]. Having trained a classifier from the above combination of labeled samples, we combine it with the pre-existing rule-based classification system as follows. If the XGBoost classifier manages to assign a non-null label to a given transaction (in the testing set), we keep this label. If it assigns a null label to a transaction, but there exists a user-independent rule that assigns a non-null label, we use the label assigned by the user-independent rule. If neither the XGBoost classifier nor the user-defined labels can classify the transaction, we leave it with a null label. We call the resulting combined classifier the *hybrid classifier*.

5   Evaluation Results

This section describes the results of our proposed classifier compared to the existing rule-based system. We access the quality of our classier in terms of three performance measures, namely (1) coverage, (2) AUC score and, (3) overriding score. In the following three subsections, we first define these measures before discussing the evaluation results for each of them.

5.1   Coverage

We measure the coverage in order to understand to what extent our proposed model covers the set of whole transactions compared to the baseline model. We define coverage as the percentage of transactions to which a model (rule-based and hybrid) can assign a known label and is formally defined as $Cov = \frac{N_+}{N}$, where N_+ is the number of non-zero labels and N is the total size of the dataset. For the hybrid model, in case the ML component is not able to assign a label then, a rule-based label is taken into consideration.

Table 3. Coverage scores of the classifier per group

Dataset	Coverage for rule-based model	Coverage for hybrid model
AP	76.4%	87.4%
CP	99.2%	99.8%

We calculate coverage on a random sample of 200,000 transactions from the whole dataset. Table 3 provides the information about the coverage being observed in both AP and CP datasets for the existing approach being employed by the financial institution (Column 1) as well as for our proposed hybrid approach (Column 2). We can see the improvement in all cases by using our proposed classifier. Particularly, in the case of AP dataset, the model has achieved an improvement of 11%, which is a significant improvement.

5.2   AUC Score

In addition to coverage, we also measure accuracy to evaluate how well the labels can be predicted using our hybrid model compared to the true labels. Because of the presence of class imbalance (some classes are rare), we measure accuracy by the means of AUC score.

In line with standard practice, we used 5-fold cross-validation to calculate the AUC scores. In each iteration, we train the model on 80% of the samples in the dataset and then we validate our model on the remaining 20%. All the reported AUC values are averaged over 5 folds. Also, we applied hyper-parameter optimization using grid search. Specifically, we varied two key hyper-parameters of XGBoost: the learning rate from 0.05 to 0.2 in steps of 0.05 and the maximum tree depth from 4 to 16 in steps of four. We selected the combination of hyper-parameters that led to the highest AUC averaged over 5 folds.

AUC is normally defined in the context of binary classification, but in our case we are dealing with a multi-class classification problem. Accordingly, we calculate the AUC for each class separately, and then we aggregate the class-specific AUCs into a total AUC measure. Specifically, we define total AUC as $AUC = \sum_{i=1}^{L} p_i \frac{N^i}{N_+} AUC_b^i$, where L is the number of labels (65 without "unknown"), N^i

is the number of i_{th} labels in the training set, N^+ is the number of labels (without "unknown") in the training set. AUC_b denotes a binary AUC function for i_{th} label and is defined as $AUC^b = \int_{\infty}^{-\infty} TPR^i(T)\left(-FPR^{i'}(T)\right) dT = P(X_1^i >$ $X_0^i)$, where TPR is true positive rate, FPR is false positive rate, X_1, X_0 are the events that correspond to i_{th} label having true and false labels.

Table 4 presents the total AUC scores for AP and CP datasets for two cases: (1) without enrichment, i.e., when we only use manually labeled transactions and (2) with enrichment, i.e., by also including a sample of the rule-based labels in our training set.

Table 4. AUC scores with and without enrichment

AUC score	AP	CP
Without enrichment	0.81	0.80
With enrichment	0.92	0.98

As expected, the AUC on the dataset without enrichment is lower than the AUC on the dataset with enrichment. This happens because in the dataset without enrichment there are less regularities – none of the labels comes from used-defined rules, but only from manually assigned labels, which in addition are sometimes inconsistent with others. In contrast, the enriched dataset has more regularity because part of the dataset is labeled using rules. Meanwhile, the lower score for CP in the non-enriched dataset is justified by the fact that the manual relabeling in CP occurs only when rule-based labels are wrong as compared to AP, when a manual label can also be assigned to transactions with no rule-based labels which are more populous in AP.

Table 5. AUC scores over the individual category groups

Code	Category group name	Without enrichment		With enrichment	
		AP	CP	AP	CP
Fo	Food	0.88	0.82	0.95	0.99
Ut	Utility, telecommunication	0.88	0.71	0.95	0.99
Ho	Household	0.77	0.75	0.90	1.00
Tr	Transportation	0.90	0.91	0.96	0.99
Cl	Clothing	0.83	0.85	0.93	0.99
Le	Leisure, travelling, spare time	0.66	0.78	0.85	0.97
Ed	Education, healthcare, beauty	0.78	0.85	0.91	1.00
Ch	Children	0.76	0.84	0.90	0.99
In	Insurance	0.98	0.76	0.99	0.96
Sa	Savings and investments	0.85	0.83	0.94	0.86
Lo	Loans and financial services	0.92	0.82	0.97	1.00
Ot	Other	0.67	0.73	0.83	0.97

Table 5 provides information about the averaged AUC score for each category. We observe that for categories like Insurance with a small number of merchants and regular payments the AUC over manually labeled dataset is high.

5.3 Overriding Score

We also measure the difference between hybrid model and rule-based label's output for the same set of transactions after the dataset enrichment. To do that we define an overriding measure, that showcases the changes in the hybrid model's prediction compared to the rule-based model's prediction for the same transaction. We define overriding measure as $Ov = \frac{N_{dif}}{N_+}$, where N_{dif} denotes the number of cases where the hybrid model predicts a different label compared to the rule-based model and, N^+ represents the number of known labels.

This overriding measure essentially captures the refinement that our proposed model has introduced over rule-based approach. We can consider this score as a measure of refinement due to the fact that the ML model's output learns exceptions to the rules from manually labeled dataset, and thus, enhancing the predictive capability of the hybrid system over rule-based approach. This is based on the fact that manual labels represents the ground truth as they have explicitly overridden the rule based output. The instances where the ML model outputs no label are filled assigned using the rule-based labels, thus, they count for N^+ and not in N_{dif}. It is computed on the enriched dataset used for training. We achieve an overriding score of 26.4% on the AP dataset and 11.9% on the CP dataset, which indicates a high level of improvement over the existing rules.

5.4 External Validation

To complement the validation reported above, we conducted a small-scale validation with the help of six employees of the financial institution. The employees classified their own personal transactions during a one-month period (subsequent to the period covered by the dataset used for training the model). The resulting dataset consists of 109 labeled payments.

To measure model accuracy on this dataset, we use the *hit ratio measure*, i.e. the percentage of transactions to which a model (rule-based and hybrid) assigns a correct most likely label. It is formally defined as $Acc = \frac{TP+TN}{N}$, where N is the total size of the dataset, TP is the number of true positive labels and TN is the number of true negative labels. The rule-based classifier achieves a hit ratio of 39%, while the hybrid classifier scores 56%, which shows a major improvement. We acknowledge that the small size of the dataset is a threat to validity. On the other hand, this external dataset is free from the potential biasing and reliability concerns related to the assignment of labels.

6 Conclusion

In this paper, we presented a hybrid approach, which exploits rule-based system as well as the crowdsourced data provided by customers, to automatically classify C2B payments. We evaluated our model on a real but anonymised dataset consisting of customers' transactions across three Northern-European countries and consists of two transactions types: (1) wire transfers (AP) and (2) card payments (CP). On the AP dataset, our model achieves an AUC of 0.92 and achieves an improvement of 11% in coverage, and provides overriding of 26.4%, compared to the existing rule-based approach. On the CP dataset, our model achieves an AUC of 0.98 and achieves a slight improvement of 0.6% in coverage, as well as providing overriding of 11.9%, compared to the existing rule-based approach.

We have multiple future directions for this work. We would like to investigate the problem using larger dataset as well as including user created text based rules as an additional feature in our model, which will allow us to measure improvements more clearly. We also plan to perform external validation using a larger real labeled dataset in order to check the accuracy of our model.

Acknowledgments. This work is supported by an unnamed financial institution and the European Regional Development Funds. We thank the employees of the financial institution who volunteered to create the external validation dataset.

References

1. Bengtsson, H., Jansson, J.: Using classification algorithms for smart suggestions in accounting systems. Master thesis, Chalmers University of Technology Gothenburg, Sweden (2015)
2. Bonald, T., Combes, R.: A streaming algorithm for crowdsourced data classification. CoRR, abs/1602.07107 (2016)
3. Chen, T., Guestrin, C.: XGBoost: a scalable tree boosting system. In: Proceedings of the 22nd ACM SIGKDD, pp. 785–794 (2016)
4. Duda, M., Haber, N., Daniels, J., et al.: Crowdsourced validation of a machine-learning classification system for autism and ADHD. Transl. Psychiatry **7**(5), e1133 (2017)
5. Etaiwi, W., Biltawi, M., Naymat, G.: Evaluation of classification algorithms for banking customer's behavior under apache spark data processing system. Procedia Comput. Sci. **113**, 559–564 (2017)
6. Folkestad, O.E.E., Vollset, E.E.N.: Automatic classification of bank transactions. Master thesis, Norwegian University of Science and Technology, Trondheim (2017)
7. Kurniawan, D.A., Wibirama, S., Setiawan, N.A.: Real-time traffic classification with twitter data mining. In: 2016 8th International Conference on Information Technology and Electrical Engineering (ICITEE), pp. 1–5, October 2016
8. Lesiv, M., Moltchanova, E., Schepaschenko, D., et al.: Comparison of data fusion methods using crowdsourced data in creating a hybrid forest cover map. Remote Sens. **8**(3), 261 (2016)
9. Li, Y., Yang, J., Song, Y., et al.: Learning from noisy labels with distillation. CoRR, abs/1703.02391 (2017)
10. Natarajan, N., Dhillon, I.S., Ravikumar, P.K., Tewari, A.: Learning with noisy labels. In: Burges, C.J.C., Bottou, L., Welling, M., Ghahramani, Z., Weinberger, K.Q. (eds.) Advances in Neural Information Processing Systems, vol. 26, pp. 1196–1204. Curran Associates Inc. (2013)

11. Nielsen, D.: Tree boosting with XGBoost. Master's thesis, NTNU, Trondheim, Norway (2016)
12. Noren, D.P., Long, B.L., Norel, R., et al.: A crowdsourcing approach to developing and assessing prediction algorithms for AML prognosis. PLoS Comput. Biol. **12**(6), e1004890 (2016)
13. Salehian, H., Howell, P., Lee, C.: Matching restaurant menus to crowdsourced food data: a scalable machine learning approach. In: Proceedings of the 23rd ACM SIGKDD, pp. 2001–2009 (2017)
14. Skeppe, L.B.: Classify Swedish bank transactions with early and late fusion techniques. Master thesis, KTH, Sweden (2014)
15. Suganthan, P., Sun, C., Gayatri, K.K., et al.: Why big data industrial systems need rules and what we can do about it. In: Proceedings of ACM SIGMOD, pp. 265–276 (2015)
16. Wu, B., Lyu, S., Ghanem, B.: ML-MG: multi-label learning with missing labels using a mixed graph. In: IEEE ICCV, pp. 4157–4165, December 2015

BIOC – Blockchains
for Inter-Organizational Collaboration

First Workshop on Blockchains
for Inter-Organizational Collaboration
(BIOC 2018)

The BIOC workshop addresses recent research efforts in the field of blockchain technology use for cross-organizational collaboration. The workshop focuses on the application of information and communication technology in order to enable organizational and governmental service provisions. The resulting technology-mediated processes are changing the delivery of private and public services as well as the broader interactions between citizens, governments, and organizations. More and more countries are considering e-governance solutions as a tool to improve the efficiency and transparency of their services. However, there is a gap in understanding the support of trust and reputation via blockchain solutions that allow for immutable event traceability.

The First Workshop on Blockchains for Inter-Organizational Collaboration (BIOC)[1], which was held in conjunction with the CAiSE 2018 conference in Tallinn, Estonia, focused on exploring systematic approaches for developing and interrelating blockchain-technology-supported services as well as increasing issues concerning blockchain-technology-enabled security and privacy of personal data use. In addition, technological advances in the field of big data analysis, blockchains for distributed application deployment, smart contracts, the Internet of Things, agent technologies, etc., offer new research directions in the blockchain-technology space for further improvements of existing solutions. More specifically, the accepted papers presented the following contributions.

The paper "Combining Artifact-Driven Monitoring with Blockchain: Analysis and Solutions"' by Giovanni Meroni and Pierluigi Plebani presents a pilot application that enables embargo documents to be published and distributed within a document management system with the guarantee of confidentiality, availability, and reliability of all information registered on the blockchain. The blockchain also facilitates the process of monitoring and controlling changes in the documents.

The paper "Toward Collaborative and Reproducible Scientific Experiments on Blockchain" by Dimka Karastoyanova and Ludwig Stage discusses adaptable scientific choreographies with blockchains facilitating decentralized choreographies in a position paper. To enable trust among collaborating scientists, the authors identify potential approaches for combining adaptable scientific choreographies with blockchain platforms, discuss their advantages, and point out future research questions.

The paper "Towards a Design Space for Blockchain-Based System Reengineering" by Marco Comuzzi, Erdenekhuu Unurjargal, and Chiehyeon Lim defines the design space, i.e., the set of options available to designers when applying blockchain to reengineer an existing system. The authors use a practice-driven bottom–up approach

---

[1] https://www.ttu.ee/projects/lss/events-23/bioc18/.

by analyzing existing blockchain use cases and show hands-on experience in real-world design case studies.

The paper "Ensuring Resource Trust and Integrity in Web Browsers Using Blockchain Technology" by Clemens H. Cap and Benjamin Leiding shows that current Web technology allows for the use of cryptographic primitives as part of server-provided Javascript that pose security problems with Web-based services. The authors present a solution based on human code reviewing and on CVE (common vulnerabilities and exposures) databases. Thus, existing code audits and known vulnerabilities are tied Javascript files with a tamper-proof blockchain approach and are signaled to the user by a browser extension.

Finally, the paper "Document Management System Based on a Private Blockchain for the Support of the Judicial Embargoes Process in Colombia" by Julian Solarte-Rivera, Andrés Vidal-Zemanate, Carlos Cobos, José Alejandro Chamorro-Lopez, and Tomas Velasco presents a pilot application that enables embargo documents to be published and distributed within a document management system. The application guarantees the confidentiality, availability, and reliability of all information registered in a blockchain. The latter facilitate not only the availability and distribution of the documents, but also the process of monitoring and controlling changes in that each participant in the network always obtains an accepted version of revised documents.

We sincerely thank the Program Committee members of the BIOC 2018 workshop for their time and support throughout the reviewing process.

April 2018   Alex Norta
                                                            Dirk Draheim

Workshop Organization

Organizing Committee

Alex Norta   Tallinn University of Technology, Estonia
Dirk Draheim   Tallinn University of Technology, Estonia

Program Committee

Benjamin Leiding	University of Göttingen, Germany
Dirk Draheim	Tallinn University of Technology, Estonia
Alex Norta	Tallinn University of Technology, Estonia
Han van der Aa	Vrije Universiteit Amsterdam, The Netherlands
Mark Staples	CSIRO, Australia
Stefan Schulte	TU Wien, Austria
Claudio Di Ciccio	Vienna University of Economics and Business, Austria
Schahram Dustdar	TU Wien, Austria
Tijs Slaats	University of Copenhagen, Denmark
Xiwei Xu	UNSW Sydney, Australia
Cristina Cabanillas	Vienna University of Economics and Business, Austria
Jan Mendling	Vienna University of Economics and Business, Austria
Barbara Weber	Technical University of Denmark, Denmark
Søren Debois	IT University of Copenhagen, Denmark
Matthias Weidlich	Humboldt University of Berlin, Germany
Guido Governatori	CSIRO, Australia
Mathias Weske	Hasso Plattner Institute, University of Potsdam, Germany
Manfred Reichert	University of Ulm, Germany
Florian Daniel	Politecnico di Milano, Italy
Marcello La Rosa	Queensland University of Technology, Australia
Stefanie Rinderle-Ma	University of Vienna, Austria

Combining Artifact-Driven Monitoring with Blockchain: Analysis and Solutions

Giovanni Meroni[(✉)] and Pierluigi Plebani

Dipartimento di Elettronica, Informazione e Bioingegneria, Politecnico di Milano,
Piazza Leonardo da Vinci, 32, 20133 Milano, Italy
{giovanni.meroni,pierluigi.plebani}@polimi.it

Abstract. The adoption of blockchain to enable a trusted monitoring of multi-party business processes is recently gaining a lot of attention, as the absence of a central authority increases the efficiency and the effectiveness of the delivery of monitoring data. At the same time, artifact-driven monitoring has been proposed to create a flexible monitoring platform for multi-party business processes involving an exchange of goods (e.g., in the logistics domain), where the information delivery does not require a central authority but it lacks of sufficient level of trust. The goal of this paper is to analyze the dependencies among these two areas of interests, and to propose two possible monitoring platforms that exploit blockchain to achieve a trusted artifact-driven monitoring solution.

Keywords: Artifact-driven monitoring · Trusted process monitoring
Cyber-physical systems

1 Introduction

To promptly satisfy the ever-changing needs of their customers, organizations must become more flexible and open to changes and opportunities. The *servitization* paradigm [8] goes into this direction: instead of owning corporate assets, be them physical goods, human resources, or business activities, an organization establishes contracts with other organizations, named service providers, that, in exchange for a periodic fee, grant the use of such assets together with value-added services (e.g., maintenance).

As a consequence of servitization, many business processes that were internal now cross the boundaries of single organizations, thus becoming *multi-party*. This also affects the goods that participate in the process, that could be now manipulated and possibly altered by multiple organizations when the process is executed. Additionally, the identity of the service providers involved in these multi-party processes is subject to frequent changes. In fact, short-term contracts with service providers that best fit the needs of a specific process instance are more and more preferred to long-term contracts that span among all the instances of a given business process.

© Springer International Publishing AG, part of Springer Nature 2018
R. Matulevičius and R. Dijkman (Eds.): CAiSE 2018 Workshops, LNBIP 316, pp. 103–114, 2018.
https://doi.org/10.1007/978-3-319-92898-2_8

Despite the previously mentioned advantages, servitization also requires organizations involved in a multi-party process to *trust* each other: i.e., to ensure that the portion of the process assigned to a party is executed as agreed with the other parties and, in case of problems, deviations are correctly reported to properly identify the cause of failures.

In our previous research work, we proposed a novel approach to monitor multi-party business processes, named artifact-driven monitoring [5]. By exploiting the Internet of Things (IoT) paradigm, artifact-driven monitoring makes physical objects *smart*, that is, makes them aware of their own conditions. Based on the conditions of these smart objects, it is then possible to identify when activities are executed and if they are executed as expected, promptly alerting the organizations when a violation occurs. Since smart objects can monitor activities regardless of the organization responsible for their execution, they can take both the orchestration (i.e., the execution of process portions internal to an organization) and the choreography (i.e., the coordination among different organizations) into account.

Although artifact-driven monitoring solves the problem of keeping track of the execution of processes that span across multiple organizations, it does not fully solve the problem of trust among organizations. In particular, the owners of the smart objects are responsible for properly configuring them by specifying which process has to be monitored, based on which physical conditions are activities identified as being executed, and with which other smart objects should monitoring information be exchanged. Therefore, organizations could intentionally misconfigure smart objects in order not to detect violations caused by them.

To guarantee the required level of trust when implementing an artifact-driven monitoring solution, this paper proposes to adopt blockchain technology that, by definition, provides a trusted environment that perfectly suits the needs of multi-party business process monitoring. Moreover, this paper introduces and compares two possible artifact-driven monitoring platforms relying on a permissioned blockchain to propagate monitoring information.

The remainder of this paper is structured as follows: Sect. 2 introduces a motivating example justifying the need for artifact-driven monitoring, which is briefly described in Sect. 3. In Sect. 4 the architecture of the two possible blockchain-based solutions are presented and compared. Finally, Sect. 5 surveys related work and Sect. 6 draws the conclusions of this work and outlines future research plans.

2   Motivating Example

To better understand the importance of a reliable and trusted process monitoring solution, a case study concerning the shipment of dangerous goods is adopted. The actors are a manufacturer M, a customer C, and a truck shipper S that is involved when potentially explosive chemicals must be delivered from M to C.

The delivery process is organized according to the Business Process Model and Notation (BPMN) model shown in Fig. 1. To avoid possible accidents during the execution of this process, the following countermeasures must be put in place. Firstly, if a leakage of the chemical is detected when M is filling a tank, no matter how modest, M must empty and replace the tank. Secondly, if the tank gets overheated while it is being shipped, S must immediately abort the shipment, notify the authorities about this potential hazardous occurrence, and wait for them to intervene.

Like in every multi-party business process, also in this case each organization is in charge only of the activities included in their pools, thus nobody has full control on the whole process. Consequently, being able to identify when activities are performed and if they are performed as expected is required to determine who caused the process not to be executed as expected. This becomes particularly important if an accident occurs, as depending on which portion of the process was not executed as expected, the organization to blame for the accident varies. For example, if the chemical explodes while the tank is being unloaded from the truck, it could be determined by a multitude of causes. Firstly, the tank may have been overheated and S decided to ignore that event and go on shipping it. Alternatively, the tank may have had a leakage and have not been replaced by M.

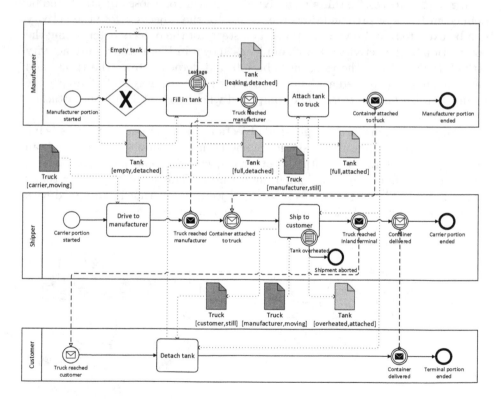

Fig. 1. BPMN diagram of the motivating example.

3   Artifact-Driven Monitoring

Nowadays, several organizations rely on a Business Process Management System (BPMS) to manage their processes, as it enacts the execution of business activities, monitors the process, and identifies potential issues. When a process includes human-based activities, operators are in charge of explicitly notifying the activation and completion of these activities. This way, the BPMS has knowledge about if, and when, those activities are performed. Consequently, the organizations have to trust the operators to provide timely notifications that reflect the actual execution of the process. In addition, when a multi-party process takes place, organizations are required to federate their own BPMS to be able to monitor the whole process. Alternatively, a centralized BPMS must be put in place, and fed with notifications sent by all the participating organizations. In both cases, relevant system integration efforts must be undertaken, and each organization have to trust the other ones.

To solve these issues, artifact-driven monitoring [5] relies on a completely different approach. Instead of requiring organizations to actively monitor a process, it moves the monitoring tasks onto the physical objects (i.e., artifacts) participating in the process. To this aim, activities operating on those objects should be defined in terms of pre-conditions (i.e., status of the objects before the activity can be executed) and post-conditions (i.e., status of the objects determining the completion of the activity). For example, as shown in Fig. 1, to execute activity *Attach tank to truck* the tank must be full and detached from the truck, and the truck must be located at the manufacturer plant and stay still. Similarly, we assume *Attach tank to truck* to be completed when the tank is full and attached to the truck.

Therefore, as long as those physical objects *(i)* are aware of the process being performed, *(ii)* can autonomously determine their own conditions, and *(iii)* can exchange this information with the other objects, they can passively monitor the process without requiring human intervention. This is made possible thank to the IoT paradigm, that makes physical objects smart, that is, equipped with sensors, a computing device, and a communication interface.

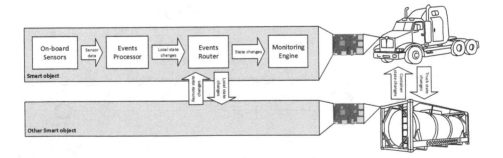

Fig. 2. Architecture of an artifact-driven monitoring platform.

Figure 2 shows the current architecture of an artifact-driven monitoring platform [5]. Firstly, the physical characteristics of a smart object are captured by *On-board Sensors*. Then, sensor data are processed and discretized by the *Events Processor* module, in order to assign to the smart object a single state from a finite set, representing its current conditions according to the possible states defined in the BPMN process model (e.g., empty, leaking). Whenever a change in the state of the smart object is detected by the *Events Processor*, this information is forwarded by the *Events Router* to the other smart objects participating in the process. As soon as the *Events Router* receives a change in the state of a smart object, either local or remote, it forwards it to the *Monitoring Engine* module, that uses this information to actively monitor the process. To do so, the *Monitoring Engine* relies on an Extended-GSM (E-GSM) model[1], which contains a formal representation of the process agreed among the organizations, enriched with information on the physical objects and states required by and altered by the business activities composing the process. This way, whenever the *Monitoring Engine* determines that an activity is being carried out or that the process is not executed as agreed, it can promptly inform the organizations participating in the process.

4   Approach

Artifact-driven monitoring allows to continuously and autonomously monitor multi-party business processes. However, it does not solve the problem of trust among organizations. In fact, organizations are in charge of configuring their own smart objects with the process to monitor, and deliberately erroneous configuration could be not detected.

For example, still referring to the accident described in Sect. 2, if the tank detects that it was overheated while being shipped, S could argue that M (the owner of the tank) incorrectly implemented the monitoring platform, or worse, it intentionally omitted, from the agreed process model, to monitor the portion responsible for detecting a leakage. In this case, an independent authority would typically have to investigate on the actual cause of such an accident, and on the correct implementation and configuration of the monitoring platform. However, this task could be really difficult. For example, the explosion may have completely destroyed the smart objects, so the authority could no longer rely on monitoring information to determine the real cause.

To solve these issues, we propose to combine artifact-driven process monitoring with blockchain. A blockchain provides a shared immutable ledger, which guarantees that each entry *(i)* has to be validated before being stored, *(ii)* is persistently stored, *(iii)* is replicated along multiple nodes, and *(iv)* is immutable. This way, by storing monitoring information on a blockchain, such an information can be accessed and validated by all the participants of a process both during its execution and after it is completed. In addition, independent auditors

---

[1] We refer you to [5] to understand the advantages of E-GSM over other process modeling languages when doing runtime process monitoring.

can also access and validate monitoring information even if the smart objects are no longer accessible, as the needed information has been distributed to the several ledgers composing the blockchain environment.

Sections 4.1 and 4.2 present two possible architectures of an artifact-driven monitoring solution integrating a blockchain, discussing the advantages and disadvantages of each solution.

Regardless of the specific approach, the adoption of a blockchain protocol to support the artifact-driven monitoring approach has the advantage of providing a native, trusted, and reliable environment for sharing monitoring information among the parties. Moreover, we propose the adoption of a permissioned blockchain [12] instead of a public one, such as Ethereum[2]. A public blockchain allows anyone to read and write entries to it, requiring the participants to manually manage the encryption of entries in case they want them to be kept confidential. Instead, a permissioned blockchain natively supports access control mechanisms to ensure that only authorized participant can read and/or write blocks on the blockchain. This way, only organizations and smart objects participating in the process can be granted write access. Also, read access can be restricted in case the participants of a multi-party process do not want information on the execution of the process be available to anyone. Moreover, adopting Ethereum as blockchain protocol gives also the possibility to define the so-called *smart contracts*, that can be defined as functions, coded using languages like Solidity[3], whose execution determines either the acceptance or the refusal of a block to be written in the chain. Since the blocks to be written concerns the status of the smart objects, we assume that smart contracts could be inferred from the initial process model. In fact, once a process instance is created (and the corresponding monitoring infrastructure properly configured), the process specification contains all the information needed to determine under which conditions smart objects change their state.

As one of the main drawbacks of blockchain concerns the performances, especially in terms of throughput and latency, both architectures adopts multiple chains to reduce space, bandwidth and computational requirements [11]. In order to work, a blockchain requires all the participants to keep track of all the entries that were written to it. Therefore, if a single chain is used by all the organizations implementing our artifact-driven monitoring solution, each smart object and organization would have to also store entries that are completely unrelated to the process they are currently monitoring. This causes the hardware and network requirements to grow proportionally to the number of entries that are written to the blockchain, and it is one of the issues that limit the scalability of a blockchain. To mitigate this issue, multiple chains based on the same blockchain protocol can be deployed. In particular, before a new execution of a process takes place, we propose to deploy a new chain and instruct the smart objects and organizations participating in that specific execution to use that chain. By doing so, each chain contains only entries that are specific to the current process

---

[2] See https://www.ethereum.org.
[3] See https://solidity.readthedocs.io/en/develop/.

execution, thus sensibly limiting the hardware and network requirements of the smart objects.

Focusing on the definition of smart contract, we propose to add a block to the chain only when a smart device detects a change in its state, and we envision two alternatives concerning the content of a block. In the first case, the block contains only the new state. Consequently, the smart contract only checks if the smart object adding the block is the one whose state changed (see Sect. 4.1). In the second case, the block contains both the new state and the series of sensor data causing the smart object to detect the change of state. In this case, the smart contract has to encode rules to verify that the change of state is compatible with the sensor data (see Sect. 4.2). As the information to be stored in a block is generated by different elements of the artifact-driven monitoring platform, these two alternatives have an impact on the configuration of the platform.

4.1   State-Oriented Block

A first approach is named state-oriented blockchain, as a new block is added whenever a smart object realizes that its state has changed.

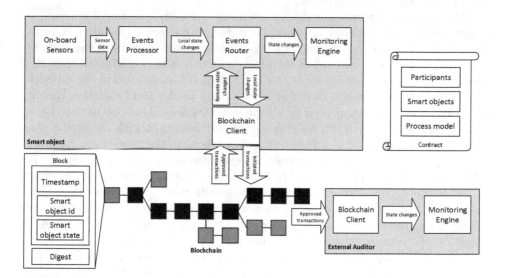

Fig. 3. State-oriented blockchain.

Figure 3 shows the reference architecture, where the blockchain is used to let smart objects exchange information on their current state. Instead of directly communicating with the other smart objects, the *Events Router* module relies on a new module, named *Blockchain Client*. The *Blockchain Client* is responsible for writing a new block whenever the current smart object changes state, and for sending a notification to the *Events Router* whenever a new block is written by the other smart objects.

Before the process starts, the identity of the organizations participating in the process and of the smart objects owned by them is extracted from the E-GSM model and formalized in a smart contract, which is written to the blockchain and approved by all the participants. The E-GSM model is also included in the description of the smart contract, to make all participants, including smart objects and external auditors, aware of the process they have to monitor.

The payload of each block in the blockchain contains a timestamp, the identity of the smart object producing the block, and the current state of the smart object. To ensure that the block was produced by the smart object it refers to, a Public Key Infrastructure (PKI) is put in place. Each smart object owns a private key, which is used to sign the block and kept private, and a public key, which is distributed among all the participants in the process. This way, thank to the PKI and the smart contract, each node approves the block only if *(i)* the signature matches the payload, and *(ii)* the smart object writing the block is actually owned by the participating organizations. Since a permissioned blockchain is adopted and, consequently, the identity of the participants is known, there is no need to put in place computationally expensive consensus algorithms, such as proof of work. Instead, simpler algorithms, such as Practical Byzantine Fault Tolerance (PBFT), are sufficient.

This architecture presents several advantages. Firstly, external auditors can easily monitor the process, either while it is being executed or after it completed. Thank to smart contracts, they can be sure that changes in the state of the smart objects were written to the blockchain only if they originated from the same smart object. In addition, as the E-GSM model is enclosed in the description of the smart contract, they can trust such a model and be certain that it represents the process approved by all the organizations. Then, by instructing a *Monitoring Engine* with the E-GSM model and feeding it with changes in the state of the smart objects extracted from the blocks in the blockchain, auditors can independently verify if the process was executed as agreed. For example, still referring to the example described in Sect. 2, if this architecture is implemented by M, S and C, the authorities can easily identify the organization responsible for the accident, even if the smart objects were destroyed. In fact, authorities can simply query the blockchain to obtain the E-GSM process and all the changes in the state of the smart objects, being sure that this information was not altered once it was written to the blockchain. Then, they can instruct a *Monitoring Engine* with the E-GSM model, and replay the state changes to detect which portion of the process was incorrectly executed.

However, this architecture also presents one limitation. By design, the blockchain does not store information on how to determine from sensor data the state of the smart objects. Consequently, organizations could argue that smart objects incorrectly determined their state, thus providing unreliable monitoring data. For example, when instructing the monitoring platform running on its tanks, M could have intentionally left out information on how to determine when the tank is leaking. Therefore, even if a leakage occurs, the monitoring platform would never be able to detect and write to the blockchain this information.

As a consequence, based only on the information on the blockchain, external authorities would not be able to notice that the process was not executed as expected.

4.2   Sensor-Oriented Block

To address the limitation of the previous approach, a new one, named sensor-oriented blockchain, is introduced. This approach also makes use of smart contracts. However, besides formalizing the organizations participating in the process and the identity of the smart objects, each smart contract also defines the rules to detect from sensor data when the smart objects change state. This makes it possible for all participants to agree on how the state of the smart objects should be detected. For example, to detect when a truck assumes the state *moving*, all participants will require the GPS coordinates of the truck to vary of at least 0.01 degrees per minute.

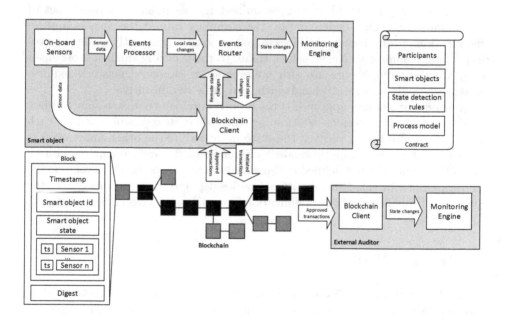

Fig. 4. Sensor-oriented blockchain.

To support this approach, the reference architecture shown in Fig. 4 is proposed. In this case, the *Blockchain Client* also receives data from the *On-board Sensors*, and encloses this information to the blocks written to the blockchain. Like in the previous architecture, a new block is written to the blockchain whenever the smart object assumes a new state. However, besides containing a timestamp, the identity of the smart object producing the block, and the current state of the smart object, each block also contains a list of sensor values, together with a timestamp, that were collected since when the previous state was detected. For example, a block written by the truck when it transitions from *moving* to *still* will contain the state *still*, the date and time when *still* was detected, the identifier of the truck, and all the GPS coordinates that the truck assumed since when the state *moving* was previously detected. Also in this case, the architecture relies on a PKI infrastructure to ensure that the block was produced by the smart object it refers to.

With respect to the previous approach, this one achieves an even greater level of trust. In fact, thank to the smart contract, every participant can autonomously verify if the state detected by a smart object is reflected by the sensor data and, if not, discard the corresponding block. Since the rules to determine this information are defined in the smart contract, and are approved by all organizations before the process takes place, nobody can argue that the process is incorrectly monitored.

However, this approach also presents some issues that are not present in the previous one. Firstly, it makes a much more intensive use of the blockchain. In fact, the size of each block can be quite large, as it also contains a set of sensor data. Therefore, depending on the sampling rate of the sensors and on the duration of the process, the blockchain can grow significantly while the process is being monitored. Nevertheless, thank to the typically small size of sensor data, storage requirements are still quite modest. However, network requirements, especially in terms of bandwidth, can grow significantly.

Another issue of this approach is the higher workload that each smart object must handle. In fact, besides determining the state of its own smart object, each smart object also has to verify if the state indicated by the other smart objects is correct. Thus, the computational requirements of the architecture depend on the total number of rules defined in the smart contract, and on their complexity. To compensate for this issue, additional nodes deputed to the verification of the blocks can be deployed on the organizations' premises, thus freeing smart objects from this task.

5   Related Work

Given the recent affirmation of blockchain in many domains, the Business Process Management (BPM) research community is also investigating the impact of this technology on all the phases of the BPM lifecycle. In [4] an exhaustive analysis of the implications of introducing blockchain in inter-organizational processes are discussed, and a list of seven possible future research directions is identified. Among them, the goal of this paper is mainly "developing a diverse set of execution and monitoring frameworks on blockchain", albeit the proposed solution may also affect other directions. To this aim, particular emphasis is given on a solution that is able to deal with some of the main aspects, namely throughput and size, that could hamper the adoption of blockchain in BPM. In fact, the proposed solution distributes the workload to several chains, resulting in a reduced amount of transactions per single chain, with consequent low hardware and network requirements. In addition, the two alternatives discussed in the paper further decrease the computational effort to be done on the blockchain by moving some of the computation to off-chain, as also suggested in [2].

Focusing on the usage of blockchain to monitor a supply chain, the literature is currently investigating this issue according to different perspectives. For instance, [3] analyses the possible grind between a blockhain infrastructure with the information management infrastructure currently adopted in the shipping domain. Moreover, in [10] a framework for process monitoring based on several private blockchain installations, globally managed by a public blockchain, is presented. In some way, the idea of having several chains to increase the confidentiality of the information among the stakeholders is similar to what it is proposed in this paper. Nevertheless, [10] considers monitoring as a centralized element, while in our approach it is distributed among the smart objects.

An interesting report, [7], proposes two different approaches: the first one relies on a common blockchain to collect all the events coming from the different stakeholders involved in the supply chain, while the second one is based on the usage of smart contracts. In both cases, the approach assumes to start from the complete definition of the choreography to configure the blockchain. As discussed in the paper, this introduces a significant problem related to the encryption of the data stored in the ledgers, as not all the information can be read by all the participants in the blockchain. In our approach, each process execution relies on a specific chain, which is accessible only by the organizations participating in that specific process execution. This solves the problem of the data confidentiality, as the data stored in one of the blockchains should be visible by all the participants. Finally, [6] proposes an interesting solution for run-time verification of business process execution based on Bitcoin, thus, with a public and very specific solution where smart contracts are not allowed.

6   Conclusions and Future Work

This paper presented how artifact-driven monitoring can benefit from blockchain to monitor multi-party processes in a trusted way. Thank to a permissioned blockchain, monitoring information is stored immutably and persistently, allowing external auditors to independently verify if the process was performed as expected, either at runtime or after the process completed.

One of the disadvantages of our approach concerns the initial set-up, as having several blockchains requires the configuration of all of them. To solve this limitation, we plan to adopt the approach proposed in [9] for configuring a blockchain-based solution starting from the choreography model.

Another potential disadvantage of this approach consists in the limited speed of blockchain. In fact, writing, approving, and distributing a new block to all the participants takes seconds for a permissioned blockchain, or even several minutes for a public one. Nevertheless, research efforts to speed up operations on a blockchain are currently being taken by both academics and the industry, so we expect this issue to be eventually solved or scaled back.

Our future research work will consist in implementing a prototype of both architectures, and validating it with real-world processes and sensor data. In addition, we will also consider the introduction of side-chains [1] to allow smart objects to monitor multiple processes at the same time, and to integrate process monitoring with automatic payment and escrow mechanisms. Finally, being the artifact-driven monitoring a nomadic infrastructure, the impact of the lack of connectivity in a blockchain solution will be investigated.

Acknowledgments. This work has been partially funded by the Italian Project ITS Italy 2020 under the Technological National Clusters program.

References

1. Croman, K., et al.: On scaling decentralized blockchains - (A position paper). In: Clark, J., Meiklejohn, S., Ryan, P.Y.A., Wallach, D., Brenner, M., Rohloff, K. (eds.) FC 2016. LNCS, vol. 9604, pp. 106–125. Springer, Heidelberg (2016). https://doi.org/10.1007/978-3-662-53357-4_8
2. Eberhardt, J., Tai, S.: On or off the blockchain? Insights on off-chaining computation and data. In: De Paoli, F., Schulte, S., Broch Johnsen, E. (eds.) ESOCC 2017. LNCS, vol. 10465, pp. 3–15. Springer, Cham (2017). https://doi.org/10.1007/978-3-319-67262-5_1
3. Jabbar, K., Bjørn, P.: Infrastructural grind: introducing blockchain technology in the shipping domain. In: GROUP 2018, pp. 297–308. ACM, New York (2018)
4. Mendling, J., et al.: Blockchains for business process management - challenges and opportunities. ACM Trans. Manage. Inf. Syst. **9**(1), 4:1–4:16 (2018)
5. Meroni, G., Baresi, L., Montali, M., Plebani, P.: Multi-party business process compliance monitoring through IoT-enabled artifacts. Inf. Syst. **73**, 61–78 (2018)
6. Prybila, C., Schulte, S., Hochreiner, C., Weber, I.: Runtime verification for business processes utilizing the Bitcoin blockchain. Future Gener. Comput. Syst. (2017)
7. Staples, M., Chen, S., Falamaki, S., Ponomarev, A., Rimba, P., Tran, A.B., Weber, I., Xu, X., Zhu, J.: Risks and opportunities for systems using blockchain and smart contracts. Technical report, Data61 (CSIRO) (2017)
8. Vandermerwe, S., Rada, J.: Servitization of business: adding value by adding services. Eur. Manage. J. **6**(4), 314–324 (1988)
9. Weber, I., Xu, X., Riveret, R., Governatori, G., Ponomarev, A., Mendling, J.: Untrusted business process monitoring and execution using blockchain. In: La Rosa, M., Loos, P., Pastor, O. (eds.) BPM 2016. LNCS, vol. 9850, pp. 329–347. Springer, Cham (2016). https://doi.org/10.1007/978-3-319-45348-4_19
10. Wu, H., Li, Z., King, B., Ben Miled, Z., Wassick, J., Tazelaar, J.: A distributed ledger for supply chain physical distribution visibility. Information **8**(4), 137 (2017)
11. Xu, X., Pautasso, C., Zhu, L., Gramoli, V., Ponomarev, A., Tran, A.B., Chen, S.: The blockchain as a software connector. In: WICSA 2016, pp. 182–191. IEEE (2016)
12. Xu, X., Weber, I., Staples, M., Zhu, L., Bosch, J., Bass, L., Pautasso, C., Rimba, P.: A taxonomy of blockchain-based systems for architecture design. In: ICSA 2017, pp. 243–252. IEEE (2017)

Ensuring Resource Trust and Integrity in Web Browsers Using Blockchain Technology

Clemens H. Cap[1] and Benjamin Leiding[2(✉)]

[1] Department of Computer Science, University of Rostock, Rostock, Germany
`clemens.cap@uni-rostock.de`
[2] Institute of Computer Science, University of Göttingen, Göttingen, Germany
`benjamin.leiding@cs.uni-goettingen.de`

Abstract. Current web technology allows the use of cryptographic primitives as part of server-provided Javascript. This may result in security problems with web-based services. We provide an example for an attack on the WhisperKey service. We present a solution which is based on human code reviewing and on CVE (Common Vulnerabilities and Exposures) data bases. In our approach, existing code audits and known vulnerabilities are tied to the Javascript file by a tamper-proof Blockchain approach and are signaled to the user by a browser extension. The contribution explains our concept and its workflow; it may be extended to all situations with modular, mobile code. Finally, we propose an amendment to the W3C subresource recommendation.

Keywords: Browser resource integrity · Code poisoning
Software delivery · Blockchain · Code review

1 Introduction

Despite the popularity and widespread use of Javascript in web-development, client-side execution of cryptography-focused Javascript remains a serious security issue. The user cannot trust the functionality downloaded from the server, since the service provider may incorrectly apply cryptographic primitives, include backdoors or even access private keys stored on the client. The service provider may do so voluntarily for criminal reasons, or involuntarily due to a court order, in forced collaboration with surveillance institutions. Several web-based messenger applications such as ChatCrypt[1] and WhisperKey[2] still deal with this problem, whereas Cryptocat[3] already moved away from in-browser Javascript execution and instead uses a browser plug-in model [10,27].

---

[1] https://www.chatcrypt.com.
[2] https://www.whisperkey.io/.
[3] https://crypto.cat/.

© Springer International Publishing AG, part of Springer Nature 2018
R. Matulevičius and R. Dijkman (Eds.): CAiSE 2018 Workshops, LNBIP 316, pp. 115–125, 2018.
https://doi.org/10.1007/978-3-319-92898-2_9

Even though many web-applications are available for review on repository websites such as GitHub[4] or GitLab[5], they still do not prevent the service provider from serving tampered files to the end-user. To prevent such an attack, each user would have to review the code himself/herself. Even for small scripts, this is only an option for skilled experts. Moreover, reviewing incoming Javascript files each time before execution is cumbersome and not feasible. In addition, this approach works only for small scripts and is not applicable for complex applications. Finally, code obfuscation techniques make this task even more difficult.

We propose to combine blockchain technology and openly accessible code reviews of static code files in order to prevent server-side code poisoning attacks. Developers push their files to an online repository, such as GitHub or GitLab, and make them available to external reviewers. At the same time, the hash of the files is published to a blockchain, for example the Bitcoin blockchain, where it is stored as permanent and tamper-free reference. Code reviewers post their reviews and secure them by including the hash of their review as well as of the reviewed code in the same blockchain. As soon as the browser of the end-user receives the Javascript code, it checks the hash of the received files against the blockchain entry. The code is executed only if the hashes match and no negative reviews indicate a security risk.

This work addresses the identified gap by introducing a concept to detect and prevent server-side code poisoning attacks, thereby answering the question of how to prevent manipulation of static in-browser files using a blockchain-based peer review system. In this contribution we shall describe the general workflow of our proposal, the specifics of the code review process, and finally the mechanisms that ensure the trustworthiness of this process. As we shall explain by a security analysis of the WhisperKey service, the security gap is a real one and endangers existing services.

WhisperKey (see footnote 2) offers secure messaging within the browser. According to their web page and our analysis it works as follows: The recipient loads a particular URL of the portal, which has the browser generate a (public, private) key pair. The private key is stored in unencrypted form in the local storage of the browser, whereas the public key is sent to the WhisperKey server, where it is stored together with further identifiers, so called magic words. The recipient forwards these magic words to the person from which she wants to receive a message. The sender provides the WhisperKey server with the magic words he obtained from the recipient and in turn his browser receives the associated public key. When typing the message, the browser of the sender encrypts the plain text and forwards the cypher text to the WhisperKey server, which again forwards it to the receiver. The receiver is identified by the magic words. Finally the receiver uses her private key to decrypt the message. The complete process is a bit more involved and employs hybrid encryption.

Besides security limitations such as short RSA keys, coincidental collisions of magic words or implementation issues, the most serious security issue is a

---

[4] https://github.com/.
[5] https://gitlab.com/.

classical man in the middle attack by the WhisperKey server. In this attack (see Fig. 1), WhisperKey distributes Javascript, which extracts the private key of the user from browser local storage and sends the private key back to WhisperKey.

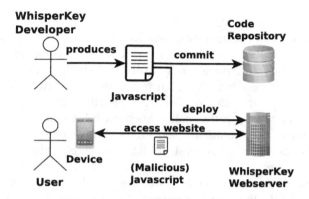

Fig. 1. Illustration of a server-side code poisoning attack.

The remainder of this paper is structured as follows: Sect. 2 provides some technical background and describes related work. Section 3 introduces the general workflow of our proposal. Afterwards, Sect. 4 expands on the peer-reviewing process. Finally, Sect. 5 concludes this contribution and provides an outlook on future work.

2   Technical Background and Related Work

In recent years, the blockchain concept majored and spread in popularity. Besides the initial Bitcoin blockchain, several other architectures emerged, e.g., Ethereum[6], Qtum[7], or RSK[8]. Moreover, a variety of applications and use-cases for blockchains have been proposed, e.g., as a platform for IoT (Internet of Things) applications [8,12], in the legal industry [18], in the finance sector [17,26] or as part of security and authentication protocols [11,13,20].

A blockchain consists of a chronologically ordered chain of blocks, where each block consists of a number of validated transactions. Each block links to its predecessor by a hash reference, so that changing the content of one block also changes all succeeding blocks and hence breaks the chain. All blocks are stored on and verified by all participating nodes. The blockchain concept, also referred to as distributed ledger system, is most noticeably known for providing the foundation of the peer-to-peer (P2P) cryptocurrency and payment system Bitcoin [16]. It consists of quite a number of minor additional protocol elements,

---

[6] https://ethereum.org/.

[7] https://qtum.org/.

[8] http://www.rsk.co/.

for example providing a trustworthy time-base and scaling the difficulty of the proof-of-work to the number of participating nodes. The current market capitalization of crypto-currencies serves as pragmatic proof of their security.

In our application, we use the fact that information encoded into a blockchain cannot be tampered with at a later moment. In Bitcoin this can be achieved somewhat artificially using the OP_RETURN script instruction, it is limited to 80 bytes [3] and produces considerable costs in transaction fees. Ethereum offers more flexibility, but still has high fees for some aspects of our use case; [6] describes a possibility to reduce the fees using off-chain storage. IOTA has an even more natural structure with regard to tamper-protecting hashed data [21] and works without per-transaction fees. [19] describes alternative architectures and suggests special-use private chains. Such an infrastructure could be operated by the open source community and protect the delivery of security critical software on the web for the general public, completely without the need for transaction-based fees.

The problem of server-side code poisoning is well known from content distribution networks (CDN), the deployment of which usually requires are careful balancing of trust, performance, and security issues [29]. CDNs do not offer protection against server-side code poisoning but further exemplify the size of the problem. The W3C subresource integrity recommendation [1] provides techniques to ensure that the CDN delivers that code for inclusion of subresources which the author of the main document expects. For example, style-sheets or Javascript libraries may be included by a main document; the including tag in the main document may provide hash-codes for the subresources. This enables the browser to check whether the (CDN-served) subresources are really what the author of the (provider-served) main document expected. However, this approach does not preclude an intentional attack by the service-provider and lacks the connection from the load process to known component vulnerabilities.

3   Concept Overview

The following section provides a general overview on the workflow of our solution. Figure 2 illustrates our approach in general. Its left hand side presents the current state of the art as discussed previously in Sect. 2, whereas the right hand side of the figure presents our proposal that extends the current workflow.

The WhisperKey developer writes the code for WhisperKey and deploys the resulting application on the WhisperKey webserver. The source code is pushed to the developers public code repository, on GitLab or GitHub. The user accesses the WhisperKey application using a suitable device and executes the Javascript code provided by the webserver. Thus far, the user is still prone to server-side code poising or other vulnerabilities that might be caused by the Javascript file.

In order to prevent this attack, we propose an expert-driven, decentralized peer-review process. As illustrated in Fig. 2, a reviewer that is interested in analyzing the WhisperKey application pulls a copy of the latest source code from the corresponding public code repository. The results of the code analysis

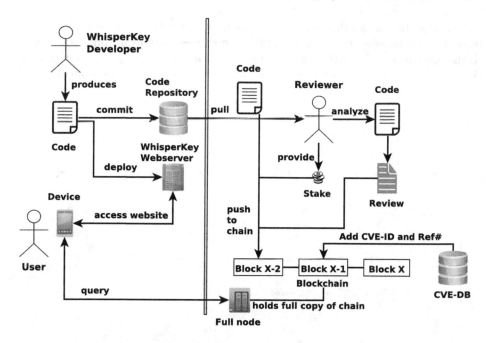

Fig. 2. General overview of the protocol workflow.

are stored in an audit report. This report either states that the reviewer is confident that the code is secure and recommended for daily use, or it describes the identified security issues.

In order to be eligible to publish code reviews, the reviewer has to provide a financial stake in form of a pre-defined cryptocurrency, such as Bitcoin, Ether, Litecoin or others. The stake is locked up for a defined time period. In case the review turns out to be wrong, the stake is lost. A detailed description of the full peer review process as well as the incentive system for participating reviewers is provided in Sects. 4.1 and 4.3. After the review, the git hash of the reviewed code version, as well as the reviewer's stake and the final review report (or the value of a cryptographic hash function on this report) are posted to the blockchain ($block_{x-2}$). Our solution does not require a specific blockchain architecture, as long as it is possible to store string encoded information as part of a transaction.

In order to enable users of the WhisperKey application to utilize the reviews available on the blockchain, we propose a web browser extension that interacts with the corresponding blockchain. Figure 3 provides a BPMN [4] illustrations of a local user's client requesting and processing an incoming file that has been reviewed by a reviewer. For this purpose, the user interacts with a small number of full blockchain nodes; the user does not have to run a full blockchain node herself but relies on a majority vote of a small number of those nodes. The browser extension regularly queries these full nodes for updates on reviews (e.g. $block_x$) and stores a list of files with their latest review results on the local user device. In case an incoming file from the WhisperKey website is marked as insecure, the browser prevents the execution of the file and outputs a warning to the user; if no information or positive reviews are found, the extension signals this appropriately. The rewards for the reviewers depend on the popularity of the reviewed file – the more clients report queries for a specific file, the higher the reward for the reviewer. Details of the incentive mechanism are discussed in Sect. 4.3.

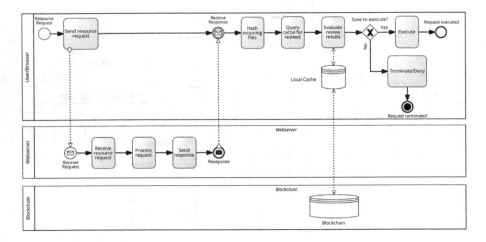

Fig. 3. BPMN representation of the local client requesting and processing an incoming file.

Finally, we need a mechanism to prove code vulnerability in order to invalidate existing positive reviews. Despite human-based conflict resolution mechanisms as discussed later in Sect. 4.3, an indisputable source of discovered vulnerabilities is the CVE system[9]. The CVE system lists publicly known cybersecurity vulnerabilities with a unique identification number, a description as well as at least one public reference for each vulnerability. In case a new CVE entry for a previously reviewed file is listed, the CVE-ID with a reference ID for the affected review is posted to the blockchain ($block_{x-1}$) resulting in a lost stake for the reviewer as well as a new negative review for the concerned file.

4 Peer-Reviewing Process

A peer-review based analysis of the provided resource, e.g., a Javascript file, is one of the main components of our proposal. Especially in software development and academic research, the process of transparent peer-reviewing is a common practice for quality assurance, e.g., [2,22–25]. We illustrate the peer-review process in Sect. 4.1, the conflict resolution mechanism in Sect. 4.2 as well as the incentive mechanisms for all involved entities in Sect. 4.3.

---

[9] https://cve.mitre.org/.

4.1 Peer-Reviewing

As briefly outlined in Sect. 3, a reviewer that is interested in reviewing a specific resource, for example a Javascript file hosted on GitHub, pulls the version that he/she is interested in reviewing. Afterwards, the reviewer performs a detailed and thorough analysis of the code and compiles a review report. Among others, the report contains the following information: Project name, project description, link to resource repository, hash of the committed version that has been reviewed, the resource itself, information about the reviewer as well as a detailed description of the review results. Finally, the report also contains a boolean value that indicates whether the reviewer suggests that the resource is secure and recommended for daily use or not - *true* in case the resource is secure and otherwise *false*. The inclusion of these meta-data as part of the report makes it available to the browser extension and to further automated processing and decision algorithms.

After completing the review process, the reviewer posts a short version or a hash of the report to a specified blockchain; the detailed report is stored in a decentralized and distributed file system (such as IPFS[10] [9]) as a reference. The short version contains the git commit hash, the project name, the resource hash and the boolean value indicating a secure or insecure file. When posting the review report to the chain, the reviewer also makes a deposit that is locked up as a stake for a predefined time period. In case the submitted review turns out to be wrong, the reviewer loses the stake. Further reviewers might add additional reviews for of the same resource thereby providing a peer-based security evaluation.

4.2 Conflict Resolution

Assuming that a certain resource receives multiple reviews, we may end up in a situation where either all reviewers agree or in a scenario with divergent results. Given the case that we have two reviews declaring a resource as secure and two other reviews claiming the exact opposite, we have to decide how to treat the resource when a browser queries the reviews for this file. Is it secure or not? A conservative approach is to tag all files as insecure that received a single negative review. The downside of this solution is a potential denial of service scenario where an attacker posts a negative review to undermine the trustworthiness of a competitor. Hence, an independent and trusted conflict resolution mechanism is required.

As described in Sect. 3, CVEs are a potential solution for the issue described above. A software that is referenced in the CVE system as vulnerable can be marked as insecure. Hence, a resource version that corresponds to an entry in the CVE system is by default not secure and the reviewers that posted a positive review lose their stakes. The problem with the CVE system is, that it does not list all existing vulnerabilities for each application or software produce, for

---

[10] https://ipfs.io/.

example, a Cross-Site-Scripting (XSS) vulnerability on a private website. Thus an alternative solution is required.

Semada[11] is a decentralized and autonomous platform that enables a reputation-driven meritocracy with a domain expert focused reputation system [5]. Experts with knowledge in a specific domain can sign up and provide proofs-of-expertise for the domain. Experts act as validators who make stakes to answer validation requests, e.g., questions targeting a specific field of expertise. The experts bet their stakes in a betting pool depending on their point-of-view on a specific issue and a majority vote decides the answer to the validation request. A Semada-like platform with software security experts might be an alternative conflict resolution platform to decide on the (in)security of a reviewed resource.

4.3 Incentive Mechanism

Finally, we introduce an incentive mechanism for our proposed concept. First, the incentive for the user that runs a client on his device in order to avoid executing insecure code, the incentive for using the system is quite simple - enhanced security. Similar applies to the developer of the used application: Code reviews of external reviewers significantly increase the security of software code [7,14,15].

The incentive for the reviewers is manifold. First, we propose a Steemit-like[12] incentive system for reviews. The Steem network continually creates new tokens that reward content creators and curators of the platform [28]. Similarly, we propose to incentivize reviewers by rewarding tokens based on the popularity of reviewed code, e.g., one million user clients queried the review for a specific file results in a certain amount of reward tokens. The reward is locked up together with the reviewers stake for some time and released over time. In case a vulnerability is found, the stake as well as the reward tokens are lost. In order to avoid millions of reviews for popular files and no reviews for less popular resources, the reward tokens are split among all reviewers. In addition, we propose to incentivize the first reviewers of a specific resource be awarding new minted tokens to them, thereby increasing the incentive to providing at least a few reviews to less popular files. Furthermore, interested users can also offer bounties for unreviewed files that would like to see reviewed, resulting in a further incentive.

Stakes and rewards that are lost due to a discovered vulnerability in a positively reviewed file might be burned, send to a non-profit organization such as the Linux foundation[13] or MOSS[14], or are awarded to the reviewer that discovered the vulnerability.

5 Conclusion and Future Work

We have provided concepts how blockchain technology can make the distribution of mobile code more secure. *First,* tampering with the reviewed status of

---

[11] http://semada.io/.
[12] https://steemit.com/.
[13] https://www.linuxfoundation.org/.
[14] https://www.mozilla.org/en-US/moss/.

Javascript code is prevented when the downloaded code is bound to a hash-value which is encoded into the blockchain. The browser can check that it is in fact receiving the same code base as it is held available in a public repository, such as GitHub or GitLab, which is mentioned in the metadata of a review. *Second*, code quality reviews may be bound to the hash of the file and ensure that the application has been analyzed by a person who has a stake in the correct functioning of that particular code. *Finally*, we believe that our concept is useful for and can be adapted to every situation where software or documents are downloaded from various different locations.

As *short-term future work* we plan to transform our contribution from the level of a conceptual workflow scheme (as in Fig. 2) into a semi-formally specified REST-Api and to provide experimental implementations on top of the Ethereum blockchain and the IOTA tangle system. On the client side, we intend an implementation in the form of a browser extension, which interacts with blockchain nodes. Moreover, we believe that web browser security in general would benefit from a standardized interface through which trusted subresources of a page can be loaded and connected to open repositories as well as review and reputation sites. The subresource integrity recommendation of the W3C [1] already realizes most of this but need to be amended by a mechanism connecting subresources to reviews and validation mechanisms.

Moreover, we identify the following *long-term research questions* for the blockchain community in general. Current consensus technology seems to work well when it boils down to checking facts which may be verified algorithmically, such as checking whether a Bitcoin transaction has been signed by a private key belonging to a public key whose hash equals the address, or ensuring that a certain event had been raised by an authenticated party to a smart contract. In our use case we can ensure that a reviewer had written a positive review for a file with a specific content and that the review subsequently was invalidated by an entry into a CVE data base. However, we still have a trust gap between intended and realized human behavior. How do we ensure that a reviewer invests sufficient time to produce a good review or generates a reasonable CVE entry? In Bitcoin the incentive structure is much simpler, but while it provides sufficient motivation to miners for generating blocks, its translation to traditional economics is far from clear as can be recognized from the high volatility of the Bitcoin course as well as from an unending stream of warnings, comparisons with the tulip bubble, and claims that it is a ponzi scheme.

Finally, future developments might focus on creating a distributed autonomous organization (DAO) that enables the resource review system. Users participating in the DAO build their reputation in the same way as described in this work, but in addition they follow a common review protocol as well as best practices that are contentiously enhanced by the DAO's members. Disputes are resolved in a Semada-like manner using a validation betting pool.

Acknowledgments. The authors would like to thank Craig Calcaterra for providing feedback, valuable insights into reputation- and incentive mechanisms as well as thoughts on a review DAO.

References

1. Akhawe, D., Braun, F., Marier, F., Weinberger, J.: Subresource integrity W3C recommendation. https://www.w3.org/TR/SRI/ (2016). Accessed 31 Jan 2017
2. Armstrong, J.S.: Peer review for journals: evidence on quality control, fairness, and innovation. Sci. Eng. Ethics **3**(1), 63–84 (1997)
3. Bartoletti, M., Pompianu, L.: An analysis of bitcoin OP_RETURN metadata. CoRR abs/1702.01024 (2017). http://arxiv.org/abs/1702.01024
4. Business Process Model: Notation (BPMN) Version 2.0. OMG Specification, Object Management Group (2011). Accessed 1 Feb 2018
5. Calcaterra, C., Kaal, W.A., Vlad, A.: Semada technical white paper - a decentralized platform for verified reputation - version 0.3. https://docs.google.com/document/d/1rMpcaO5rlXw5RxUCDy_e_his6DSdrDfUS9qwcgWHAAw/edit (2017). Accessed 25 Feb 2018
6. Didil (Pseudonym): Off-chain data storage: Ethereum & IPFS - saving on gas. https://medium.com/@didil/off-chain-data-storage-ethereum-ipfs-570e030432cf (2017). Accessed 31 Jan 2018
7. Felderer, M., Büchler, M., Johns, M., Brucker, A.D., Breu, R., Pretschner, A.: Security testing: a survey. In: Advances in Computers, vol. 101, pp. 1–51. Elsevier (2016)
8. Huckle, S., Bhattacharya, R., White, M., Beloff, N.: Internet of Things, blockchain and shared economy applications. Procedia Comput. Sci. **98**, 461–466 (2016)
9. Benet, J.: IPFS - content addressed, versioned, P2P file system. https://ipfs.io/ipfs/QmR7GSQM93Cx5eAg6a6yRzNde1FQv7uL6X1o4k7zrJa3LX/ipfs.draft3.pdf (2017). Accessed 17 Jan 2018
10. Kobeissi, N.: Cryptocat blog - moving to a browser app model. https://web.archive.org/web/20130206114001/blog.crypto.cat/2012/08/moving-to-a-browser-app-model/ (2012). Accessed 3 Nov 2017
11. Leiding, B., Cap, C.H., Mundt, T., Rashidibajgan, S.: Authcoin: validation and authentication in decentralized networks. In: The 10th Mediterranean Conference on Information Systems - MCIS 2016, Cyprus, CY, September 2016
12. Leiding, B., Memarmoshrefi, P., Hogrefe, D.: Self-managed and blockchain-based vehicular ad-hoc networks. In: Proceedings of the 2016 ACM International Joint Conference on Pervasive and Ubiquitous Computing: Adjunct, pp. 137–140. ACM (2016)
13. McCorry, P., Shahandashti, S.F., Clarke, D., Hao, F.: Authenticated key exchange over bitcoin. In: Chen, L., Matsuo, S. (eds.) SSR 2015. LNCS, vol. 9497, pp. 3–20. Springer, Cham (2015). https://doi.org/10.1007/978-3-319-27152-1_1
14. McGraw, G.: Software security. IEEE Secur. Priv. **2**(2), 80–83 (2004)
15. McGraw, G.: Automated code review tools for security. Computer **41**(12), 108–111 (2008)
16. Nakamoto, S.: Bitcoin: a peer-to-peer electronic cash system. https://bitcoin.org/bitcoin.pdf (2008). Accessed 17 Jan 2018
17. Nguyen, Q.K.: Blockchain - a financial technology for future sustainable development. In: International Conference on Green Technology and Sustainable Development (GTSD), pp. 51–54. IEEE (2016)
18. Norta, A., Vedeshin, A., Rand, H., Tobies, S., Rull, A., Poola, M., Rull, T.: Self-aware agent-supported contract management on blockchains for legal accountability. https://docs.agrello.org/Agrello-Self-Aware_Whitepaper-English.pdf (2017). Accessed 17 Jan 2018

19. O'Leary, D.E.: Configuring blockchain architectures for transaction information in blockchain consortiums: the case of accounting and supply chain systems. Intell. Syst. Account. Finan. Manag. **24**(4), 138–147 (2017)
20. Ouaddah, A., Elkalam, A.A., Ouahman, A.A.: Towards a novel privacy-preserving access control model based on blockchain technology in IoT. In: Rocha, Á., Serrhini, M., Felgueiras, C. (eds.) Europe and MENA Cooperation Advances in Information and Communication Technologies. AISC, pp. 523 533. Springer, Cham (2017). https://doi.org/10.1007/978-3-319-46568-5_53
21. Popov, S.: The tangle, version 1.3. https://pdfs.semanticscholar.org/13ec/26512f6602a5184aa3beb6193694dc8c9974.pdf (2017). Accessed 7 Feb 2018
22. Rennie, D.: Editorial peer review: its development and rationale. Peer Rev. Health Sci. **2**, 1–13 (2003)
23. Rigby, P.C., German, D.M., Storey, M.A.: Open source software peer review practices: a case study of the apache server. In: Proceedings of the 30th International Conference on Software Engineering, pp. 541–550. ACM (2008)
24. Rigby, P.C., Storey, M.A.: Understanding broadcast based peer review on open source software projects. In: Proceedings of the 33rd International Conference on Software Engineering, pp. 541–550. ACM (2011)
25. Rowland, F.: The peer-review process. Learn. Publish. **15**(4), 247–258 (2002)
26. SALT Technology Ltd.: Salt - blockchain-backed loans. https://membership.saltlending.com/files/abstract.pdf (2017). Accessed 17 Jan 2018
27. Schneier, B.: Cryptocat - Schneier on security. https://www.schneier.com/blog/archives/2012/08/cryptocat.html (2012). Accessed 3 Nov 2017
28. Steemit Inc.: Steem - an incentivized, blockchain-based, public content platform. https://steem.io/SteemWhitePaper.pdf (2017). Accessed 19 Dec 2017
29. Teridion Blog: CDN security: are CDNs safe? https://www.teridion.com/2017/02/are-cdns-safe/ (2017). Accessed 31 Jan 2018

Document Management System Based on a Private Blockchain for the Support of the Judicial Embargoes Process in Colombia

Julian Solarte-Rivera[1], Andrés Vidal-Zemanate[1], Carlos Cobos[1(✉)],
José Alejandro Chamorro-Lopez[2], and Tomas Velasco[3]

[1] University of Cauca, Popayán, Cauca, Colombia
{julianesolarter, lenelvidal, ccobos}@unicauca.edu.co
[2] Password Consulting Services, New York, USA
jose.chamorro@password.com.co
[3] Primart Studios, Cali, Valle del Cauca, Colombia
tomas@primartstudios.com

Abstract. In recent years, the conglomeration of financial and governmental entities with responsibility for the judicial embargoes process in Colombia has met with serious problems implementing an efficient system that does not incur major cost overruns. Given the large number of participants involved, development of a centralized document management system was always deemed to be unsuitable, so that the entire process of sending and receiving documents of attachments is still carried out today in physical form, by postal mail. This article presents the development of a pilot application that instead enables embargo documents to be published and distributed within a document management system that nevertheless guarantees the confidentiality, availability and reliability of all information registered in the blockchain. On developing this solution, the very nature of blockchain was found to facilitate not only the availability and distribution of the documents, but the process of monitoring and controlling changes in them. As a result, each participant in the network always obtains an accepted version of revised documents, thus reducing costs and facilitating a greater collaboration among the participating entities.

Keywords: Blockchain · Multichain · Document management system

1 Introduction

An embargo consists of the retention, by judicial order, of a good belonging to a person to assure payment of a debt, payment of judicial expenses, or of fees due to criminal acts. In Colombia, Government notification of embargoes to financial entities is currently an extensive and complex process, involving a great many public, private, or mixed economy organizations. Many state entities such as governorships (28), mayorships (1122) and hospitals (45) have the power to impose embargoes in different localities throughout the country. However, the judges who formalize the initiation of the embargo process are distributed in 3,256 courts within all jurisdictions, levels, and specialties. Recipient entities, meanwhile, comprise a large, financial group that

© Springer International Publishing AG, part of Springer Nature 2018
R. Matulevičius and R. Dijkman (Eds.): CAiSE 2018 Workshops, LNBIP 316, pp. 126–137, 2018.
https://doi.org/10.1007/978-3-319-92898-2_10

currently consists of 23 banks, 187 cooperatives, and 27 fiduciaries located throughout Colombia with the capacity to carry out embargoes against citizens or legal residents.

In the first stage of the process, through the courts, the governmental entities issue an embargo notice. The notice is distributed to all receiving entities, without exception. Once the notice arrives at a particular recipient entity, each must execute the garnishment order for all the persons indicated and prepare a response letter indicating the details of the garnishment action performed.

During the process, a number of problems highlight the inefficiency in its execution and generate a series of cost overruns. First, there is not a complete systematization of the process. Each entity involved carries out its tasks in an isolated, different way. Although existing information systems aim to support the process, these are specific to each entity and do not interoperate one with another. Secondly, since these documents are not converted into a digital format, the embargo and response notices have to be delivered physically between the different headquarters of each entity, sent by postal mail, resulting in the additional cost of shipping to each entity. These costs affect the receiving entities to an even greater extent, since they must pay to send garnishment notices to each ID or NIT (Tax ID of a company) listed in the embargo. A third major drawback is that although most financial institutions have as clients only 2% of the people who are being embargoed, they nevertheless need to verify and provide information on the remaining 98% of the people listed in the embargo.

The receiving entities (287 in total that includes banks, cooperatives, and fiduciaries) currently receive an average of 5,000 embargo notices per month, each with a shipping cost close to USD $0.7. This generates an approximate total cost of USD $3,500 per entity per month. The process implies an average monthly cost for the receiving entities of USD $1,004,500, plus the cost of shipment from the courts that corresponds to the same value, leading to an approximate global value of US $2,009,000 per month.

The communication mechanism between the different affected entities is far from optimal. In the first place, sending notices in physical form by postal mail does not guarantee that these will always arrive on time. The situation is aggravated for the issuing entities since the people embargoed can withdraw the money just before the bank receives the notice. Another major problem is evidenced by the fact that there is no mechanism to verify if an embargo action was already executed in another entity at some point, thus all entities are obliged to execute the embargo independently of it already having been executed in another entity. This affects all the clients in these entities since once the terms of the lien are clarified they must go to each of the different financial entities remaining to request the refund of their money. Therefore, if a person has three bank accounts in different entities with balances greater than $1,000 USD and receives an embargo of $500 USD, all three banks will be forced to garnish $500 regardless of whether another entity has already executed the embargo.

The state and its entities have not implemented a technological mechanism to reduce costs in this process because they have not decided on a suitable technology that ensures factors such as availability, security, and integrity of information. Given the above factors and the characteristics of the problem, where there is a large number of financial and governmental organizations with the need to participate and validate together each step of the embargo process, the implementation of a centralized system would not be entirely efficient since its implementation involves additional costs and efforts. Achieving the required availability in a centralized system implies the use of replication of mechanisms in several servers in different geographical locations and with the need to implement mechanisms for their constant synchronization. In terms of how much security is needed in the centralized systems, there are users that have the ability to modify information without any restriction, giving opportunity to possible fraud that can compromise the integrity of the information. Considering what has been described, the objective of this article is to present a solution based on blockchain to reduce costs and increase the efficiency of the embargo process, as well as to improve collaboration between the entities involved in said process [13, 14].

Forthcoming in Sect. 2, we present the developed solution, explaining the design decisions and the architecture of the system followed with more details of the components of the system and their interaction. Finally, in Sect. 3, we present the conclusions and future actions that the team recommends be carried out.

2   Proposed Solution

2.1   Solution Approach

To solve the various problems associated with the embargoes notification process described above, we chose to design a pilot application developed in a virtual environment and then deployed to a private network. The proposed application allows a document associated with an embargo order to be published and distributed to a set of users with the necessary credentials to represent a receiving financial entity, which in turn can generate and record documents with answers for each ID or NIT listed within the garnishment notice [5].

The system has been designed so that each embargo notice, annex documents and response documents are associated and managed by their own metadata, as well as connected to the users of the system that manages it. The objective of the system is to use the potential of blockchain to propose a document management system that simplifies each of the stages of the process, allowing each task to be carried out in an efficient manner, reducing cost overruns and delays in the process [11, 12].

To make an adequate decision on which blockchain platform to use for development, different aspects were analyzed, including: (1) the nature of the blockchain, (2) the number of transactions and the traffic supported by the network, (3) the ease of development, (4) the deployment, and (5) the costs involved. Additionally, there is great convenience to using a private blockchain and a public one [2].

2.2   Public Blockchain vs Private Blockchain

Considering that a blockchain network can be divided into two clear models: the public blockchain implementation model, and the permitted or private blockchain model, a study was made of the advantages of each one, based on the infrastructure used by the different participants of the process.

Although initially the possibility of using a public blockchain network was considered, instead we decided to use a platform that would allow the implementation of a private blockchain for various reasons. In the first place, the proposed solution mainly seeks to manage user permissions by providing restricted and confidential access to the data stored within the blockchain. It is much more viable to implement within a private blockchain that is guided under the concept of privileges, than in a public use blockchain where in theory any user can connect to the network and access the information.

Secondly, the ability to adapt the storage form, structure and content of transactions based on the system's own needs and the rules of the process provided by the implementation of a private blockchain was considered.

Another important aspect that was considered is related to the consensus algorithms within the network, where work or stake test algorithms are generally highlighted in public blockchain networks, which contribute a greater degree of control over the network on possible attacks, but they require participating nodes with a high computing capacity with the aim of being able to mine within the blockchain. In the field of private blockchain, these algorithms may vary depending on the needs and requirements of the network and the transactional system itself, implementing more efficient mechanisms in terms of computational resources for consensus among the different participating nodes, a situation that is important when considering the heterogeneous infrastructure that the participating institutions have [1, 3].

2.3 Selection of the Blockchain Platform

By adopting the private blockchain model for the development of the prototypes, the next step was focused on choosing a suitable platform among several available options. In this aspect, different options were considered, opting at the end for the Multichain platform.

Multichain is an open source platform with support for the development of private blockchains and oriented to financial transaction systems sponsored by a broad set of companies in the sector. In addition, through previous experimentation, it demonstrated a good ease of deployment adaptable to the architecture defined in the design of the prototypes.

Table 1 presents a comparison between some of the different blockchain options considered, including the comparison between Multichain with public-facing blockchains, among which are some well-known ones such as Bitcoin or Ethereum [6–9].

2.4 Architecture and Deployment

The pilot application was designed to work on a Web environment. At the architectural level it is possible to distinguish two main components: the client, in charge of interacting with the end users of the system; and the server, in charge of containing the logic to interact with the blockchain and attend to the different requests sent from the client. Both client and server are deployed in separate environments with similar hardware and software aspects, on servers running the Apache 2.4 version and supported on a GNU/Linux operating system in the Ubuntu version 16.04.

Table 1. Comparative table of blockchain platforms considered

Aspect	Multichain	Public blockchains	Hyperledger	Chaincore
Cost	Infrastructure only	Cost for each transaction	Infrastructure only	Infrastructure only
Permission administration	Different permission settings	Each user individually	Different permission settings	Different permission settings
Privacy options	Both public and private	Public only	Both public and private	Both public and private
Compatibility	Compatible with bitcoin core	Usually not compatible with more blockchains	Not compatible with more blockchains	Not compatible with more blockchains
Consensus	"MiningDiversity"	Proof-of-work	PBFT	Federated Consensus Protocol
Availability of information	Available only with user permissions	For all the users of the blockchain	Available only with user permissions	Available only with user permissions

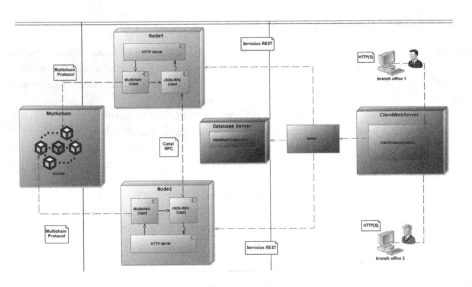

Fig. 1. System architecture

In Fig. 1 the main components of the system are presented and then a general description of their interaction is presented.

An entity connects to the web application (ClientWebApplication) making a connection to the server by sending a request for registration or reading, the server sends this request to a node (Node 1, Node 2, ..., Node N) which is responsible for registering in the blockchain, after this the blockchain is synchronized and all the participants are informed of the new record.

It is important to emphasize that the operation of the blockchain does not depend on any centralized database; the centralized database is used when reports are requested, and it is required to gather information from the blockchain.

Considering the architecture presented in Fig. 1, the client used the Java programming language and the JSF framework together with the MVC model. This component was organized in packages (see Fig. 2) where the facades package is in charge of making the connection with the server sending JSON requests to obtain or record information; the drivers package is responsible for communicating with the facades to obtain the necessary information and convert it into the types of data to be used. Finally, the Views use the controllers to obtain the necessary data. The package models make a representation of the information in the blockchain as a class and the package utilities are classes used for different purposes.

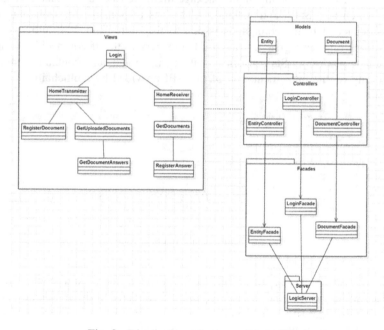

Fig. 2. Distribution of components to Client

Regarding the server application (see Fig. 3), PHP was used. The implemented REST API is divided into two main directories; the first, called 'logic', are the files with the classes responsible for taking the requests, analyzing the validity of the data and applying the logic of the business for the registration and reading of a transaction or set of transactions structuring a response that can be sent to the client in the front-end. The second directory, called 'cli-multichain', contains a set of classes whose function is to allow the communication of the REST API with the multichain API, allowing to perform read and write operations in the blockchain.

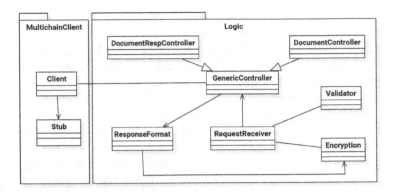

Fig. 3. Server component distribution

On the server in the 'cli-multichain' package there are two classes that have greater relevance, which are 'Stub' and 'Client'. 'Client' is responsible for isolating details directly associated with the commands issued to the multichain API, allowing these operations to be done in a generic way and being very useful if you decide to change the blockchain platform. 'Stub' works as its complement and contains commands dependent only on the implementation of the API provided by multichain.

```
public function multichain($method) // other params read from func_get_args()
{
    $args=func_get_args();

    return $this->json_rpc_send($this->multichain_chain['rpchost'],
    $this->multichain_chain['rpcport'],
    $this->multichain_chain['rpcuser'],
    $this->multichain_chain['rpcpassword'], $method, array_slice($args, 1));
}
```

Fig. 4. "Multichain" function code

Figure 4 shows the source code of the function called 'multichain' contained in the 'Stub' class, which allows one to issue commands directly to the multichain API by specifying a host address, a port number, and a user with its respective password through which it is possible to connect to the 'multichain daemon'.

As a complement, the 'multichain' function is invoked by various functions contained in the 'Client' class, in Fig. 5, the sample 'getDatosTransaccion' function is taken as an example, which allows obtaining the metadata of a specific transaction identified by its transaction identifier or 'txId'.

Internally within the function 'getDatosTransaccion' the 'multichain' function is invoked to specify the 'getrawtransaction' command proper to the multichain API, which queries and returns the metadata associated with the transaction with the specified 'txId'. Once the metadata is obtained, these are converted from hexadecimal format to plain text, and are encoded in a JSON object, which is returned to the 'logic' package controllers, which add the final headers, encrypt it and return it to the client.

```
public function getDatosTransaccion($txid)
{
    $retorno=array('error' => 'No se pudo consultar. Compruebe sintaxis');
    $resultado=$this->stub->multichain('getrawtransaction',$txid,1);

    if($resultado['error']==NULL)
    {
        $datoshexa=$resultado['result']['data'][0];
        $arraydatos=json_decode($this->stub->hex2Str($datoshexa),true);
        $retorno = array('result' => $arraydatos);
    }
    else
    {
        if($resultado['error']['code']==-8)
        {
            $retorno= array('error' => 'txid no existe');
        }

    }
    return $retorno;
}
```

Fig. 5. Source code function "getDatosTransaccion"

It is important to note that in the implementation of the REST API within the servers there are no components in charge of data storage in any relational database since all the record and reading of documents are handled directly according to the rules of storage in the blockchain. However, the solution uses a relational database that contains data that may be susceptible to being changed over time; for example, information associated with personal customer data and/or contact data between entities. It is considered that storing this data within the blockchain is inappropriate at the conceptual level.

With the proposed solution, a series of improvements are achieved during all stages of the embargo process. In the first place, the delivery times of the documents associated with notification and response of embargo requests would be greatly reduced given that these documents would no longer be issued physically and distributed by postal mail, and instead will be issued in digital form using blockchain as a support to distribute them to all the participants in the process through a network. In addition, implementing the proposed solution will exponentially reduce costs in the embargoes process. The costs associated with sending the documents by postal mail could be suppressed, as well as reducing the cost overruns generated by the fines incurred by the receiving financial entities by the untimely notification of the documents responding to the requests for embargoes [10].

The above benefits will also generate effective collaboration between all the organizations involved, optimizing the communication process between them, and directly benefiting the customers of financial institutions. For example, a client of two or more of these entities would no longer be affected by the execution of a compulsory seizure action from all financial entities where they have funds and would avoid the arduous process of requesting the reimbursement of their assets once this has been done.

The problem is solved with the government entity that issued the order for embargo enforcement. This is possible because through the implementation of the system, organizations will have knowledge of the execution of embargo actions executed for each of their clients at any time during the process.

2.5 Roles and Permissions

Information in MultiChain is saved by means of Streams that enable a categorization of the information and a level of permissions for these categories. As such, the following roles are defined in the system for managing the respective permissions in the network [4]:

- **Sender**: The sender features the following privileges: (1) "Connect", which enables it to connect with other nodes and see the contents of the blockchain; (2) "Send", which allows it to write information only in the Streams to which it is subscribed - in this case the sender is subscribed only to the "generated_documents" Stream and is thus permitted to upload information to this Stream only; and (3) "Create", which permits it to create a Stream. Each time a document is uploaded, a Stream is created so that the responses of the receivers can be recorded there.
- **Receiver**: The receiver has the privileges of "Connect" and of "Send" only in the Streams to which it can upload a response.
- **Administrator**: The administrator has the option of granting and revoking all the permissions available in the network, such as "Connect", "Create", "Send" and "Mine". The latter allows the selection of which nodes will be miners in the blockchain.

This system of permissions functions analogously to authentication, as is the case in BitCoin, generating a public key and a private key as follows:

- Each node presents its identity as a public address in the list in which the permissions are defined. This list is contained by all the nodes in the network.
- Each node verifies that the applicant's address is on its own list of permissions, in order to ensure a consensus.
- Each node sends a challenge message to the other party.
- Each node returns a signature of the challenge message, which shows its ownership of the private key corresponding to the public address they presented.
- If there is any irregularity in any of the nodes, the peer-to-peer connection will be aborted.

2.6 How Does It All Begin?

The miner of the first block, called the Genesis block, automatically receives all the privileges. This participant is in charge of managing all the privileges for the other participants. The privileges that are granted or revoked are recorded as a transaction to keep track of these activities. When there are more than two administrators in the blockchain and a change is required in the privileges of a participant in the role of administrator or miner, a consensus will be needed wherein all of the administrators approve the change.

When a new node is prepared to be part of the blockchain, this node saves both a public and a private key. The administrator subsequently gives connection permissions to the new node using its public key.

2.7   Encryption in Streams

To achieve confidentiality in the Streams, the data is encrypted before being stored in the blockchain. The password to read the encrypted data is only available to a subset of blockchain participants; the others cannot read it. This task can be carried out quite efficiently by using a combination of symmetric and asymmetric cryptography.

"The method makes use of three blockchain streams, whose purposes are as follows:

- One stream, which we call pubkeys, is used by participants to distribute their public keys under the RSA public-key cryptography scheme.
- A second stream, which we call items, is used to publish large pieces of data, each of which is encrypted using symmetric AES cryptography.
- A third stream, which we call access, provides data access. For each participant who should see a piece of data, a stream entry is created which contains that data's secret password, encrypted using that participant's public key." (taken from MultiChain whitepaper, see https://www.multichain.com/developers/stream-confidentiality) [6].

3   Conclusions

Through the implementation of the solution, we sought to present a cost-efficient alternative for the document management problems associated with the embargoes process in Colombia. Blockchain is an emerging technology that allows transparency at the level of transactions, adding features that improve the scalability, availability and integrity of data. The implemented solution allows another perspective with respect to traditional information systems usually based on a large database contained in a high-capacity server, transferring the system to a distributed database through a network point to point, where all the participants are responsible for the control and supervision of the data. This allows the system to have a higher level of availability since it will change from depending on the correct operation of a single central server, to the operation of a set of components made up of all the nodes that interact and relate to the blockchain.

Additionally, the characteristics of the blockchain networks allow for considerably improved aspects related to the security of the system and increase the availability of the proposed solution against different types of attacks such as DDoS since it does not have a single point of failure compared to the applications guided by conventional distributed architectures. Another improved aspect regarding the security of the system includes the integrity of the data, which are stored and verified by means of specific consensus mechanisms and, in theory, not modified or eliminated once written in the blockchain.

In the field of document management, it was found that the very nature of blockchain facilitates the availability and distribution of documents, as well as the monitoring and process of controlling changes in them, allowing each participant in the network to always obtain an accepted and revised version of the documents of interest in an efficient way, given that once a document is registered within the system it is immediately available to all interested parties who automatically seek to keep an updated copy of the blockchain. This is undoubtedly much more optimal than the physical distribution of documents by postal mail, or digitally using a conventional centralized system where the central server would usually be responsible for the extra task of sending update notifications to each of the clients, or on the contrary, clients saturate the server with requests for constant actualization. In addition, the use of blockchain allows the system not to depend solely on a large database that stores all the transactional information, having large workloads and consuming a large amount of space within the network equipment, which translates to a possible reduction of the costs of acquisition and maintenance of database servers in contrast to a traditional centralized document management system.

In contrast, databases store a smaller set of data associated with data mostly prone to change and/or be eliminated over time; these databases in turn should have a much simpler and more efficient relational structure that allows to optimize the processes of consultation and reading of the information.

One of the main objectives of the project team in the short term is to implement the proposed solution in a small set of entities as a pilot test in order to obtain feedback, find gaps, or possible needs not covered within the initial proposal. As a result, we will obtain a well-structured and robust solution that allows its generalized deployment in all the organizations involved in the process of embargoes in Colombia.

References

1. Morabito, V.: Business Innovation Through Blockchain. The B³ Perspective. Springer, Cham (2017). https://doi.org/10.1007/978-3-319-48478-5
2. Chuen, D., Deng, R.: Handbook of Blockchain Digital Finance and Inclusion, vol. 1. China Tech, Mobile Security, and Distributed Ledger, USA (2017)
3. Gupta, M.: BlockChain for Dummies. Wiley, USA (2017)
4. Brunnler, K.: A logic of blockchain updates, Scopus. In: Conference Papper (2017)
5. Davidson, S., de Filippi, P., Potts, J.: Blockchains and the economic institutions of capitalism. J. Inst. Econ., 1–20 (2018). https://doi.org/10.1017/S1744137417000200
6. Greenspan, G.: Multichain Private BlockChain White Paper. https://www.multichain.com/download/MultiChain-White-Paper.pdf
7. Nakamoto, S.: Bitcoin: A Peer-to-Peer Electronic Cash System. https://bitcoin.org/bitcoin.pdf
8. HyperLedger Foundation: HyperLedger Architecture, vol. 1. https://www.hyperledger.org/wp-content/uploads/2017/08/Hyperledger_Arch_WG_Paper_1_Consensus.pdf
9. ChainIng: Chain Protocol Whitepaper. https://chain.com/docs/1.2/protocol/papers/whitepaper

10. Haughwout, J.: Tracking medicine by transparent blockchain. Pharm. Process. **33**(1), 24–26 (2018). https://www.scopus.com/inward/record.uri?eid=2-s2.0-85041910404&partnerID= 40&md5=612062b1d6063ef645c89cff7c793d93

11. Dagher, G.G., Mohler, J., Milojkovic, M., Marella, P.B.: Ancile: privacy-preserving framework for access control and interoperability of electronic health records using blockchain technology. Sustain. Cities Soc. (2018). https://doi.org/10.1016/j.scs.2018.02.014

12. Pazaitis, A., De Filippi, P., Kostakis, V.: Blockchain and value systems in the sharing economy: the illustrative case of Backfeed. Technol. Forecast. Soc. Chang. **125**, 105–115 (2017). https://doi.org/10.1016/j.techfore.2017.05.025

13. Ying, W., Jia, S., Du, W.: Digital enablement of blockchain: evidence from HNA group. Int. J. Inf. Manage. **39**, 1–4 (2018). https://doi.org/10.1016/j.ijinfomgt.2017.10.004

14. Ølnes, S., Ubacht, J., Janssen, M.: Blockchain in government: Benefits and implications of distributed ledger technology for information sharing. Gov. Inf. Quart.y **34**(3), 355–364 (2017). https://doi.org/10.1016/j.giq.2017.09.007

Towards a Design Space for Blockchain-Based System Reengineering

Marco Comuzzi$^{(\boxtimes)}$, Erdenekhuu Unurjargal, and Chiehyeon Lim

Ulsan National Institute of Science and Technology, Ulsan, Republic of Korea
{mcomuzzi,eeg1123,chlim}@unist.ac.kr

Abstract. We discuss our ongoing effort in designing a methodology for blockchain-based system reengineering. In particular, we focus in this paper on defining the design space, i.e., the set of options available to designers when applying blockchain to reengineer an existing system. In doing so, we use a practice-driven approach, in which this design space is constructed bottom-up from analysis of existing blockchain use cases and hands-on experience in real world design case studies. Two case studies are presented: using blockchain to reengineer the meat trade supply chain in Mongolia and blockchain-based management of ERP post-implementation modifications.

Keywords: Blockchain · System design · Reengineering

1 Introduction

A blockchain is a shared ledger through which different parties can verify and store any kind of records and transactions in blocks. A block has the hash information of the previous block and the blocks are connected with the hash information and form a chain. Owing to cryptographic techniques, a blockchain is immutable and tamper-proof by design and, as such, it creates trust among involved parties without the need for intermediaries to verify the validity of transactions. Although blockchain is recognised as a potentially revolutionary technology for all industries, deployment of blockchains outside finance and, specifically, cryptocurrencies and related applications, is still largely experimental. For instance, all papers in a special issue on blockchain and information systems research recently published in BISE[1] considered only applications of blockchain in risk management and finance.

In the literature, we recognise some efforts to look at blockchain as a design tool for reengineering existing systems. Benefits of applying blockchain in a system span from removing intermediaries and lowering transactional costs to

---

This work was supported by UNIST research fund, project number 1.180055.

[1] http://www.bise-journal.com/?p=1243.

© Springer International Publishing AG, part of Springer Nature 2018
R. Matulevičius and R. Dijkman (Eds.): CAiSE 2018 Workshops, LNBIP 316, pp. 138–143, 2018.
https://doi.org/10.1007/978-3-319-92898-2_11

increasing agility and security, and creating trust among partners. Kshetri [5] has recently analysed the potential impact of blockchain on supply chain reengineering. Their analysis, however, is limited to benefits and drawbacks and only marginally focuses on blockchain as a design element of a supply chain. In the field of software architecture, Xu et al. [9] provide a thorough taxonomy of blockchain-based systems for architecture design. The analysis, however, is situated at a technical, developer-oriented level, focusing on protocol design and computational efficiency. Nevertheless, as shown later, many of the considerations made by Xu et al. have also inspired our work.

Based on our analysis instantiated above, we argue that more research is needed about blockchain as a tool for system reengineering. In this paper we aim at giving an overview of our ongoing research in this direction. In particular, we describe our efforts in defining a methodology for blockchain-based system reengineering. Virtually any type of system where information is exchanged by multiple parties can be reengineered using blockchain. The wide applicability of blockchain as a reengineering paradigm makes it impossible to develop a top-down approach that could fit any possible scenario. Conversely, in this work we take a bottom-up, practice-driven approach, in which the design space of blockchain-based system reengineering is built by considering the features required by different real design cases analysed by the authors (see [7] for a similar process followed by the authors in the context of defining big data to advance service). At this nascent stage of blockchain literature, this empirical approach would be useful to derive theoretical implications. We concur with the Action Research philosophy [2] that close observation and understanding is possible only through action. Nothing helps understand blockchain-based system reengineering better than the reengineering of one made by the researchers.

In this paper, we present a first iteration in developing a blockchain-based system reengineering design space. This is based on a preliminary analysis of several blockchain use cases in different industries, and, most importantly, on two case studies that we are currently developing. These two case studies are briefly presented in the next section. Section 3 introduces the design space. Section 4 discusses ongoing and future work while drawing the conclusions.

2   Case Studies

Case 1 refers to reengineering the livestock supply chain in the Mongolian meat market; case 2 refers to using blockchain for managing post-implementation changes in ERP implementations. Before initiating the two case studies, we analysed existing use cases of blockchain (e.g., in finance [3], energy [4], consumer electronics [6], and manufacturing [1]) to initially identify some dimensions of system design that have been tested and extended through our own design case studies.

Case 1: Blockchain-Based Livestock Supply Chain in Mongolia
The total number of livestock (sheep, goat, cow, horse and camel) in Mongolia is about 60 million units, that is, about 20 times the country's population.

Mongolian livestock is mostly owned by herders, who roam seasonally in the vast Mongolian countryside. Most of the meat consumption, however, occurs in the country's capital Ulanbataar, where about 40% of the country's population lives. The trade between herders and the capital's meat sellers, e.g., supermarkets and local markets, is mediated by so-called *dealers*. Dealers are middlemen, usually family-based, with enough manpower to either transport large livestock quantities to the capital or slaughter livestock in the countryside and transport the carcasses to the capital.

This current meat trade supply chain has several problems. The system is not regulated and dealers have a staggering bargaining power, since they are the only ones that can match supply and demand. This is a problem particularly for herders, who cannot negotiate prices that would allow them to have decent standards of living. Meat sellers, on the other hand, have no visibility on the supply chain and rely completely on information from dealers, which has major issues for tracking delivery dates and quantities and guaranteeing the source of the meat. While the role of dealers cannot be physically eliminated, this is a typical scenario in which blockchain-based reengineering can clearly reduce the power of dealers and dramatically increase the level of data transparency and trust among actors in the supply chain.

The solution that we envision in this case considers multiple blockchains, one for each identified supply chain, i.e., a set of herders, middlemen and meat sellers repeatedly doing business together. The content of blocks is fairly straightforward, since only basic information about traded livestock and provenance has to be recorded. Simple smart contracts to adjust traded stock levels can also be included. Blockchains can be also used to track payments, possibly involving external actors such as banks or escrow services. In order to maintain trust among partners, a new block can be added to blockchains only if all parties involved in the supply chain agree to it. A further development of applying blockchain in this scenario concerns the creation of one global higher level blockchain that the national government can use to study and apply regulations to this key market in the Mongolian economy. This global blockchain may involve meat companies and authorities and scale up the scenario. It can then be used to enforce regulation, such as stricter controls and reporting policies for herdsmen and dealers exceeding certain levels of gross trade, or verification of meat seller provenance information based on data stored in the blockchain.

Case 2: Blockchain to Manage ERP Post Implementation Changes

Most organisations worldwide have already gone through one or more ERP implementations and found themselves in the so-called post-implementation phase. In this phase, the ERP systems may require changes beyond traditional corrective maintenance to address emerging business requirements, e.g., new government regulations or different warehouse management policies. These changes bear an impact on the static design structure and runtime of an ERP system. A change of a business object, for instance, may not be compatible with functions using it, making them practically unusable. In turn, these functions may be used in business processes. The instances currently running of these processes may run into trouble if they have not passed the execution point at which these unusable new functions are required. Managing ERP post-implementation changes helps to avoid chaotic evolution of the system, therefore increasing ERP system and data quality.

In previous work, the authors have already proposed and evaluated a tool-supported methodology to manage ERP post-implementation changes effectively [8]. Following the principle of engineering change management, a change to an ERP system is first proposed. Then, before being approved, it is evaluated in terms of its design- and run-time impact on the existing system. Based on its impact, a change can be either approved or refused. Once approved, a change is then executed. Execution involves the actual implementation of changes and the transition of running process instances affected by the change to a safe termination.

The methodology described above can clearly benefit from a blockchain-based reengineering. In particular, for any given ERP installation, we envision a single blockchain keeping track of all post-implementation changes occurred since the go-live of the system. A block should contain all information related with a change, such as the business requirement addressed, the persons involved in the change (approval, implementation etc.), the impact of the change, and details about what has been changed and how, e.g., whether the ERP code base has been modified or simply some ERP configuration parameters have been changed. A block should also include smart contracts to enforce the safe termination of running process instances affected by a change. Finally, the consensus rules in place to accept a new block in the blockchain should embed the evaluation of the impact of a proposed change. In particular, we envision a combination of automated and voting-based consensus. The impact of a change can be evaluated automatically and a change may be automatically refused if it has a too large impact on the existing system. At the same time, however, a voting system can be implemented to keep into account the human aspect in this decision making process: a proposed change, for instance, although of limited impact on the system, may be rejected by managers because not aligned to other organisational policies. Alternatively, a change may be rejected if a sufficient share of the users involved in the processes affected by the change do not agree with it, for instance because it would be modify current practice too radically.

Compared to existing methodologies, blockchain-based implementation brings a set of additional benefits to this scenario. The history of post-implementation changes of an ERP system can be documented fully in a traceable and immutable way. Most importantly, the blockchain would allow to track not only *what* has been done, but also *how* a change has been implemented, e.g., both the process followed to propose and approve a change and the smart contracts that have been enforced after the change implementation would also be stored safely in the blockchain.

3   Design Space

Based on the case studies introduced above, we organise the blockchain-based system reengineering design space into a set of design dimensions, which belong to two areas, i.e., *Structure* and *Interaction*. The former groups design concerns related to the static content of blockchain(s) in a system, whereas the latter identifies concerns related with the behaviour of actors in a system when using the blockchain.

In the *Structure* area, we identify the following 4 design dimensions:

Cardinality. Concerns the numbers of blockchain to be implemented in a given domain. In case study 1, one blockchain for each *trade network*, i.e., group of trading herders, dealers, meat sellers, can be created; a global blockchain can be created with aggregated information to support regulation enforcement at government level. In case study 2, one particular blockchain is created for each ERP installation to track all changes occurred to it. Note that one organisation may run multiple ERP installations from different vendors at once.

Type. Concerns whether public/permissioned or private blockchains are considered. Private and permissioned blockchains can increase security and resiliency by leveraging public computational resources to assess block validity. Case study 1 can benefit from using public/permissioned blockchains because it concerns a more open scenario, in which dealers and meat sellers can dynamically join, whereas case study 2 represents a typical private case, in which information should only be shared within a specific organisational domain.

Content of Blocks. Concerns the information recorded in blocks; In case 1, records are simply about livestocks and trades, with elementary smart contracts adjusting trade balances and stock levels; in case 2, the content is more complex and smart contracts should be deployed to ensure safe termination of running process instances affected by process change.

Block Determination. Concerns the way in blocks are determined. Case study 1 may adopt a temporal approach, similar to the one adopted by cryptocurrencies, in which blocks are written at a given frequency to include all transactions occurred in a given time interval; changes in case study 2 may occur at a much lower frequency than transactions in case study 1, so case study 2 may adopt an event-based paradigm, in which a new block is written for each ERP change.

In the *Interaction* area, we identify the following 4 design dimensions:

Validation. Concerns the (possibly automated) rules to validate the content of a block. In case 1, these are simple conditions on account balances and stock levels . In case 2, more complex rules to evaluate the validity of a proposed change and its impact on the existing ERP system should be considered.

Consensus. Concerns the way in which parties reach consensus before including a new valid block in a blockchain. In case 1, all parties should agree to new block creation; in case 2, a voting system giving more importance to the opinion of users/managers with more experience should be in place.

Incentives. Concerns the method to motivate and promote the participation and interactions of network participants. In case 1, a token may be used for monetary incentives to the participants; in case 2, a token may not be appropriate because the blockchain should be fully private.

Permissions. Concerns the scheme regulating the ability of actors to propose and access content of a blockchain. In case 1, dealers, sellers and herders can propose new transactions, possibly manually, while government has a read-only access to data in blockchains. In case 2, a more complex scheme regulates access, i.e., only process owners and technical managers may propose new ERP changes, while users can only read information about past changes.

4   Conclusions

The work presented in this paper is currently being developed. On the one hand, we are defining more case studies to extend/refine the design space definition. In particular, we are considering blockchain-based reeengineering of several initiatives in our university campus, such as the reengineering using blockchain of research notebooks in natural sciences and a campus-wide cryptocurrency to secure and facilitate dorm fees payment and on-campus student subsistence. On the other hand, we are developing the methodology beyond the design space definition, to support system design on top of the defined design method. We are currently developing systematic guidelines to define alternative design configurations and an optimisation method to choose the optimal configuration based on notion of utility (e.g. selecting the combination of design options that maximizes the utility function of one specific participant or that balances the utility functions of different participants).

References

1. Abeyratne, S.A., Monfared, R.P.: A Blockchain Application in Energy. Loughborough University (2017)
2. Avison, D.E., Lau, F., Myers, M.D., Nielsen, P.A.: Action research. Commun. ACM **42**, 87–94 (1999)
3. Guo, Y., Liang, C.: Blockchain application and outlook in the banking industry. Financ. Innov. **2**, 24 (2016)
4. Hukkinen, T., Mattila, J., Ilomäki, J., Seppala, T.: A Blockchain Application in Energy. The Research Institute of the Finnish Economy (2017)
5. Kshetri, N.: Blockchain's roles in meeting key supply chain management objectives. Int. J. Inf. Manag. **39**, 80–89 (2018)
6. Lee, J.H., Pilkington, M.: How the blockchain revolution will reshape the consumer electronics industry. IEEE Consum. Electron. Mag. **6**, 19–23 (2017)
7. Lim, C., Kim, K., Kim, M.J., Heo, J.Y., Kim, K.J., Maglio, P.P.: From data to value: a nine-factor framework for data-based value creation in information-intensive services. Int. J. Inf. Manag. **39**, 121–135 (2018)
8. Parhizkar, M., Comuzzi, M.: Impact analysis of ERP post-implementation modifications: design, tool support and evaluation. Comput. Ind. **84**, 25–38 (2017)
9. Xu, X., Weber, I., Staples, M., Zhu, L., Bosch, J., Bass, L., Pautasso, C., Rimba, P.: A taxonomy of blockchain-based systems for architecture design. In: 2017 IEEE International Conference on Software Architecture (ICSA), pp. 243–252. IEEE (2017)

Towards Collaborative and Reproducible Scientific Experiments on Blockchain

Dimka Karastoyanova[1(✉)] and Ludwig Stage[2]

[1] Information Systems Group, University of Groningen, Groningen, The Netherlands
d.karastoyanova@rug.nl
[2] SySS GmbH, Tübingen, Germany
bpm@stage.syss.de, bpm@ludwig-stage.de

Abstract. Business process management research opened numerous opportunities for synergies with blockchains in different domains. Blockchains have been identified as means of preventing illegal runtime adaptation of decentralized choreographies that involve untrusting parties. In the eScience domain however there is a need to support a different type of collaboration where adaptation is essential part of that collaboration. Scientists demand support for trial-and-error experiment modeling in collaboration with other scientists and at the same time, they require reproducible experiments and results. The first aspect has already been addressed using adaptable scientific choreographies. To enable trust among collaborating scientists in this position paper we identify potential approaches for combining adaptable scientific choreographies with blockchain platforms, discuss their advantages and point out future research questions.

Keywords: Flexible scientific choreographies · Reproducibility
Trust · Blockchain · Collaboration · Adaptive smart contracts

1 Introduction

Currently the blockchain technology has a significant impact on Business Process Management (BPM) research and is considered to be the main disruptor in this field. Challenges and opportunities of blockchains for BPM [3] have been identified and abundant research work has been reported towards identifying the best use of blockchains for enabling decentralized collaborative processes. Initial results have been demonstrated towards bridging the gap between the convenient process modeling provided by BPM systems and the "possibilities opened by blockchain platforms" [2], in particular related to the charm of keeping immutable trace of transactions without the need of a third party. The major opportunity to exploit is therefore the promise to enable trusted collaborations between "mutually untrusting parties" [2].

In this position paper we focus on only one of the aspects of BPM, namely *runtime adaptation of processes*. The discussion in [3] about how blockchain

© Springer International Publishing AG, part of Springer Nature 2018
R. Matulevičius and R. Dijkman (Eds.): CAiSE 2018 Workshops, LNBIP 316, pp. 144–149, 2018.
https://doi.org/10.1007/978-3-319-92898-2_12

relates to the BPM life cycle identifies the opportunity to utilize blockchains as one means of preventing illegal adaptation in order to ensure correct process execution, and ensuring the conformance with a model and rules defined in the contract among parties.

In this work we focus our research on the *synergies of the fields runtime adaptation of choreographies, blockchains and eScience*. Our motivation comes from the fact that in eScience, and in particular scientific workflows, there is a need for *adaptable or flexible choreographies* to support scientists in their trial-and-error manner of scientific exploration. We claim that scientists need enabling systems for a completely different type of collaboration when modeling their in-silico experiments. We identify the need for trusted, reproducible, collaborative adaptation of the in-silico experiments. Our position is that this need can be attended to by adaptable blockchain-based choreographies that allow collaborating scientists to track the provenance of the adaptation steps made in addition to the provenance of data, analyses and results. The other opportunity we identify is that adaptable blockchain-based choreographies can provide the means towards both RARE research (Robust Accountable Reproducible Explained) [1,4] and FAIR publishing (Findable Accessible Interoperable Reusable results).

With this position paper we want to identify the possible approaches to employ blockchain platforms for collaborative, adaptable and reproducible in-silico experiments. In Sect. 2 we will provide background information about the eScience requirements and the "Model-as-You-Go for Choreographies" approach that addresses only some of these requirements. In Sect. 3 we identify potential solutions, discuss their capabilities and identify open research questions to be overcome in future research on the synergies of BPM and blockchains in the field of eScience. We conclude the paper in Sect. 4.

2   Flexible Choreographies in eScience

Here we only discuss the two aspects of scientific experiments which are influencing our envisioned research the most: (1) the need to enable collaborative explorative research allowing scientists to interleave modeling and execution of experiment steps and (2) the aspect of reproducibility of experiments necessary in order to establish trust in the research method, data and obtained results.

Workflow technology offers a design and implementation approach for in-silico experiments and recent research results evidence considerable developments and broad acceptance of the concept scientific workflows. Scientists use scientific workflows to specify the control and data flow of experiments and orchestrate scientific software modules and services. The use of workflow technology in eScience fosters improvements in scientific collaboration through software services reuse. However, scientists have additional requirements on workflow modeling and enactment to ones of users in the business domain. Scientists often demand support for *trial-and-error experimentation* where (a) experiments are being modeled, started, paused, extended and resumed and (b) parts of the experiment are created and executed by different scientists on their own execution infrastructure. On the one hand scientists want to be able to start executing incomplete, partially defined workflow models; add, remove and skip experiment steps to complete the model while it is being executed; reverse and repeat the execution of experiment steps with different parameters [7]. On the other hand all these operations are required to be performed in collaboration. Here, natural scientists are both the designers and users of a workflow model [8]. In our recent work we address these requirements with an approach called *Model-As-You-Go for Choreographies* [7]. The approach is based on runtime adaptation of processes, an interactive scientific Workflow Management System (sWfMS) [7] and a special middleware (called ChorMiddleware) coordinating the adaptation of choreographies [9] (see Fig. 1). The system supports the life cycle of scientific workflows. A modeling and monitoring environment is used to: (a) model collaborative experiments using choreographies with the ChorDesigner, (b) generate the visible interfaces of all participating workflows in the collaboration (Transformer component), (c) refine the internal workflow logic of the individual participant workflows and (d) serve as a monitoring tool. Scientists use the modeling tools to perform adaptation steps on the choreography that models the overall experiment or on the individual workflows, or both, and these changes are propagated to the running process instances on the workflow engines. In answer to the demand of scientists to monitor the state of the experiment that is currently being modeled and executed, we show the monitoring information directly in the modeling tools, as well as all adaptation steps. The workflow execution is performed by a set of sWfMS. The coordination is done by the ChorMiddleware implementing corresponding algorithms and coordination protocols.

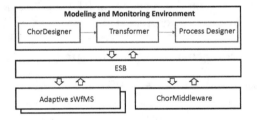

Fig. 1. Architecture of the Model-as-You-Go system (adapted from [9])

Another critical eScience requirement is *provenance*, which is the basis for *reproducible research* [4]. Computing environments used for scientific research are required to track the provenance of data, analyses and results with the purpose of ensuring reproducibility and repeatability of research, comparison of results and methods, preservation of the whole experiment and peer review [1]. In eScience this implies that all new tools and systems must enable provenance and need to expand recording, reporting, and reproduction of methods, data and results [4]. To enable *trust* among scientists in collaborative work on experiments, tracking provenance becomes even more important [1]. Consequently, the Model-as-You-Go approach has to ensure that the adaptive nature of all experiments is captured and reproducible on the level of both the individual adaptive workflows and the choreography. Establishing provenance is not only necessary for the data used but also for the changes made by each of the scientists in the collaboration and the adaptation. Therefore there is a need to capture the changes made that have led to the final choreography model and that would help scientists understand what combination of software services and data have been used, in what sequence, thus document all their steps. This need could be addressed in a traditional way using an audit trail component of sWfMS, however the trend in scientific research towards more trusted scientific results calls for an approach more suitable for collaborative environments where no single party should have control over the adaptation ledger. As indicated above and in literature, blockchain could be the technology suitable to provide a solution to establish trust and support provenance and reproducibility of research [5].

3   Approaches for Reproducible, Collaborative and Adaptable Experiments

Considering the original focus of our work, namely the use of flexible choreographies in support of collaborative experiment modeling, and the available, standard-based system realization, we envision two approaches of employing blockchain.

The *first approach* (see Fig. 2, left) would be to reuse as much as we can from our existing realization system and combine it with a blockchain platform purely as a ledger. Supporters of blockchain for research suggest that it could improve "reproducibility and the peer review process by creating incorruptible data trails and securely recording publication decisions" [5]. Realizing this approach would mean that the audit trail (i.e. the history of workflow and choreography execution) is stored on a blockchain. The issue here is that typical audit trails are huge amounts of data, and in eScience by default the amounts of data we deal with is big anyhow. Storing data on the blockchain is very expensive, so it remains to be investigated how much of the historical data should be stored on the blockchain and how much on some other storage so that the reproducibility of the experiment can be guaranteed. Note that the history of all adaptation steps that is produced by our system has to be recorded too, which means that all the information we currently collect from workflow engines, the coordination middleware and the modeling tools that are the interface of scientists to the system has to appear on the audit trail.

In order to enable the FAIR publishing of the research results, which should also demonstrate the reproducibility of the experiment, the audit trail on the blockchain and the rest of the information necessary for that, but not more than the scientists would like to disclose, has to be read out from the system and presented appropriately. The visualization techniques necessary for that have to be delivered, too. The advantages of this approach are that we can reuse as much as possible of the existing sWfMS and because of this fact we would have a system capable of recording the trace of adaptations in place much faster. Such an approach may be appropriate enough for some scientific research efforts [5].

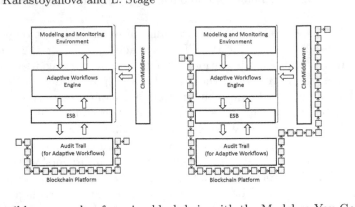

Fig. 2. Possible approaches for using blockchain with the Model-as-You-Go system

The disadvantage that we foresee from the current stand point is the fact that smart contracts, which enable blockchains to be more than just logs, would not be utilized and hence the capabilities they possess would remain unexplored.

The *second approach* is to investigate how a blockchain BPM system, such as [2], can be used instead of the workflow engine that is in place now and the adaptation mechanisms it implements, together with the middleware coordinating the adaptation of choreographies (see Fig. 2, right). This approach requires a new concept of *adaptable smart contracts*, because processes on a blockchain-based BPM system are deployed as smart contacts. Research in adaptable smart contracts will have to focus on the following activities: (a) Define the concept of adaptable smart contracts and identify the mechanisms of how smart contracts can be adapted; abundant research in process adaptation like [6] can be used as a systematic guideline to address this issue. (b) Investigate how adaptable collaborative scientific choreographies are represented on a blockchain BPM system using smart contracts. (c) As smart contracts stand for a "transaction protocol that executes the terms of a contract" [2], it has to be evaluated if the coordination protocols for choreography adaptation need to be designed, deployed and run as smart contracts as well. The system architecture of an enabling system may have different topologies featuring different functional components or parts of components on a blockchain. Investigation and evaluation of what the best architectural topology is for certain scientific domains must be carried out and at the same time consider the placement of data on the blockchain and the user's security and privacy preferences. The consideration about how the design of the audit trail should look like is the same as with the first approach, however the monitoring capability may require a more complex architecture to be realized, since the monitoring information has to be made available directly into the choreography and workflow modeling tools. Publishing of the experimental results needs to be enabled with this approach, too. Advantages of this approach are that all steps in experiments and all adaptations performed will be stored in an immutable trace and that the coordination of adaptation will be a trusted protocol execution. For collaborative scientific explorations where reproducibility and trust are of utmost importance, this approach has a huge potential.

A disadvantage is the admittedly higher integration effort and complexity of the system and of the adaptation mechanisms.

4   Conclusions

In this paper we state our position that the combination of collaborative adaptable choreographies and the blockchain technology is a very promising one and qualifies as a solution for enabling trusted collaboration in eScience. We identified two possible courses of action for future research: the first approach uses blockchain platforms as a ledger only to store information relevant for the reproducibility of collaborative experiments and their results, and their publishing, whereas the second approach proposes using blockchain platforms for the execution of adaptive scientific choreographies and workflows through the notion of adaptive smart contracts. We have also identified the open research questions both approaches are facing and indicated their advantages and disadvantages. Admittedly, there are more open questions for future research. Some examples are the user friendliness of the potential realizations of either approach, their performance characteristics, and the access control mechanisms that will satisfy the demands of scientists to disclose only the minimum of information allowing for reproducibility.

References

1. Goble, C.: Results vary: the pragmatics of reproducibility and research object frameworks, keynote. iConference (2015). https://www.slideshare.net/carolegoble/i-conference2015-goblefinalupload
2. López-Pintado, O., et al.: Caterpillar: a blockchain-based business process management system. In: Proceedings of the BPM Demo Track and Dissertation Award (BPM 2017) (2017). http://ceur-ws.org/Vol-1920/BPM_2017_paper_199.pdf
3. Mendling, J., et al.: Blockchains for business process management - challenges and opportunities. CoRR abs/1704.03610 (2017). http://arxiv.org/abs/1704.03610
4. Mesirov, J.P.: Accessible reproducible research. Science **327**(5964), 415–416 (2010). http://science.sciencemag.org/content/327/5964/415
5. van Rossum, J.: Blockchain for research. Science, November 2017. https://figshare.com/articles/Blockchain_for_Research/5607778
6. Weber, B., et al.: Change patterns and change support features - enhancing flexibility in process-aware information systems. Data Knowl. Eng. **66**(3), 438–466 (2008)
7. Weiss, A., et al.: Model-as-You-Go for Choreographies: rewinding and repeating scientific choreographies. IEEE Trans. Serv. Comput. **PP**(99), 1 (2017)
8. Weiß, A., Karastoyanova, D.: Enabling coupled multi-scale, multi-field experiments through choreographies of data-driven scientific simulations. Computing **98**(4), 439–467 (2016)
9. Weiß, A., Andrikopoulos, V., Sáez, S.G., Hahn, M., Karastoyanova, D.: ChorSystem: a message-based system for the life cycle management of choreographies. In: Debruyne, C., et al. (eds.) OTM 2016. LNCS, vol. 10033, pp. 503–521. Springer, Cham (2016). https://doi.org/10.1007/978-3-319-48472-3_30

COGNISE – Cognitive Aspects
of Information Systems Engineering

6th International Workshop on Cognitive Aspects of Information Systems Engineering (COGNISE 2018)

Preface

Cognitive aspects of software and information systems engineering have received increasing attention in the literature and at conferences in recent years, acknowledging that these aspects are as important as the technical ones, which have traditionally been in the center of attention. This workshop serves as a stage for new research and lively discussions on this topic, involving both academics and practitioners.

The goal of this workshop is to provide a better understanding and more appropriate support of the cognitive processes and challenges practitioners experience when performing information systems development activities. Understanding the challenges and needs, educational programs, as well as development supporting tools and notations may be enhanced for a better fit to our natural cognition, leading to better performance of engineers and higher systems quality.

The workshop aims to bring together researchers from different communities such as requirements engineering, software architecture, modeling, design and programming, and information systems education, who share an interest in cognitive aspects, for identifying the cognitive challenges in the diverse development-related activities and for proposing for relevant solutions.

The sixth edition of this workshop, held in Tallinn on June 12, 2018, was organized in conjunction with the 30th International Conference on Advanced Information Systems Engineering (CAiSE 2018) and in collaboration with the working conference on Exploring Modelling Methods for Systems Analysis and Development (EMMSAD), this year named EMMSAD++ (in conjunction with COGNISE and ASDENCA).

This edition of COGNISE attracted eight international submissions. Each paper was reviewed by three members of the Program Committee. Of these submissions, four papers were accepted for inclusion in the proceedings (50%). The papers presented at the workshop provide a mix of novel research ideas, presenting full research or research in progress. In addition, the workshop hosted a keynote speech by Prof. Walid Maalej: "Requirements 4.0 from Systematic User Involvement to System Adaptation."

We hope that the reader will find this selection of papers useful to be informed and inspired by new ideas in the area of cognitive aspects of information systems engineering, and we look forward to future editions of the COGNISE workshop following the six editions held to date.

April 2018

Irit Hadar
Irene Vanderfeesten
Barbara Weber

COGNISE 2018 Organization

Organizing Committee

Irit Hadar	University of Haifa, Israel
Irene Vanderfeesten	Eindhoven University of Technology, The Netherlands
Barbara Weber	Technical University of Denmark, Denmark

Program Committee

Banu Aysolmaz	Vrije Universiteit Amsterdam, The Netherlands
Daniel M. Berry	University of Waterloo, Canada
Jan Claes	Ghent University, Belgium
Kathrin Figl	Vienna University of Economics and Business, Austria
Stijn Hoppenbrouwers	HAN University of Applied Sciences, Arnhem, The Netherlands
	Radboud University, The Netherlands
Marta Indulska	University of Queensland, Australia
Meira Levy	Shenkar College of Engineering and Design, Israel
Jeffrey Parsons	Memorial University, Canada
Geert Poels	Ghent University, Belgium
Maryam Razavian	Eindhoven University of Technology, The Netherlands
Alexander Serebrenik	Eindhoven University of Technology, The Netherlands
Sofia Sherman	University of Waterloo, Canada
Pnina Soffer	University of Haifa, Israel
Dirk van der Linden	University of Bristol, UK
Anna Zamansky	University of Haifa, Israel

The Origin and Evolution of Syntax Errors in Simple Sequence Flow Models in BPMN

Joshua De Bock and Jan Claes[(✉)]

Department of Business Informatics and Operations Management, Ghent
University, Tweekerkenstraat 2, 9000 Ghent, Belgium
{joshua.debock, jan.claes}@ugent.be

Abstract. How do syntax errors emerge? What is the earliest moment that potential syntax errors can be detected? Which evolution do syntax errors go through during modeling? A provisional answer to these questions is formulated in this paper based on an investigation of a dataset containing the operational details of 126 modeling sessions. First, a list is composed of the different potential syntax errors. Second, a classification framework is built to categorize the errors according to their certainty and severity during modeling (i.e., in partial or complete models). Third, the origin and evolution of all syntax errors in the dataset are identified. This data is then used to collect a number of observations, which form a basis for future research.

Keywords: Conceptual modeling · Business Process Management
Process · Model · Process of process modeling · Quality · Syntactic quality
Syntax error

1 Introduction

Conceptual models are frequently used in practice and therefore it should come as no surprise that people are interested in the improvement of their quality [1, 2]. Therefore, we decided to study how quality issues arise and evolve during the modeling process. With this research we hope to provide a first insight into possible evolutions and the detection of syntax errors in early stages, as to improve the quality of process models. Because many factors influence the quality of conceptual models (e.g., the modeling goal, the domain of interest, the modeling language, the intended audience), this is a complex study domain and it was decided to limit the scope of the research in this initial phase. One of the oldest and most influential frameworks about the quality of conceptual modelling is the *SEQUAL* framework [2]. This framework makes a distinction between **syntactic quality** (symbol accordance with the modelling language syntax and vocabulary), **semantic quality** (correctness and completeness of the model in relation to reality), and **pragmatic quality** (understanding correctness of the model by its users).

Methodologically, it makes sense to first investigate syntactic quality. In contrast to for example semantic and pragmatic quality, syntactic quality can be measured more accurately because syntax errors can be detected and valued relatively more objectively [3]. Also, there is already a large body of knowledge related to syntactic quality. It

© Springer International Publishing AG, part of Springer Nature 2018
R. Matulevičius and R. Dijkman (Eds.): CAiSE 2018 Workshops, LNBIP 316, pp. 155–166, 2018.
https://doi.org/10.1007/978-3-319-92898-2_13

appears to be included in most model quality frameworks (e.g., SEQUAL [3], CMQF [4]), reliable and valid metrics exist that measure syntactic quality (e.g., soundness of process models), and a high number of model editors contain features to prevent or detect syntax errors (e.g., Rational System Architect, ARIS). Although one may argue that it is less useful for practice to focus on syntax errors because tools help to avoid them, the practical value of this research lies exactly in the support for the development of such tools. The insights in the origin and evolution of syntax errors may bring forward the moment that tools can interact with the user about current or future syntax issues.

Next, mainly for practical reasons (i.e., the availability of a specific dataset), the scope of this paper is also reduced to only sequence flow process models, using a very limited subset of only 6 constructs from the popular BPMN language. The advantage is that the complexity of the research is reduced to its bare minimum. Obviously, this comes at the cost of a limited internal and external validity. Nevertheless, as you will be able to discover further in this paper, we still collected non-trivial observations that form a solid basis for future research.

The research was performed in three phases. First, based on the specification of the selected BPMN constructs, a comprehensive list was composed of potential syntax errors. Second, a classification framework was built that is used to categorize these potential errors according to their certainty and severity. Third, using the list and framework, the origin and evolution of the syntax errors that were made during a modeling session with 126 modelers was investigated in order to collect observations. As such, this paper describes 11 observations about the origin and evolution of syntax errors during modeling. They describe valuable insights, but they also illustrate the potential of the applied research method for future, more extensive, research.

This paper is structured as follows. Section 2 presents related work. Section 3 describes the construction of the list with syntax errors. Section 4 discusses the framework that can be used to classify syntax errors based on certainty and severity. Section 5 presents the collected observations. Section 6 provides a conclusion.

2   Related Work

To the best of our knowledge, this is the first work to study the origin and evolution of syntax errors in conceptual models throughout the construction process. Nevertheless, this work builds further on studies about the quality of conceptual models and on research about conceptual modeling that takes a process orientation.

The prominent *SEQUAL* framework has been adapted and extended multiple times (e.g. by Krogstie et al. [3], who make a distinction between 10 different types of quality). A more recent effort, is the *Conceptual Modelling Quality Framework* (CMQF), which further extends the aforementioned frameworks [4]. As such, it synthesizes the above-mentioned *SEQUAL* extension and the *Bunge-Wand-Weber* (BWW) framework [5].

In order to put the study towards the origin and evolution of syntax errors into perspective, it can be considered in a stream of research that takes a process-oriented view on modeling. Hoppenbrouwers et al. describe the main variables in what is called the **process of conceptual modeling** [6]. Wilmont et al. add a cognitive level to this research and focus on individual differences as a key factor in the variation of errors between modeling efforts [7]. At the same time, Soffer et al. lay the foundation for the study of the **process of process modeling**, focusing on only one particular type of conceptual models (i.e., process models) [8]. This initiated a popular research stream about various aspects of the process of process modeling [9–11]. With insights in the origin and evolution of syntax errors, our research could improve the process of process modeling by assisting the modeler during the process.

3 Construction of the List of Potential Syntax Errors

This section describes the creation of the list with potential syntax errors within the scope of the research (i.e., sequence flow models with a simplified BPMN syntax).

3.1 Approach

The BPMN 2.0 specification [12] was used to look up the definition and usage constraints of the sequence flow constructs of our tool. The six available constructs in the tool are (1) start event, (2) end event, (3) XOR (split or join) gateway, (4) AND (split or join) gateway, (5) activity, and (6) sequence flow. These are considered to be essential for sequence flow modeling and they were selected because they are most used in BPMN models [13]. Then, based on the specification, a list was built with the potential syntax errors (i.e., wrong usage of the symbols). Finally, the list was completed with other syntax issues that are similar to the real errors, but which are not wrong according to the syntax (cf. Sect. 4.3).

3.2 Results

Table 1 presents the composed list. It is an extension of the list by Claes et al. [14]. The syntax issues that are not erroneous are marked in grey. From here on, we refer to *syntax errors* to indicate all issues in Table 1 that are not marked in grey and we use *syntax issues* to refer to all issues in the list (including the *syntax errors*).

Table 1. List of syntax issues with six constructs in BPMN 2.0

Construction	Code	
Contains no start event	0s	(0 start events)
Contains no end event	0e	(0 end events)
Contains multiple start events	S	(multiple starts)
Contains multiple end events	E	(multiple ends)
Sequence flow to start event	Bs	(between)

(continued)

Table 1. (*continued*)

Construction	Code	
Sequence flow from end event	Be	(between)
Sequence flow from start event missing	Ms	(missing edges)
Sequence flow to end event missing	Me	(missing edges)
Not all of the paths are closed (missing end event?)	P	(path not closed)
Multiple parallel sequence flows from non-gateway	Sa	(missing AND split)
Multiple optional sequence flows from non-gateway	Sx	(missing XOR split)
Multiple parallel sequence flows towards non-gateway	Ja	(missing AND join)
Multiple optional sequence flows towards non-gateway	Jx	(missing XOR join)
Contains no gateways at all (but does contains multiple paths)	G	(no gateways)
No join gateways in case of optional iterations	I	(wrong iteration)
One gateway combines a join and split feature	C	(combination)
Wrong type of join combined with a certain split	W	(wrong type)
Gateway with only one incoming and one outgoing sequence flow	1	(1 edge in/out)
Wrong nesting of gateways	N	(wrong nesting)
AND and XOR are joined together in one join gateway	T	(joined together)
Infinite Loop	IL	(infinite loop)
Deadlock	DL	(deadlock)
Sequence flow between activities missing	Ma	(missing edges)
Sequence flow between gateways missing	Mg	(missing edges)
No label for activity	La	(missing label)
No label for edge departing from XOR splits	Lx	(missing label)

4   Construction and Application of the Classification Framework

This section presents and discusses the classification framework that was built to categorize the *syntax issues* according to their certainty and severity.

4.1   Approach

Since we are interested in the evolution of errors (and related issues) during the modeling process, we were faced with the difficulty to recognize the *syntax issues* in an incomplete model. This is more challenging than one may expect at first sight. Let us illustrate this with an example. In sequence flow models, each element needs to be connected in the model in order to specify the order in which they should be considered (i.e., the sequence flow). In most modeling tools (including the one that was used for this research, cf. Sect. 5.1), a sequence flow arrow can be placed only between two existing components. Therefore, the modeler first has to create these two components and only then they can be connected with the arrow. But what if the connection of the two elements by placing the arrow is postponed? Since we do not know if this would be deliberate, it is (temporarily) hard to make a distinction between a planned delay and an actual *syntax issue*. Therefore, one dimension of the framework is the ***certainty*** of *syntax issues* in a partial or complete model.

Further, unfortunately, the specification of the BPMN 2.0 language [12] is not always completely consistent. For example, whereas it is explicitly stated that it is allowed to use a gateway that combines a join and a split function (*"a single Gateway could have multiple input and multiple output flows"*, p. 90), it is not fully clear what the meaning is of this construction. The specification explains only the meaning of diverging and of converging gateways in detail. Furthermore, even when certain combinations of symbols are explicitly allowed and defined by the specification, because of the popularity of best practices and guidelines, modeling experts may still consider them to be wrong (e.g., omitting the AND split or XOR join gateway in certain cases). On the contrary, combinations also exist that are clearly not allowed according to the specification, but it is easy to guess what is meant (e.g., joining two *parallel* paths directly in an activity). These are often (mistakenly) considered to be correct. Therefore, the other dimension of the classification framework is the ***severity*** of *syntax issues* in a partial or complete model.

4.2   Certainty Dimension

A distinction is made between ***wrong combinations of symbols*** and ***missing symbols*** during modeling. The former are *syntax issues* that can be resolved only by changing or removing something in the model, whereas the latter can be resolved by only adding symbols to the model. In case of wrong combinations of symbols, it is certain that a *syntax issue* exists. In the second case, the distinction between temporary planned incompleteness and unconsciously missing symbols cannot be made based on only the inspection of the partial model. Therefore, we introduce the notion of partial completeness to help assess the certainty of *syntax issues*. Every part in the model that is considered complete, will then by definition contain only ***definite*** *issues*. On the other hand, when a part of the model is considered incomplete, only the wrong combinations of symbols are considered *definite issues*, whereas missing symbols are considered ***uncertain*** *issues*.

We define ***completed parts*** of an incomplete sequence flow model as:

- the parts of the model between an opened split gateway that has been closed again by a join gateway, AND
- the parts of the model that are connected to an end event (in the direction of the sequence flows).

A number of remarks still need to be made. (1) When a model is sent to a model reader, it is considered to be complete and all parts are considered complete (even if the conditions for partial incompleteness are met). (2) This means that complete models cannot contain *uncertain issues*. Every *syntax issue* in a complete model is a *definite issue*. (3) All *uncertain issues* will thus eventually evolve into *definite issues* unless the modeler adds the missing symbols or changes the erroneous construction.

4.3   Severity Dimension

Since there can be a discussion whether a *syntax issue* is a real error in certain cases, we also make a distinction between different severity levels. We define three severities of *syntax issues*.

- First, an **error** is when the *syntax issue* is clearly wrong according to the specification.
  Are considered an error: 0s, 0e, Bs, Be, Ms, Me, Ma, Mg, P, Ja, 1, W, T, IL.
- Second, an **irresolution** is when the specification is not completely clear or when it is inconsistent.
  Are considered an irresolution: D, G, I, C, N, La, DL.
- Third, a **confusion** is when the *syntax issue* is clearly correct according to the specification, but nevertheless it is widely considered a bad practice because it hinders the (ease of) understanding.
  Are considered confusing: Jx, Sx, S, E, Sa, Lx.

4.4   Transformations

The two levels of certainty – uncertain (U) and definite (D) – and the three levels of severity – error (E), irresolution (I), and confusion (C) – provide six combinations: uncertain error (UE), uncertain irresolution (UI), uncertain confusion (UC), definite error (DE), definite irresolution (DI), and definite confusion (DC). Not every transformation between these types is possible. The *uncertain* types can evolve into *definite* types (e.g., when the part is completed without correcting the *issue*) or they can be resolved by the modeler. They cannot transform (directly) into another *uncertain* type. On the other hand, *definite* types can transform into other *definite* types or they can be resolved. They cannot transform (again) into an *uncertain* type. Table 2 presents an overview. Possible transformations are marked with an "X", and "/" refers to 'no issue'.

Table 2. Possible transformations between the types of syntax issues, marked with an "X"

From \ To	UE	UI	UC	DE	DI	DC	/
UE	–			X	X	X	X
UI		–		X	X	X	X
UC			–	X	X	X	X
DE				–	X	X	X
DI				X	–	X	X
DC				X	X	–	X
/	X	X	X	X	X	X	–

5   Investigation of the Origin and Evolution of Syntax Issues During Modeling

This section discusses how the list and classification framework were used to analyze the origin and evolution of *syntax issues* during modeling.

5.1   Approach

For this research, an existing data set was used (the same as by Claes et al. [14]). It contains the data of a modeling experiment in which the participants were instructed to construct a sequence flow model based on a textual description of a process (at a certain point in the experiment task flow, cf. [14]). The participants were 126 master students of Business Engineering at Ghent University who were enrolled in a Business Process Management course in which they learned the BPMN 2.0 syntax and how to create models within this language. The tool used to collect the data, is the Cheetah Experimental Platform[1]. It contains a simplified BPMN modeling editor offering the six constructs described above (cf. Sect. 3.1). It was selected for its features to log every operation of the user in an event log and to replay the modeling afterwards. This latter feature was used to evaluate after each operation of the user whether a *syntax issue* arose, and which was the kind and type of the *syntax issue*. For each of the 126 modeling instances, we thus complemented the dataset with the timing, kind, and type of *syntax issues* during modeling. This allowed performing a number of interesting analyses, which are discussed below.

5.2   Syntax Issues During and After Modeling

First, it was examined which types of *syntax issues* were made during modeling. On average, each sequence flow model contained 2.4 UEs, 1.0 UIs, 4.3 UCs, 3.2 DEs, 2.3 DIs, and 5.5 DCs during modeling. Since certain of these *issues* can evolve into others, this does not mean that each model contained on average 18,7 different *syntax issues* during modeling (the sum of the aforementioned numbers). After modeling, there are on average 0.5 DEs, 2.2 DIs, and 3.6 DCs.

Figure 1 shows more details on the spread of *syntax issues* during and after modeling. Based on Fig. 1, a number of observations can be made:

Obs1.   The minimum occurrence of each *syntax issue*, both during and after modeling, is 0. The dataset confirms that 2 of the 126 (1.5%) did not have any *syntax issue* during the whole modeling process.

Obs2.   Even when ignoring the outliers, the variance of the occurrence of *syntax issues* is relatively high (0 to ≥ 5 for most types).

Obs3.   Confusions (UC and DC) occur more than the other types of *syntax issues*

---

[1] Download and info at http://bpm.q-e.at/?page_id=56 (dd. 16/03/0218).

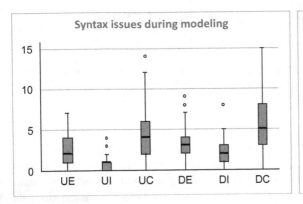
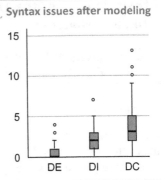

Fig. 1. Boxplots of the number of syntax issues per model during and after modeling

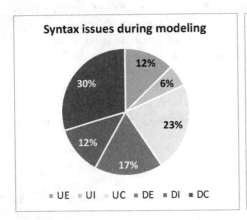
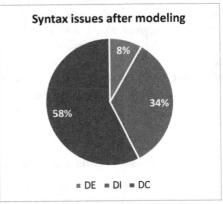

Fig. 2. Types of syntax issues during and after modeling

Next, the *relative* occurrence of each type of *syntax issue* during and after modeling is presented in Fig. 2.

Obs4. Also in Fig. 2 it can be noticed that confusions occur more than the other types of *syntax issues* (cf. Obs3)

5.3   The Origin of Syntax Issues During Modeling

In order to investigate the origin of a *definite syntax issue*, we examined what happened at the time of the operation that caused the *issue*. When another type of *issue* disappeared with that same operation, the operation is considered to have transformed one type into another type (with the restriction that no *issue* can evolve into an(other) *uncertain issue*). If no other *issue* type disappeared at the same time, the *definite syntax issue* was considered to be initiated at that exact point in time (denoted with origin "/").

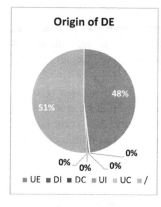
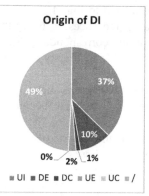
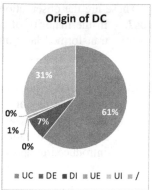

Fig. 3. The origin of syntax issues during modeling

Figure 3 shows an overview of the origins of the *definite syntax issues* during modeling. Again, a number of interesting observations can be made:

Obs5. A *definite issue* often has its origin in an *uncertain issue* of the same severity (orange slices). In this case, the *issue* could thus already be detected in an incomplete part of the partial model.

Obs6. In the other cases, they mostly are created directly (green slices). Only rarely they originate from another type of *definite issue* (red slides, ≤ 10%) or from another type of *uncertain issue* (yellow slices, ≤ 2%)

5.4   The Evolution of Syntax Issues During Modeling

Based on the first of the previous set of observations (i.e., Obs5), one may wonder if an *uncertain* type of *syntax issue* always evolves into a *definite* type of the same severity. Therefore, it is interesting to see in which other types the *uncertain* types evolve during modeling, which is represented in Fig. 4.

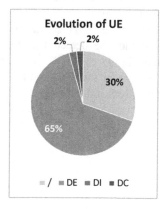
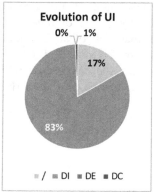
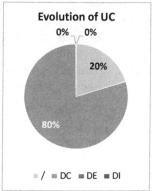

Fig. 4. The evolution of uncertain syntax issues during modeling

These are the observations related to Fig. 4:

Obs7.   In the majority of cases (red slices, ≥ 65%) the *uncertain syntax issue* was transformed later on in the corresponding *definite* type of *issue*. This means that the *syntax issue* can indeed already be detected in an incomplete part of the partial model (cf. Obs5).

Obs8.   In a smaller number of cases (green slices, 17–30%), the *issue* was resolved before the model part was completed (because then it would be transformed into a *definite issue*, which are the red slices). Potentially, they were never a real *issue*, but rather the manifestation of the postponement of actions, which introduced temporary *syntax issues*

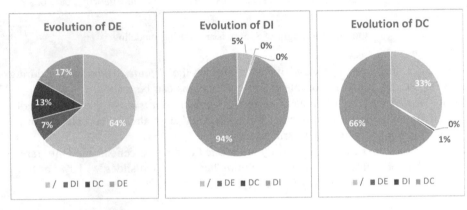

Fig. 5. The evolution of definite syntax issues during modeling

Further, it is also interesting to see what happens with the *definite syntax issues* during modeling. Figure 5 shows in what other types of *issues* they evolved. It can be observed:

Obs9.   Most (64%) of the *definite errors* (DE) are resolved before completing the model. Nevertheless 17% of these errors remain in the final model. Some others turn into an irresolution (7%) or a confusion (13%).

Obs10.   In contrast, the majority (94%) of *definite irresolutions* (DI) are never resolved. Remember that 37% of all DIs could already be detected in an incomplete part of the partial model (cf. Obs5 and Fig. 3).

Obs11.   Similarly, 66% of de *definite confusions* (DC) remain in the final model, whereas 61% of all DCs can be detected early (cf. Obs5 and Fig. 3)

6 Conclusion

Based on the specification of the BPMN 2.0 syntax for process modeling, we derived a list of potential syntax errors and related issues that can occur in simple sequence flow models. As already proposed by Natschläger et al., the definitions of constructs are scattered over different pages of the BPMN specification and they are not always unambiguously defined [15]. Therefore, a classification framework was constructed to categorize the issues in the list according to the certainty (uncertain or definite) and severity (error, irresolution, confusion). Further, we analyzed the data of 126 modeling instances and added the timing, kind (i.e., according to the list), and type (i.e., according to the framework) of each detected issue to the data.

The results are provisional (cf. limitations below), but interesting. Most (64%) of the real syntax errors (DE) that were made during the modeling session from the dataset were corrected. They were not present anymore in the final model. Only 17% remained (the other 19% were transformed in other issues). Moreover, 48% of all the real errors (DE) during modeling could be detected at an early stage, when the part of the model in which they occurred was still not completed.

Further, except for real errors (DE), we also collected information about irresolutions (DI), which are syntax issues for which experts would not agree if they are actually correct or not (for example a single gateway combining a join and split function). Irresolutions (DI) were seldom corrected (only 5%). Interestingly, 37% of them could be detected at an early stage. Similarly, confusions (DC) are constructions that are definitely correct, but that should advisably be avoided (such as certain occasions of multiple arrows arriving or originating in an activity without using an explicit gateway). Not less than 66% of them are never removed after originating. Yet, 61% can be detected early. An average model from the dataset contained 3.2 errors (DE), 2.3 irresolutions (DI), and 5.5 confusions (DC) during modeling (of which on average 0.5 DE, 2.2 DI, and 3.6 DC remained in the final model).

These conclusions indicate that it could be useful to study the origin and evolution of syntax issues in more detail. This can advance the tool features that aim to detect and prevent syntax issues. It may also produce interesting knowledge for modeling teachers, because in a learning context it is always better to focus on the root cause of problems. Therefore, we propose that future research focuses on dealing with the limitations of this study on the one hand and on extending the scope of the research on the other hand.

Being an explorative study that aims to reveal initial insights in the origin and evolution of syntax issues in conceptual models, this study has a number of limitations. First, the dataset is an arbitrary dataset, which is definitely not representative for all modelers (for example it contains only data of student observations). Next, the used list and the used framework are not evaluated. There is a real chance that they are not complete. Further, the analysis was performed by a limited number of people. Since the coding of syntax issues was very labor-intensive, the probability of mistakes is real. On the other hand, the dataset is considered big enough to warrant a certain degree of reliability of the results.

Finally, we plan to extend the study in several ways. Whereas the current analysis is limited to the evolution of the three generic severity types, in future work the evolution analysis will focus on all the different kinds of issues in the list. Future work may also include an extension towards other (process) modeling languages (including the full set of BPMN constructs) and towards other types of quality.

References

1. Rockwell, S., Bajaj, A.: COGEVAL: applying cognitive theories to evaluate conceptual models. Adv. Top. Database Res. **4**, 255–282 (2005)
2. Lindland, O.I., Sindre, G., Solvberg, A.: Understanding quality in conceptual modeling. IEEE Softw. **11**, 42–49 (1994)
3. Krogstie, J., Sindre, G., Jørgensen, H.: Process models representing knowledge for action: a revised quality framework. Eur. J. Inf. Syst. **15**, 91–102 (2006)
4. Nelson, H.J., Poels, G., Genero, M., et al.: A conceptual modeling quality framework. Softw. Qual. J. **20**, 201–228 (2012)
5. Wand, Y., Weber, R.: An ontological model of an information system. IEEE Trans. Softw. Eng. **16**, 1282–1292 (1990)
6. Hoppenbrouwers, S.J.B.A., (Erik) Proper, H.A., van der Weide, T.P.: A fundamental view on the process of conceptual modeling: how do people do it? In: Delcambre, L., Kop, C., Mayr, H.C., Mylopoulos, J., Pastor, O. (eds.) ER 2005. LNCS, vol. 3716, pp. 128–143. Springer, Heidelberg (2005). https://doi.org/10.1007/11568322_9
7. Wilmont, I., Hengeveld, S., Barendsen, E., Hoppenbrouwers, S.: Cognitive mechanisms of conceptual modelling. In: Ng, W., Storey, V.C., Trujillo, J.C. (eds.) ER 2013. LNCS, vol. 8217, pp. 74–87. Springer, Heidelberg (2013). https://doi.org/10.1007/978-3-642-41924-9_7
8. Soffer, P., Kaner, M., Wand, Y.: Towards understanding the process of process modeling: theoretical and empirical considerations. In: Daniel, F., Barkaoui, K., Dustdar, S. (eds.) BPM 2011. LNBIP, vol. 99, pp. 357–369. Springer, Heidelberg (2012). https://doi.org/10.1007/978-3-642-28108-2_35
9. Pinggera, J., Soffer, P., Fahland, D., et al.: Styles in business process modeling: an exploration and a model. Softw. Syst. Model. **14**, 1055–1080 (2013)
10. Claes, J., Vanderfeesten, I., Pinggera, J., et al.: A visual analysis of the process of process modeling. Inf. Syst. e-Bus. Manag. **13**, 147–190 (2015)
11. Claes, J., Vanderfeesten, I., Gailly, F., et al.: The Structured Process Modeling Theory (SPMT) - a cognitive view on why and how modelers benefit from structuring the process of process modeling. Inf. Syst. Front. **17**, 1401–1425 (2015)
12. OMG: Business Process Model and Notation (BPMN) version 2.0. (2011)
13. zur Muehlen, M., Recker, J.: How much language is enough? theoretical and practical use of the business process modeling notation. In: Bellahsène, Z., Léonard, M. (eds.) CAiSE 2008. LNCS, vol. 5074, pp. 465–479. Springer, Heidelberg (2008). https://doi.org/10.1007/978-3-540-69534-9_35
14. Claes, J., Vanderfeesten, I., Gailly, F., et al.: The Structured Process Modeling Method (SPMM) - what is the best way for me to construct a process model? Decis. Support Syst. **100**, 57–76 (2017)
15. Natschläger, C.: Towards a BPMN 2.0 ontology. In: Dijkman, R., Hofstetter, J., Koehler, J. (eds.) BPMN 2011. LNBIP, vol. 95, pp. 1–15. Springer, Heidelberg (2011). https://doi.org/10.1007/978-3-642-25160-3_1

Mining Developers' Workflows
from IDE Usage

Constantina Ioannou[✉], Andrea Burattin, and Barbara Weber

Technical University of Denmark, Kongens Lyngby, Denmark
{coio,andbur,bweb}@dtu.dk

Abstract. An increased understanding of how developers' approach the development of software and what individual challenges they face, has a substantial potential to better support the process of programming. In this paper, we adapt Rabbit Eclipse, an existing Eclipse plugin, to generate event logs from IDE usage enabling process mining of developers' workflows. Moreover, we describe the results of an exploratory study in which the event logs of 6 developers using Eclipse together with Rabbit Eclipse were analyzed using process mining. Our results demonstrate the potential of process mining to better understand how developers' approach a given programming task.

Keywords: Process mining · Tracking IDE interactions
Developers' workflows · Source code

1 Introduction

Increasing the productivity of software development has traditionally been an important concern of the software engineering field. This includes software development processes (e.g., agile and lean development), development principles and practices (e.g., test-driven development, continuous integration), tools like integrated development environments (IDEs), but also human factors. Considering the tremendous productivity differences between developers of 10:1 [4], there is substantial potential to better support the process of programming by better understanding how developers' approach the development of software and what individual challenges they face.

The process of programming is highly iterative, interleaved and loosely ordered [7]. Developers need to understand the requirements presented to them and form an internal representation of the problem in working memory by extracting information from external sources [3]. Based on the requirements a solution design is developed [3]. This includes at the general level the decomposition of requirements into system structures, i.e., modules and, on a more detailed level, the selection or development of algorithms to implement different modules [18]. The solution design is then implemented using a specific development environment and a particular programming language [18,21] and it is

© Springer International Publishing AG, part of Springer Nature 2018
R. Matulevičius and R. Dijkman (Eds.): CAiSE 2018 Workshops, LNBIP 316, pp. 167–179, 2018.
https://doi.org/10.1007/978-3-319-92898-2_14

evaluated whether the developed solution is suitable to solve a problem [6,9,21]. Depending on the development process used, the development principles and practices, the used IDE and programming language as well as personal preferences, experience, and capabilities the process of programming varies.

In this paper we show the potential of process mining to better understand how developers' approach the creation of a solution for a given programming task using the IDE Eclipse. The contribution of this paper is twofold. First, the paper provides adaptations of an existing Eclipse plugin, i.e., Rabbit Eclipse, to produce event logs that can be used for process mining purposes. Second, it describes the results of an exploratory study in which the event logs of 6 development sessions were analyzed. The work does not only have potential to better understand the processes developers follow to create a solution to a given programming task using the IDE Eclipse.

In the future we can use the developed plugin to compare how the usage of different development principles and practices impacts the way how developers solve a given problem and use conformance checking to identify deviations from best practices. Moreover, when integrated with eye tracking, we cannot only determine how developers interact with the IDE and the different source code artifacts, but additionally where they have their focus of attention.

2   Background and Related Work

In Sect. 2.1 we discuss existing research on tracking IDE usage. In this paper we use the IDE Eclipse together with the Rabbit Eclipse plugin to collect the interactions of developers with the IDE (cf. Sect. 2.2) that are then used for process mining (cf. Sect. 2.3).

2.1   Tracking IDE Usage

Research recording the interactions of a developer with the IDE including their analysis and visualization are related to our work. For example, [17] provides quantitative insights into how Java developers use the Eclipse IDE. Moreover, [16] developed DFlow for recording developers' interactions within the IDE Pharao including their visualization and applied it to better understand how developers spend their time. Similarly, Fluorite [23] and Spyware [19] were implemented in order to collect usage data from the Eclipse IDE and to replay and backtrack developers strategies visualizing code histories. Unlike our research the focus is on a single development session, rather than abstract behavior derived from a set of sessions. Most closely related to our work is [1] in which frequent IDE usage patterns have been mined and filtered in order to form usage smells. More precisely, this approach identifies time-ordered sequences of developer actions that are exhibited by many developers in the field. However, the focus of [1] is on developers' interactions with the IDE only. In contrast, our proposal considers the inter-relationships of interactions and source code artifacts, thus, emphasizing the way developers solve a programming task rather than how developers use the IDE.

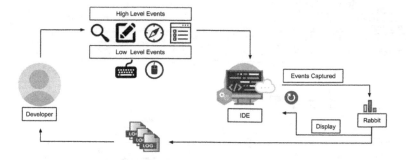

Fig. 1. Model: Rabbit Eclipse

2.2 Rabbit Eclipse

Rabbit Eclipse is a statistical plugin, capable of recording developers' interaction without interrupting their process, within the Eclipse IDE. Figure 1 gives an overview of the instrumentation approach employed in this paper.

When implementing a software within Eclipse, developers generate through their interactions with the IDE various low and high level events. Low level events are keyboard shortcuts and mouse clicks, whereas high level events are related to context menu or wizard interactions. Whenever an event is observed, Rabbit Eclipse is triggered to capture and analyze the interaction. These interactions are then stored in event logs and upon request of a developer the data collected by Rabbit Eclipse can be displayed graphically within Eclipse.

The structure of event entries are presented in Fig. 2. For each type of event entry an event log is produced. At the top of the hierarchy are the classes `DiscreteEvent` and `ContinuousEvent`, which distinguish between the main types of interactions recorded, i.e., instant and continuous interactions. `Command` and `Breakpoint` events are listed as discrete interactions. On the other hand, interactions such as switching between files, views, perspectives, launching, Java elements and session inherit from `ContinuousEvent`, since the duration for such activities is relevant.

2.3 Process Mining

Process mining is the bridge between model-based process analysis and data oriented analysis techniques such as machine learning and data mining [22]. In order to be amenable for process mining the event logs produced should conform to the minimum data model requirements [8]. These are: the case id, which determines the scope of the process, an activity which determines the level of detail for the steps and timestamp, which determines when the activity took place. Using process discovery a process model explaining the behavior of the recorded log can be derived. Moreover, using conformance checking deviations of the event log when compared to a reference behavior can be identified.

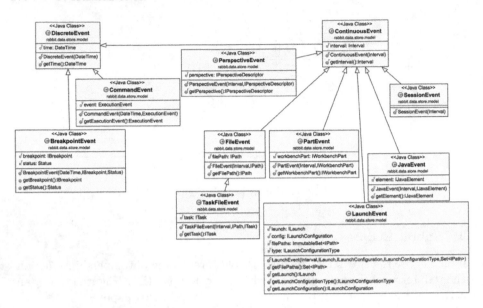

Fig. 2. UML class diagram of the hierarchy of events as recorded by Rabbit Eclipse

Closely related to our work presented in this paper is the emerging area of software process mining. With the increasing availability of software execution data, the application of process mining techniques to analyze software execution data is becoming increasingly popular. The potential of software process mining was first demonstrated by [10,20]. More specifically, source code repositories were mined to obtain insights into the software development processes development teams employed. Moreover, [2] suggests the usage of localized event logs where events refer to system parts to improve the quality of the discovered models. In addition, [11] proposes the discovery of flat behavioral models of software systems using the Inductive Miner [13]. In turn, [15] proposes an approach to discover a hierarchical process model for each component. An approach for discovering the software architectural model from execution data is described in [14]. Finally, [12] allows to reconstruct the most relevant statecharts and sequence diagram from an instrumented working system. The focus of all these works is software development processes or the understanding of the behavior of the software, while our focus is to use process mining to understand how a developer solves a programming task.

3 Extending Rabbit Eclipse for Process Mining

Although Rabbit Eclipse provides broad and profound statistical results on developers' interactions within the Eclipse IDE, the data provided are not sufficient to enable the mining of developers' interactions as envisioned. In particular, as previously highlighted, timestamp and case id notions were not included in

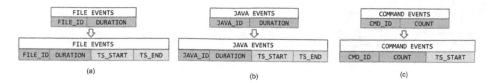

Fig. 3. Timestamp modifications on three events

the collection. Therefore, we needed to expand some events in order to enable their usage in the context of process mining. Firstly, all the event logs were customized to include timestamp and case id by modifying classes `DiscreteEvent` and `ContinuousEvent`. Further, due to the nature of Rabbit Eclipse the collected interactions have no actual relation between them. To resolve this constraint focus was given to change the interpretation of `FileEvent`, `JavaEvent`, and `CommandEvent` (cf. Fig. 2) which seemed the most promising with respect to our goal. The rest of this section presents the adjustments introduced to enable the process mining investigations envisioned.

3.1 Adaptations to Enable Process Mining

To enable the extraction of a workflow from our data, using process mining techniques, timestamps and case id needed to be included in the recordings.

As mentioned, the event logs for `ContinuousEvents` (both `FileEvent` and `JavaEvent`) contain durations, which means that entries referring to the same interaction were merged, whereas, concerning `DiscreteEvents` (i.e., `Command-Events`), event logs report the frequency of such interactions. We instrumented Rabbit Eclipse to allow the collection of all timestamps, as shown in Fig. 3. Specifically, for `ContinuousEvents` timestamps to indicate start and end time were introduces (i.e., each event represented as time interval) and for `Discrete-Events` a single timestamp was added (i.e., each event as time instant).

Additionally, Rabbit Eclipse does not have the notion of a case id. Therefore, we decided to artificially add one. Specifically, we assumed to have each developer referring to one different case id as approximation of a single development session.

With these changes in place, we were able to associate Rabbit Eclipse recordings to user's actions. Thus, we obtained a proper event log: we shifted the scope of Rabbit Eclipse from logging file changes (suitable for software process mining) to logging user's interaction with the IDE (suitable for process mining).

3.2 Mapping Commands to Resources

By default, Rabbit Eclipse has no capability to establish links between the commands and the resource where these commands were performed. Therefore, we instrumented Rabbit Eclipse to be able to take this element into account together with timing information. The result is an augmented version of the `CommandEvent`, as depicted in Fig. 4. This augmentation needed to consider

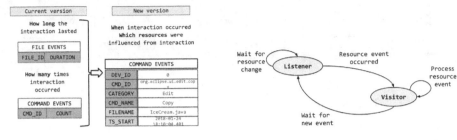

Fig. 4. Command modifications to track interactions

Fig. 5. Listener/visitor design pattern for the implemented tracker

different scenarios which are possible, including commands involving single or group of resources (such as renaming a folder or moving files). To better achieve our goal, we also implemented an interaction tracker, which listens for resource change events (see Fig. 5). Once the new tracker is triggered, it processes the event to identify and store affected commands.

3.3 Augmentation of Commands with Java Details

The version of the `JavaEvent` class available in the current version of Rabbit Eclipse was not able to provide information referring to the specific Java constructs being modified. This data, however, could contain very important information for our analysis. To extract this information, we instrumented Rabbit Eclipse to inspect the Abstract Syntax Tree (AST) of each modified Java class. This enables the Rabbit Eclipse plugin to capture the modified methods and correspondingly update the commands.

4 Exploratory Study

This section explains the exploratory study we conducted to evaluate the adapted version of the Rabbit Eclipse plugin.

4.1 Study Design and Execution

Participants. Six participants were included in the case study. One participant is a software developer in a medium sized company, while the other five are newly graduated master students from Computer Science and related fields. All of them primarily develop in C, C++ and Java, mainly for embedded systems. Their age ranges from 25 to 29, and they have between 6 months to 2 years of experience using Eclipse.

Fig. 6. Data collection and analysis procedure followed

Task. Participants had to work on a fairly simple programming task that takes around 30 min/1 h for completion. The task required the participants to first install our version of Rabbit Eclipse and then to implement an inheritance hierarchy of classes that derive from an abstract superclass using Java as a programming language. As depicted in Fig. 14, the task consists of five classes, a superclass called `DessertItem` and four derived classes, i.e., `Cookie`, `Candy`, `IceCream` and `Sundae`. Participants were provided with a description of the classes to be implemented including the class diagram (cf. Appendix A) and a test file called `DessertShop`. To avoid inconsistent naming between participants, participants were encouraged to strictly follow the class and method naming as shown in the class diagram. While working on the task participants were not allowed to ask for help or explanation since this could affect their way of thinking. After the participants finished their implementation, they were requested to send the files collected from the tool. Thereafter, the required data set for process mining was retrieved.

4.2   Data Collection and Analysis Procedure

Figure 6 illustrates the data collection and analysis procedure we employed.

Step 1: Collect Data. To collect data concerning a developer's interactions with the IDE we asked participants to install our version of Rabbit Eclipse. During the implementation of the task all interactions of the participants with the IDE were then recorded using Rabbit Eclipse.

Step 2: Prepare Data. Throughout the second step of the approach and after receiving the exported raw data sets from all participants, the data set requires refinement before it can be used for process mining. To begin with, any unrelated, captured interactions with projects in the developer's current workspace were removed from the data set. Next, since process mining requires homogeneity among the data set, any inconsistencies in the data sets were detected and adjusted. An example of inconsistency is when a participant, instead of using correctly the requested naming `Test.java`, used `test.java`. In addition, the XML formatted event logs are converted to CSV format.

Step 3: Combine Data. The refined data are combined into one file and are imported to Disco.

Table 1. Settings used for Disco to obtain the four results

#	Result's name	Participants	Event log	Activity	Attribute
1	Most common commands	5	cmds	Command	-
2	Developers' workflow	5	cmds	File	Command
3	Classes workflow	5	cmds	Command	File
4	Source code workflow	4	javas	Method and file	-

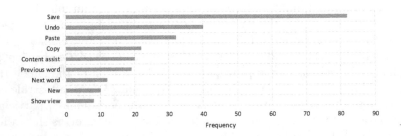

Fig. 7. Most common commands used

Step 4: Mine Process. Disco was then used to analyze the data and settings were configured so that for all experiments the case id used was the developer's id and the timestamp used was the start time of events. Further, specific settings defined for each experiment are displayed in Table 1.

All participants were able to fulfill the task within the given time frame (i.e., all programming sessions lasted between 30 min and 1 h). Most of the participants used expected methodologies and commands, however, as indicated in Table 1 for all analyses one of the participants had to be excluded because of generating a considerable amount of noise events, as well as for the fourth analysis two participants were excluded due to failed recordings from the tool.

4.3   Results

Most Common Commands. A statistical analysis of the entire sample using Disco showed that in total 323 commands were executed for all five participants (most common are shown in Fig. 7). When we observe the distribution of command interactions retrieved, we can see that only a small amount of the available Eclipse standard commands were executed. In fact, only 31 different commands occurred out of the 350 available. A possible explanation for that might stem from the simple nature of the given task. Moreover, our analysis showed that participants tend to use and repeat similar commands. Out of 31 different commands used, the most common are: Save, Undo and Paste which concurs with results of previous studies [17].

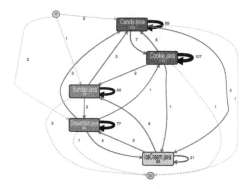

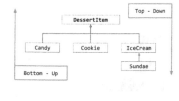

Fig. 8. Workflow diagram depicted by Disco

Fig. 9. Class outline with corresponding programming techniques

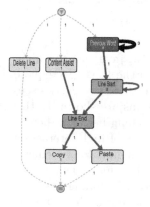

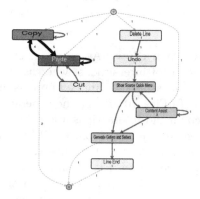

Fig. 10. Workflow diagram of Ice Cream.java

Fig. 11. Workflow diagram of Cookie.java

Developers' Workflow. Figure 8 displays the connection between file switching and command interactions. The file resources implemented throughout the task are indicated as nodes and the command interactions leading from one file to another as edges. The diagram shows that half of participants begun their implementation by interacting with `DessertItem.java` which was the superclass and then moved to the implementation of subclasses, while the other half, begun interacting with subclasses (i.e., `Candy.java`, `Sundae.java`) and then moved to the superclass. These two approaches participants followed (cf. Fig. 9) are denoted in literature [5] as "top-down" versus "bottom-up" approach. When following a top-down approach a developer begins with the main problem and then subdivides it into sub problems. Whereas when employing a bottom-up approach the developer begins with sub-problems building up to the main problem.

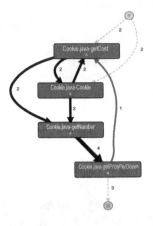

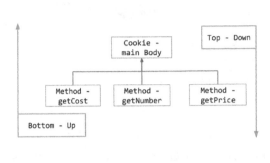

Fig. 12. Workflow diagram Cookie.java

Fig. 13. Class outline with corresponding programming techniques

Classes Workflow. As observed in Fig. 8, class `Cookie.java` has the highest amount of interactions, whereas, `IceCream.java` has the least. To explore further this aspect we applied process mining focusing on these two classes separately. In Figs. 10 and 11 the generated workflow diagrams are shown. In this case, command interactions appear as nodes and the switching between them is represented as edges. From Fig. 10 we can infer the absence of high interaction traffic and this is expected since `IceCream.java` was fairly simple to implement. On the other hand, Fig. 11 illustrates `Cookie.java` which is more demanding: this is reflected in a more complex routing of the interactions, including self loops and repetition. This suggests that there is a diversity in the approach used when dealing with classes of different difficulty level.

Source Code Workflow. In Fig. 12 an attempt to process mine the source code interactions in `Cookie.java` is displayed. The method names of the class are indicated as nodes and the arrows indicate the flow participants followed. Participants followed two patterns (cf. Fig. 13), either they begun by building the body of the class and then implementing the methods in detail or the opposite. This was observed not only within the `Cookie.java` but also in the other implemented classes. Therefore this realization, implies that the workflow techniques mentioned (top down and bottom up) are applied not only for the class design but also for the methods, showing potential in performing process mining on source code development.

5   Summary and Conclusions

In this paper we presented an extension of the Rabbit Eclipse plugin that is able to collect developers' interactions with Eclipse that can be used for process mining. Moreover, we presented the results of an exploratory study where

6 developers developed a small piece of software using Eclipse together with Rabbit Eclipse. The analysis of the data using process mining allowed us to identify the most commonly used commands. Moreover, we could observe that the participating developers employed different object oriented programming techniques, i.e., top down and bottom up, to solve the programming task. In addition, we could identify differences in creating single classes. Our results demonstrate that it is possible to mine developers' workflows from their interactions within an IDE. However, it has to be noted that the existing work is subject to several limitations such as the low number of subjects and the task difficulty.

In the future we plan to extend our study with more subjects and more complex tasks. Another avenue of future research is the integration with eye tracking, thus allowing us to complement our results with data on where developers focused their attention. In addition, future work will consider (retrospective think aloud) to obtain insights into the developer's thinking process.

A   Task Description

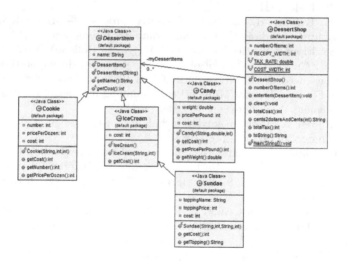

Fig. 14. The given class diagram

The task is the implementation of inheritance hierarchy of classes that derive from an abstract superclass. Please follow the task carefully and develop the required units. It is crucial to follow the given naming for your variables methods and classes as shown in Fig. 14. The following classes are required: (a) DessertItem abstract superclass. (b) Candy, Cookie, IceCream classes which derive from DessertItem superclass and (c) Sundae class which derives from IceCream class. A Candy item has a weight and a price per pound which are used to determine its cost. The cost should be calculated as (cost) * (price per pound).

A Cookie item has a number and a price per dozen which are used to determine its cost. The cost should be calculated as (cost) * (price per dozen). An IceCream item simply has a cost, and the cost of a Sundae is the cost of the IceCream plus the cost of the topping. The DessertShop class was given to developers and contained the main functions of the shop and the test for the classes.

References

1. Damevski, K., Shepherd, D.C., Schneider, J., Pollock, L.: Mining sequences of developer interactions in visual studio for usage smells. IEEE Trans. Softw. Eng. **43**(4), 359–371 (2017)
2. van der Aalst, W.: Big software on the run: In vivo software analytics based on process mining (keynote). In: Proceedings of ICSSP 2015, pp. 1–5. ACM (2015)
3. Brooks, R.: Towards a theory of the cognitive processes in computer programming. Int. J. Man Mach. Stud. **9**(6), 737–751 (1977)
4. DeMarco, T., Lister, T.: Peopleware: Productive Projects and Teams. Dorset House Publishing Co., New York (1987)
5. Konstantas, D., Léonard, M., Pigneur, Y., Patel, S. (eds.): Object-Oriented Information Systems. LNCS, vol. 2817. Springer, Heidelberg (2003). https://doi.org/10.1007/978-3-540-45242-3
6. Guindon, R., Krasner, H., Curtis, B .: Cognitive process in software design: activities in early, upstream design. In: Human-Computer Interaction, INTERACT 1987, pp. 383–388. Elsevier Science Publishers B.V. (North Holland) (1987)
7. Guindon, R., Curtis, B.: Control of cognitive processes during software design: what tools are needed? In: Proceedings of CHI 1988, pp. 263–268 (1988)
8. IEEE Task Force on Process Mining: Process mining manifesto. In: Business Process Management Workshops, pp. 169–194 (2011)
9. Kant, E., Newell, A.: Problem solving techniques for the design of algorithms. Inf. Process. Manag. **20**(1–2), 97–118 (1984)
10. Kindler, E., Rubin, V., Schäfer, W.: Incremental workflow mining based on document versioning information. In: Li, M., Boehm, B., Osterweil, L.J. (eds.) SPW 2005. LNCS, vol. 3840, pp. 287–301. Springer, Heidelberg (2006). https://doi.org/10.1007/11608035_25
11. Leemans, M., van der Aalst, W.M.P.: Process mining in software systems: discovering real-life business transactions and process models from distributed systems. In: Proceedings of MODELS, pp. 44–53, September 2015
12. Leemans, M., van der Aalst, W.M.P., van den Brand, M.G.J.: Recursion aware modeling and discovery for hierarchical software event log analysis (extended). CoRR, abs/1710.09323 (2017)
13. Leemans, S.J.J., Fahland, D., van der Aalst, W.M.P.: Discovering block-structured process models from event logs - a constructive approach. In: Colom, J.-M., Desel, J. (eds.) PETRI NETS 2013. LNCS, vol. 7927, pp. 311–329. Springer, Heidelberg (2013). https://doi.org/10.1007/978-3-642-38697-8_17
14. Liu, C., van Dongen, B.F., Assy, N., Aalst, W.M.P.: Software architectural model discovery from execution data. In: 13th International Conference on Evaluation of Novel Approaches to Software Engineering, March 2018
15. Liu, C., van Dongen, B., Assy, N., van der Aalst, W.M.P.: Component behavior discovery from software execution data. In: 2016 IEEE Symposium Series on Computational Intelligence (SSCI), pp. 1–8, December 2016

16. Minelli, R., Lanza, M.: Visualizing the workflow of developers. In: Proceedings of VISSOFT, pp. 2–5 (2013)
17. Murphy, G.C., Kersten, M., Findlater, L.: How are Java software developers using the Elipse IDE? IEEE Softw. **23**(4), 76–83 (2006)
18. Pennington, N., Lee, A.Y., Rehder, B.: Cognitive activities and levels of abstraction in procedural and object-oriented design. Hum. Comput. Interact. **10**, 171–226 (1995)
19. Robbes, R., Lanza, M.: SpyWare: a change-aware development toolset. In: Proceedings of ICSE, pp. 847–850 (2008)
20. Rubin, V., Günther, C.W., van der Aalst, W.M.P., Kindler, E., van Dongen, B.F., Schäfer, W.: Process mining framework for software processes. In: Wang, Q., Pfahl, D., Raffo, D.M. (eds.) ICSP 2007. LNCS, vol. 4470, pp. 169–181. Springer, Heidelberg (2007). https://doi.org/10.1007/978-3-540-72426-1_15
21. Tegarden, D.P., Sheetz, S.D.: Cognitive activities in OO development. Int. J. Hum. Comput. Stud. **54**(6), 779–798 (2001)
22. van der Aalst, W.M.P.: Process Mining: Data Science in Action. Springer, Heidelberg (2016). https://doi.org/10.1007/978-3-662-49851-4
23. Yoon, Y.S., Myers, B.A.: Capturing and analyzing low-level events from the code editor. In: Proceedings of the 3rd ACM SIGPLAN Workshop on Evaluation and Usability of Programming Languages and Tools - PLATEAU 2011, p. 25 (2011)

Designing for Information Quality in the Era of Repurposable Crowdsourced User-Generated Content

Shawn Ogunseye[(⊠)] and Jeffrey Parsons

Faculty of Business Administration, Memorial University of Newfoundland,
St. John's, Newfoundland & Labrador, Canada
{osogunseye,jeffreyp}@mun.ca

Abstract. Conventional wisdom holds that expert contributors provide higher quality user-generated content (UGC) than novices. Using the cognitive construct of *selective attention*, we argue that this may not be the case in some crowd-sourcing UGC applications. We argue that crowdsourcing systems that seek participation mainly from contributors who are experienced or have high levels of proficiency in the crowdsourcing task will gather less diverse and therefore less repurposable data. We discuss the importance of the information diversity dimension of information quality for the use and repurposing of UGC and provide a theoretical basis for our position, with the goal of stimulating empirical research.

Keywords: User-generated content · Information diversity
Information quality · Repurposability · Crowdsourcing

1 Introduction

The development of interactive web technologies allows organizations to access information from individuals outside, and not formally associated with, the organization. This external information is commonly known as user-generated content (UGC) – content that is voluntarily contributed by individuals external to organizations. Access to UGC is revolutionizing industry and research. UGC sourced through crowdsourcing systems – systems that enable "outsourcing a task to a 'crowd', rather than to a designated 'agent' … in the form of an open call" [1, p. 355] – have successfully been used in diverse contexts for understanding customers, developing new products, improving service quality, and supporting scientific research [2–5]. In this paper, UGC and crowdsourcing refer specifically to UGC from purpose-built *integrative crowdsourcing systems*[1] that "pool complementary input from the crowd" [6, p. 98], rather than passive UGC collected through applications such as social media.

When creating crowdsourcing systems, one important design decision sponsors[2] must make is determining the composition of an appropriate crowd [28]. This decision influences the other design decisions about crowdsourcing projects (i.e. system design,

---

[1] Crowdsourcing systems that gather distributed information for decision making [6]
[2] Owners (key design decision makers) of crowdsourcing and crowd-facing systems [17]

© Springer International Publishing AG, part of Springer Nature 2018
R. Matulevičius and R. Dijkman (Eds.): CAiSE 2018 Workshops, LNBIP 316, pp. 180–185, 2018.
https://doi.org/10.1007/978-3-319-92898-2_15

task design, and motivation of contributors). Because the quality of UGC to be collected is a concern, sponsors either require potential contributors to possess relevant knowledge of the crowdsourcing task or allow a broader spectrum of volunteers to be part of their crowds. Choosing the former implies implementing recruitment strategies that favor knowledgeable contributors and prevent less knowledgeable contributors from participating, such as training volunteers before they are allowed to participate [8, 9] and recruiting experienced contributors – people who have previously participated (or are presently participating) in a similar project [31].

By restricting participation in integrative crowdsourcing projects to trained or experienced contributors, sponsors seek to tap into contributors' proficiency and familiarity with the task to ensure high information quality [30, 31]. This practice is supported in practice and in the crowdsourcing literature. For example, Wiggins et al.'s [p. 17] survey of 128 citizen science crowdsourcing projects – which often are integrative crowdsourcing systems that engage citizens in data collection – reports that "several projects depend on personal knowledge of contributing individuals in order to feel comfortable with data quality". Likewise, [8] promotes a contributor selection strategy for "eliminating poorly performing individuals from the crowd" and identifying experts from volunteers "who consistently outperform the crowd". However, in this position paper, *we make the case against adopting strategies that restrict participation to only knowledgeable contributors.*

2 Information Quality and Repurposable UGC

Knowledge about the phenomena on which data are being collected is assumed to positively influence the key dimensions of information quality – information accuracy and information completeness. Information accuracy is defined as "the correctness in the mapping of stored information to the appropriate state in the real world that the information represents" [10, p. 203], while information completeness is the "degree to which all possible states relevant to the user population are represented in the stored information" [10, p. 203]. However, the literature contains several studies in which experts or knowledgeable contributors in the crowd have not provided more accurate information than novices. For example, three studies in an ecological context found that knowledgeable contributors did not provide more accurate data than non-experts [11–13]. Likewise, in an experiment in which participants were required to identify and provide information about sightings of flora and fauna, novices performed as well as knowledgeable contributors with respect to the study's task [9].

Similarly, even though Kallimanis et al. [13] showed that less knowledgeable contributors report less information than knowledgeable contributors based on the fitness criterion employed in their study, they also reported that less knowledgeable contributors provided more data about certain aspects of the tasks than knowledgeable contributors and made significantly more unanticipated discoveries. These findings are mostly congruent with Lukyanenko et al.'s field and lab experiments [9, 16], which showed that the conceptualization and design of a crowdsourcing system plays a role in the completeness of data provided by contributors with varying degrees of knowledge. In sum, empirical research offers evidence that knowledgeable contributors do not always provide more complete or more accurate information (i.e. higher quality information) than those with little or no domain knowledge.

While accuracy and completeness are pertinent dimensions of information quality, UGC needs to encompass diverse views and perspectives to sufficiently address the need for contributed data to be repurposable [17]. This repurposability requirement can only be met if crowdsourced data is "managed with multiple different fitness for use requirements in mind" [18, p. 11]. That is, the design choices made for integrative crowdsourcing systems should also support information diversity – the "number of different dimensions" present in data [7, p. 214] – to ensure repurposability and reusability of data. The relevant dimensions of information quality for crowdsourced UGC thus go beyond accuracy and dataset completeness and include information diversity.

Information diversity is *the ratio of the amount of distinct information in contributions about an entity to the amount of information available in the contributions. The degree of diversity between two contributions A and B, each consisting of a set of attributes, is* $\frac{(A \cup B - A \cap B)}{A \cup B}$. *The higher the ratio, the more diverse both contributions are*[3]. Information diversity promotes discoveries as it enables different users and uses of data, which may lead to unanticipated insights [17]. Information diversity helps provide a better understanding of data points, as some contributors may give details about the data point where others do not. In addition, information diversity affords flexibility to project sponsors, as data requirements may change with new insight or because projects are commissioned without clearly defined hypotheses in mind. A richer, more robust dataset can better handle such changes than a highly constrained one.

Understandably, information diversity has not received a lot of attention in the information quality literature, which has mainly focused on the quality of information collected within organizations with tight control over their information inputs, processing and outputs, and with predetermined users and uses of resulting data. Within these traditional organizational settings, described in [17] as *closed information environments*, information diversity is sometimes considered undesirable and data management processes seek to minimize or eliminate it. Moreover, in the few cases where data diversity has been considered in the context of the repurposability of UGC, research has focused on system (or data acquisition instrument) design [17–19]. Less attention has been paid to the effect of the cognitive diversity (i.e. differences in experience and task proficiency) arising from the choice of target crowds on the diversity of data generated.

3   Theoretical Foundation for Information Quality in UGC

Generally speaking, humans manage limited cognitive resources in the face of a barrage of sensory experience by paying selective attention to relevant features that aid in identifying instances of a class, while irrelevant features (those not useful for predicting class membership) can be safely ignored. Even though everyone selectively attends to

---

[3] This definition is easily extended to the case where A and B are sets of contributions.

information to some extent, our use of selective attention only covers top-down attention, i.e. "internal guidance of attention based on prior knowledge, willful plans, and current goals" [14, p. 509].

Although selective attention leads to efficient learning, it is accompanied by the cost of learned inattention to features that are not "diagnostic" in the present context [21, 22]. Training leads to selective attention to pertinent or diagnostic attributes [22, 24]. When members of a crowd have been trained, their reporting will most closely align to the information learned from their training, resulting in less diversity than would be present in data reported by members of an untrained crowd. This is particularly pronounced when the training provides specific rules for performing the task, as contributors will tend to rely on (and pay attention to) this explicit information above any implicit inference they may form themselves – a phenomenon known as salience bias [15].

Consider a citizen science scenario (adapted from [22]) where contributors who have been trained on how to identify rose bushes were requested to report their occurrences in a field of rose, cranberry and raspberry bushes. In addition, assume contributors through their training are able to distinguish rose bushes from the other bushes present in the field by the absence of berries. Their training is sufficient to ensure the data they report is accurate and complete as other attributes like the presence of thorns would not be diagnostic in this context where rose and raspberry bushes both have thorns. However, if in the future a user needs to repurpose the collected data to confirm the presence of cranberry bushes in the same field or estimate their number, the presence or absence of berries is no longer diagnostic as cranberry and raspberry bushes have red berries, and the presence of thorns becomes diagnostic as cranberry bushes do not have thorns. The data becomes inadequate requiring resources to repeat the data acquisition stage. This tendency for training to influence the information reported by contributors making contributions align with the training received while reducing their diversity thus affects repurposability and the ability to make discoveries.

Similarly, experience increases the tendency towards selective attention. The absence of the tendency for selective attention is "a developmental default" [23, 24]. Infants do not selectively attend to attributes of instances. They reason about entities by observing all the features of individual instances [20] and are, therefore, naturally comparable to novice contributors in an integrative crowdsourcing context [24, 25]. The tendency for selective attention thus forms with development to aid classification as a mechanism for coping with the deluge of information around us. For this reason, the capacity to classify is a distinguishing factor between adults and infants [20]. As experience increases, the tendency for selective attention increases correspondingly.

Knowledge of the crowdsourcing task acquired by contributors through training or experience will help them report mainly about attributes of instances they have been taught (or learned experientially) to be relevant to the task [26]; thus, they are expected to be less likely to attend to attributes irrelevant to the task than novices [27]. Ogunseye and Parsons [29] argue that knowledge therefore affects the accuracy and completeness of contributed data as knowledgeable contributors have an increased tendency to only focus on diagnostic attributes, ignoring changes to other attributes when they occur. In addition, knowledgeable contributors show more resistance to further learning [27], impeding their ability to make discoveries. We add here that since contributors with similar knowledge are expected to show similar levels of selective attention and contribute more homogeneous data than cognitively diverse contributors, knowledge (task proficiency and experience) will also reduce a crowd's capacity for information diversity.

4   Conclusion

As organizations continue to leverage the collective wisdom of crowds, interest in crowdsourced UGC will continue to grow. At the center of new discovery and insight from UGC based on integrative crowdsourcing tasks rather than selective crowd-sourcing tasks is the ability of collected UGC to accommodate the different perspectives of multiple users. This desire for repurposable UGC places a new information diversity requirement on crowdsourced information that is largely absent from traditional IS environments, where the uses of data are usually predetermined and stable. In addition to traditional dimensions of information quality, we argue for the inclusion of the information diversity dimension as a necessary dimension for crowdsourced UGC. We also explain from a cognitive perspective why training and experience will constrain information diversity and correspondingly, reduce the quality of crowdsourced UGC. Consequently, systems that seek repurposable UGC are better served if they are designed with inclusivity and openness as their core focus. Our agenda for future research includes studying how cognitive diversity impacts information diversity in different settings and how this impact affects the quality of decisions made from UGC.

References

1. Afuah, A., Tucci, C.L.: Crowdsourcing as a solution to distant search. Acad. Manage. Rev. **37**, 355–375 (2012)
2. Castriotta, M., Di Guardo, M.C.: Open innovation and crowdsourcing: the case of mulino bianco. In: D'Atri, A., Ferrara, M., George, J., Spagnoletti, P. (eds.) Information Technology and Innovation Trends in Organizations, pp. 407–414. Springer (2011). https://doi.org/10.1007/978-3-7908-2632-6_46
3. Hosseini, M., Phalp, K., Taylor, J., Ali, R.: The four pillars of crowdsourcing: a reference model. In: IEEE Eighth International Conference on Research Challenges in Information Science (RCIS) 2014, pp. 1–12. IEEE (2014)
4. Tarrell, A., Tahmasbi, N., Kocsis, D., Tripathi, A., Pedersen, J., Xiong, J., Oh, O., de Vreede, G.-J.: Crowdsourcing: a snapshot of published research. In: Proceedings of the Nineteenth Americas Conference on Information Systems, Chicago, Illinois, 15–17 August (2013)
5. Tripathi, A., Tahmasbi, N., Khazanchi, D., Najjar, L.: Crowdsourcing typology: a review of is research and organizations. In: Proceedings of Midwest Association Information System MWAIS (2014)
6. Schenk, E., Guittard, C.: Towards a characterization of crowdsourcing practices. J. Innov. Econ. Manag. **1**(7), 93–107 (2011). https://doi.org/10.3917/jie.007.0093
7. Hwang, M.I., Lin, J.W.: Information dimension, information overload and decision quality. J. Inf. Sci. **22**(3), 213–218 (1999)
8. Budescu, D.V., Chen, E.: Identifying expertise to extract the wisdom of crowds. Manag. Sci. **61**, 267–280 (2014)

9. Lukyanenko, R., Parsons, J., Wiersma, Y.F.: The IQ of the crowd: understanding and improving information quality in structured user-generated content. Inf. Syst. Res. **22**, 669–689 (2014)

10. Nelson, R.R., Todd, P.A., Wixom, B.H.: Antecedents of information and system quality: an empirical examination within the context of data warehousing. J. Manag. Inf. Syst. **21**, 199–235 (2005)

11. Austen, G.E., Bindemann, M., Griffiths, R.A., Roberts, D.L.: Species identification by experts and non-experts: comparing images from field guides. Sci. Rep. **6**, 1–7 (2016). 33634

12. Bloniarz, D.V., Ryan, H.D.P.: The use of volunteer initiatives in conducting urban forest resource inventories. J. Arboric. **22**, 75–82 (1996)

13. Kallimanis, A.S., Panitsa, M., Dimopoulos, P.: Quality of non-expert citizen science data collected for habitat type conservation status assessment in Natura 2000 protected areas. Sci. Rep. **7**(1), 1–10 (2017). 8873

14. Katsuki, F., Constantinidis, C.: Bottom-up and top-down attention: different processes and overlapping neural systems. Neuroscientist **20**(5), 509–521 (2014)

15. Lee, H.C., Ba, S., Li, X., Stallaert, J.: Salience bias in crowdsourcing contests. Inf. Syst. Res. (2018). Articles in Advance

16. Lukyanenko, R., Parsons, J., Wiersma, Y.F.: The impact of conceptual modeling on dataset completeness: a field experiment. In: 35th International Conference on Information System ICIS 2014 (2014)

17. Parsons, J., Wand, Y.: A Foundation For Open Information Environments (2014)

18. Woodall, P.: The data repurposing challenge: new pressures from data analytics. J. Data Inf. Qual. JDIQ. **8**, 11 (2017)

19. Castellanos, A., Castillo, A., Lukyanenko, R., Tremblay, M.: Repurposing Organizational Electronic Documentation: Lessons from Case Management in Foster Care (2017)

20. Best, C.A., Yim, H., Sloutsky, V.M.: The cost of selective attention in category learning: Developmental differences between adults and infants. J. Exp. Child Psychol. **116**, 105–119 (2013)

21. Colner, B., Rehder, B.: A new theory of classification and feature inference learning: an exemplar fragment model. In: Proceedings of the 31st Annual Conference of the Cognitive Science Society, pp. 371–376 (2009)

22. Hoffman, A.B., Rehder, B.: The costs of supervised classification: the effect of learning task on conceptual flexibility. J. Exp. Psychol. Gen. **139**, 319 (2010)

23. Gelman, S.A.: The development of induction within natural kind and artifact categories. Cognit. Psychol. **20**, 65–95 (1988)

24. Kloos, H., Sloutsky, V.M.: What's behind different kinds of kinds: Effects of statistical density on learning and representation of categories. J. Exp. Psychol. Gen. **137**, 52 (2008)

25. Keil, F.C.: Concepts, Kinds, and Conceptual Development. MIT Press, Cambridge (1989)

26. Harnad, S.: Cognition is Categorization. In: Cohen, H., Lefebvre, C. (eds.) Handbook of Categorization, pp. 20–42. Elsevier, Amsterdam (2005)

27. Plebanek, D.J., Sloutsky, V.M.: Costs of selective attention: when children notice what adults miss. Psychol. Sci. **28**, 723–732 (2017). 956797617693005

28. Malone, T.W., Laubacher, R., Dellarocas, C.: The collective intelligence genome. MIT Sloan Manag. Rev. **51**, 21 (2010)

29. Ogunseye, S., Parsons, J.: Can expertise impair the quality of crowdsourced data? In: Proceedings of 15th AIS SIGSAND Symposium Lubbock, Texas (2016)

30. Wiggins, A., Newman, G., Stevenson, R.D., Crowston, K.: Mechanisms for data quality and validation in citizen science. In: 2011 IEEE Seventh International Conference on e-Science Workshops, pp. 14–19 (2011)

31. Gura, T.: Citizen science: amateur experts. Nature **496**, 259–261 (2013)

Test First, Code Later: Educating for Test Driven Development

Teaching Case

Naomi Unkelos-Shpigel[✉] and Irit Hadar

Information Systems Department, University of Haifa,
Carmel Mountain, 31905 Haifa, Israel
{naomiu,hadari}@is.haifa.ac.il

Abstract. As software engineering (SE) and information systems (IS) projects become more and more of collaborative nature in practice, project-based courses become an integral part of IS and SE curricula. One major challenge in this type of courses is students' tendency to write test cases for their projects at a very late stage, often neglecting code coverage. This paper presents a teaching case of a Test-Driven Development (TDD) workshop that was conducted during a SE course intended for senior undergraduate IS students. The students were asked to write test cases according to TDD principles, and then develop code meeting test cases received from their peers. Students' perceptions towards TDD were found to be quite positive. This experience indicates that instructing SE courses according to TDD principles, where test cases are written at the beginning of the project, may have positive effect on students' code development skills and performance in general, and on their understanding of TDD in particular. These findings are informative for both education researchers and instructors who are interested in embedding TDD in IS or SE education.

Keywords: Software engineering · Requirements engineering
Test Driven Development · Education

1 Introduction

In the last two decades, as the agile manifesto [2] has been increasingly adopted in industry, the contribution of collaborative projects has been recognized, focusing on continuous review among practitioners within and among development teams. However, information system (IS) and software engineering (SE) students are typically not being trained during their studies for this type of collaborative work [15].

Project-based courses, in which students are required to develop a prototype as their final assignment, are an integral part of IS and SE degrees' curricula. The teachers of these courses face several challenges, such as ensuring equal participation of all students in the workload [12], and creating projects that will be both of high quality and utility, all in parallel to teaching a large portion of theoretical background [15].

In recent years, collaborative practices have been used in SE education, in order to enhance student participation in tasks throughout the semester. This interactive method

© Springer International Publishing AG, part of Springer Nature 2018
R. Matulevičius and R. Dijkman (Eds.): CAiSE 2018 Workshops, LNBIP 316, pp. 186–192, 2018.
https://doi.org/10.1007/978-3-319-92898-2_16

of experiencing other groups' work, while presenting their own, resulted in positive feedbacks about the projects and the assessment method [15].

Test-driven development (TDD) is a software development practice, encouraging developers to write tests prior to code development [3]. This practice has become popular in recent years in industry as a requirements specification method. However, several challenges still hinder TDD practices in both industry and education [4].

This paper presents a teaching case of a SE project-based course for IS students. Leveraging on existing examples for TDD in practice, this paper presents a teaching case of incorporating a TDD workshop into this course. While designing and executing this workshop, the following research questions arose: (RQ1) How can we provide the students with an experience that will emphasize the advantage of using TDD over traditional testing? (RQ2) How do students perceive TDD following this workshop?

The next section presents the background for our research. Section 3 details the TDD workshop. Section 4 presents the findings, and Sect. 5 discusses the conclusions and future research directions.

2 Background

2.1 Test Driven Development (TDD)

Test driven development (TDD) is a software development practice, encouraging developers to write tests prior to code development [1, 3]. In recent years, TDD has become very useful in specifying the desired software behavior [7]. As explained by Hendrickson [7]: "The TDD tests force us to come to a concrete agreement about the exact behavior the software should exhibit."

Developers who practice TDD contribute to product quality and overall productivity [4, 5]. In addition, when examining the use of TDD in academic environments and in the industry, a major improvement in product quality is observed [3, 9].

A major challenge of TDD is that it does not provide testers and developers with full guidance on which parts of the code they should focus. Instead, they are expected to understand on their own, which parts of the code they should test, and investigate why these tests fail [11]. Another challenge is related to the collaborative nature of the TDD practice; while TDD has been found to increase collaboration among developers and testers in lab environments [4], further research is needed in order to understand how collaboration contribute to practicing TDD in industry-scale projects.

2.2 Collaborative Requirements Engineering (RE)

A major concern of the current RE practice is collaboration [5, 8]. Using agile practices has led to solving many challenges of traditional RE. However, performing RE according to the agile principles is still an evolving craft. Inayat et al. [10], conducted a systematic literature review in order to understand what the main characteristics and challenges in agile RE are. Out of over 540 papers retrieved, only 21 were found to be relevant to agile practices. A key issue in the relevant papers is requirement change management, as requirements elicitation in agile development is usually based on user stories, which are frequently changing. Therefore, requirements are validated usually through prototyping, and documentation hardly takes place [10].

Several research works examined the practice of collaborative TDD. Romano et al. [11] used ethnographic research in order to study novice programmers' reaction to performing TDD in pair programming. They concluded that this practice holds several limitations to collaboration and requires tool support. They also made an interesting observation that programmers first visualize the code, and only then write the test. An additional research, which analyzed TDD practices in GitHub, found that TDD may increase collaboration among testers and programmers, but may also hinder the process, as it sets a high bar of expected results [4].

3 The TDD Workshop

The TDD workshop was designed as a teaching method, executed in two consecutive years in an advanced SE course, intended for third year undergraduate IS students. The course consisted of 59 students in fall 2016-7, and 75 students in fall 2017-8. The students worked in teams of four, building a software product. In the first three weeks of the semester, the students wrote a requirements document and constructed a rapid prototype. Following these tasks, they developed the product employing SCRUM [13] methodology.

In order to teach the students TDD, we conducted a short lecture explaining TDD and its practice. Next, we conducted a two-part workshop, as explained below.

In the first year, the workshop took place in the 6th and 7th lecture. In the first week of the workshop, the students received an assignment (see Fig. 1) and were asked to write as many automated tests as they could think of. The groups uploaded the tests into the course's website. In the second week of the workshop, each group received tests written by another group, and were asked to code functions accordingly.

---

1. Create a simple String calculator with a method int **Add(string numbers)**

- The method can take 0, 1 or 2 numbers, and will return their sum (for an empty string it will return 0) for example "" or "1" or "1,2"

- Start with the simplest test case of an empty string and move to 1 and two numbers

2. Allow the Add method to handle an unknown amount of numbers

3. Allow the Add method to handle new lines between numbers (instead of commas).

- the following input is ok: "1\n2,3" (will equal 6)
- the following input is NOT ok: "1,\n" (not need to prove it - just clarifying

---

Fig. 1. The task given in the first workshop (taken from: http://osherove.com/tdd-kata-1)

In the second year, the procedure was repeated with the following two alterations: (1) the workshop took place in the 2nd and 3rd lecture. (2) The task was different - In the first week of the workshop: the students received the task of finding valid URLs in an online chat history messages. The reason for the first change was that we wanted to see whether performing the workshop at an earlier stage in the course, would affect performance. The second change was aimed to enable the students to face a "real life" coding challenge, which they are familiar with from their online activity.

4   Students' Reflections on the TDD Workshop

At the end of the course, the students filled out a questionnaire, in which they were asked about their opinions regarding each part of the workshop. In addition, at the end of the semester, the students were asked to describe their perceptions on TDD and its challenges, based on their experience in the workshop. Figure 2 presents the main categories found in each semester (Fall 2016-7 – 52 respondents, Fall 2017-8 – 65 respondents). We analyzed the responses inductively [14] with regards to the research questions.

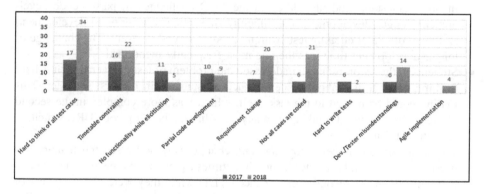

Fig. 2. TDD challenges emergent categories

RQ1 – The students referred to TDD as an interesting and beneficial, as well as a challenging experience. Referring to the first part (tests writing), they mostly addressed the challenge of writing tests without having a product or code:

- *"Very challenging – forced us to think of all possible tests"*
- *"It taught us how to deal with unfamiliar code, and how to test it"*

They also mentioned the relatedness of the task to the course project:

- *"Very good. We divided the work among team members, which was a good preparation for the project."*

Referring to the second part (code writing), the responses mostly addressed the challenge of writing code according to tests received from other groups:

- *"It was very hard to write code according to other students' tests"*
- *"Great experience! it gave us an idea of how the situation will be in the industry, because it's always going to be this way: we will get some code and we'll have to make some changes on it."*

- *"It was very surprising when we got to code test [cases], which we did not think of in the first part."*

When addressing both parts of the workshop, some students mentioned the importance of this practice to their future careers. Others addressed both parts of the task as informative and helpful in viewing tests and code tasks through the perspective of other groups.

RQ2 – In both semesters, the students addressed some challenges of TDD, which have already been discussed in the literature [6]. These include the difficulty to achieve requirements coverage, the required ongoing communication between testers and developers, and longer development duration. In the second semester, when the students performed the workshop as a requirements elicitation procedure for their project, they focused in their responses mostly on requirements coverage and requirement changes.

Some interesting observations emerged from analyzing the full responses:

- In both semesters, students addressed the TDD challenges of partial code development, longer development, the difficulty of writing tests prior to development, and the problem of eliciting tests with no product or code present. The challenge of longer development time was the one most frequently mentioned.
- Students in the second semester addressed the problem of tests' coverage ("it is hard to think of all tests") about twice as much as students in the first semester. This finding could be related to the task itself, which was more complex in the second semester, and required thinking of many possible faults (erroneous URL structure, website not found, etc.).
- The topics of requirements coverage and change were addressed much more frequently in the second semester (about three times as much). We believe that the fact that students in the second semester faced TDD while they were in the process of eliciting requirements for their project, made them more aware to the aspect of TDD as requirements specification method. Furthermore, as they faced requirements change throughout the duration of the semester, at the end of the process they were experienced at coping with these changes. They realized that tests written at the beginning of the process could not cover these changes.
- The challenge of misunderstandings between developers and testers was also mentioned more frequently (about twice as much) in the second semester. As the task was more complex in the second semester, this finding was to be expected.
- A new category, which emerged only in the second semester, is the difficulty of conducting TDD in agile projects. Since TDD is part of agile practices, this category is surprising. Students explained this challenge with the fact that agile development requires prompt results. Performing TDD "by the book", usually requires spending a substantial amount of time in the beginning of each development cycle. This is perceived as delaying code development.

5 Expected Contribution and Future Directions

In this paper, we presented a teaching case, designed to enhance students' perception and performance of TDD practices. According to our findings, performing the workshop at the beginning of the course, resulted in students enhanced understating of TDD's advantages and challenges. This finding can assist and guide instructors who are interested in embedding in their course TDD as a requirements specification method. We intend to repeat this workshop next year as well, and to add TDD tasks to the course project. This will enable to evaluate the overall project quality while performing TDD. Such an evaluation will add quantitative performance indicators to the students' self-reported perceptions elicited in this exploratory study.

References

1. Beck, K.: Test-Driven Development: by Example. Addison-Wesley Professional, Boston (2003)
2. Bissi, W., Neto, A.G.S.S., Emer, M.C.F.P.: The effects of test driven development on internal quality, external quality and productivity: a systematic review. Inf. Softw. Technol. **74**, 45–54 (2016)
3. Bjarnason, E., Sharp, H.: The role of distances in requirements communication: a case study. Req. Eng. **22**(1), 1–26 (2015)
4. Borle, N.C., Feghhi, M., Stroulia, E., Greiner, R., Hindle, A.: Analyzing the effects of test driven development in GitHub. In: Empirical Software Engineering, pp. 1–28 (2017)
5. Fucci, D., Turhan, B., Juristo, N., Dieste, O., Tosun-Misirli, A., Oivo, M.: Towards an operationalization of test-driven development skills: an industrial empirical study. Inf. Softw. Technol. **68**, 82–97 (2015)
6. Gopinath, R., Jensen, C., Groce, A.: Code coverage for suite evaluation by developers. In: Proceedings of the 36th International Conference on SE, pp. 72–82. ACM (2014)
7. Hendrickson, E.: Driving development with tests: ATDD and TDD. Starwest (2008)
8. Marczak, S., Damian, D.: How interaction between roles shapes the communication structure in requirements-driven collaboration. In: 2011 19th IEEE International Requirements Engineering Conference (RE), pp. 47–56 (2011)
9. Kurkovsky, S.: A LEGO-based approach to introducing test-driven development. In: Proceedings of the 2016 ACM Conference on Innovation and Technology in Computer Science Education, pp. 246–247. ACM (2016)
10. Inayat, I., Salim, S.S., Marczak, S., Daneva, M., Shamshirband, S.: A systematic literature review on agile requirements engineering practices and challenges. Comput. Hum. Behav. **51**, 915–929 (2015)
11. Romano, S., Fucci, D., Scanniello, G., Turhan, B., Juristo, N.: Results from an ethnographically-informed study in the context of test driven development. In: Proceedings of the 20th International Conference on Evaluation and Assessment in SE, p. 10. ACM (2016)
12. Schneider, K., Liskin, O., Paulsen, H., Kauffeld, S.: Media, mood, and meetings: related to project success? ACM Trans. Comput. Educ. (TOCE) **15**(4), 21 (2015)
13. Schwaber, K.: Agile project management with Scrum. Microsoft Press, Redmond (2004)

14. Strauss, A., Corbin, J.: Basics of Qualitative Research: Techniques and Procedures for Developing Grounded Theory. Sage Publications, Thousand Oaks (1998)
15. Unkelos-Shpigel, N.: Peel the onion: use of collaborative and gamified tools to enhance software engineering education. In: Krogstie, J., Mouratidis, H., Su, J. (eds.) CAiSE 2016. LNBIP, vol. 249, pp. 122–128. Springer, Cham (2016). https://doi.org/10.1007/978-3-319-39564-7_13

Workshop on Enterprise Modeling

Second International Workshop on Enterprise Modeling

Preface

Modern enterprises are under permanent pressure for change to cope with new competitors and to integrate emerging technologies. These changes involve adoption of processes, architectures, operations, value propositions, and the response to evolving market requirements — especially regarding the digitalization. Enterprise modeling is of primary importance for developing, analyzing, and deploying information systems that operate in today's digitalized world and for addressing some of these challenges.

The focus of the enterprise modeling workshop at CAiSE 2018 was on foundations and applications of enterprise modeling as well as on the model-based development and evolution of enterprise-wide information systems. The second edition of the enterprise modeling workshop was held in Tallinn, Estonia, co-located with CAiSE 2018. In total, the workshop attracted nine international submissions from six countries. After a thorough reviewing process, four papers were accepted as full papers to be presented at the workshop and included in the workshop proceedings. Thus, a competitive acceptance rate of 44.44% was applied.

The workshop program comprises papers that follow different research methodologies. Contributions focus on applications of enterprise modeling in diverse domains as well as foundational aspects, e.g., the development of new modeling methods and the integration of ontologies. The paper entitled "An Application Design for Reference Enterprise Architecture Models" follows a design science research methodology. The author proposes an application design for reference enterprise architectures. The applicability of the approach is demonstrated in the domain of regulatory compliance management. In "The 'What' Facet of the Zachman Framework – A Linked data-Driven Interpretation" the development of a novel modeling method that facilitates conceptual modeling while utilizing the linked data paradigm is presented. The modeling method provides a technology-agnostic lens on the "What" facet of the Zachman framework. Laurenzi et al. propose in their paper "Toward an Agile and Ontology-Aided Modeling Environment for DSML Adaptation" an innovative approach that integrates modeling and meta-modeling in a single ontology-aided environment. The ontology thereby enriches the formality of the modeling language semantics. Finally, the paper "Toward a Risk-Aware Business Process Modeling Tool Using the ADOxx Platform" presents research that targets the conceptualization and implementation of a modeling tool for risk management with the ADOxx metamodeling platform. The novelty of the approach lies in the semantic integration of risk management and business process management by conceptual modeling means.

An invited keynote complemented the scientific paper presentations. We were happy to host Prof. Kurt Sandkuhl form the University of Rostock as a keynote speaker. The keynote was entitled "Enterprise Modeling: From Expert Discipline to Common Practice."

We are thankful to all authors who submitted their research to the workshop. We want to thank all Program Committee members for their valuable and constructive feedback. A special thanks goes to Prof. Kurt Sandkuhl for delivering an interesting keynote. Finally, we want to thank the CAiSE workshop chairs for accepting the enterprise modeling workshop and thereby providing us with a stage we could occupy to further advance the field.

April 2018

Dominik Bork
Hans-Georg Fill
Dimitris Karagiannis
Matti Rossi

Workshop Organization

Organizing Committee

Dominik Bork   University of Vienna, Austria
Hans-Georg Fill   University of Bamberg, Germany
Dimitris Karagiannis   University of Vienna, Austria
Matti Rossi   Aalto University, Finland

Program Committee

Frederick Benaben   École des Mines d'Albi-Carmaux, France
Xavier Boucher   École Nationale Superieure des Mines de St. Etienne,
                                France
Osvaldo Cairó Battistutti   Instituto Tecnológico Autónomo de México, México
Luis Camarinha-Matos   Universidade Nova De Lisboa, Portugal
Elisabetta Di Nitto   Politecnico di Milano, Italy
Aurona Gerber   University of Pretoria, South Africa
Fausto Giunchiglia   University of Trento, Italy
César González-Pérez   Spanish National Research Council, Spain
Yoshinori Hara   Kyoto University, Japan
Dimitris Kiritsis   EPFL Lausanne, Switzerland
Elyes Lamine   École des Mines d'Albi-Carmaux, France
Heinrich C. Mayr   University of Klagenfurt, Austria
Selmin Nurcan   Pantheon-Sorbonne University, France
Andreas Oberweis   Karlsruhe Institute of Technology, Germany
Klaus Pohl   University of Duisburg-Essen, Germany
Claudia Pons   University of La Plata, Argentina
Kurt Sandkuhl   University of Rostock, Germany
Alta van der Merwe   University of Pretoria, South Africa
Jan Vanthienen   Katholieke Universiteit Leuven, Belgium
Francois Vernadat   European Court of Auditors, Luxembourg
Stanislaw Wrycza   University of Gdansk, Poland
Eric Yu   University of Toronto, Canada
Jelena Zdravkovic   Stockholm University, Sweden

The "What" Facet of the Zachman Framework – A Linked Data-Driven Interpretation

Alisa Harkai, Mihai Cinpoeru, and Robert Andrei Buchmann[✉]

Faculty of Economics and Business Administration, Business Informatics
Research Center, Babeş-Bolyai University, Cluj-Napoca, Romania
{alisa.harkai,mihai.cinpoeru,
robert.buchmann}@econ.ubbcluj.ro

Abstract. The recommended interpretation of the "What" facet in the Zachman Framework is that it serves as a data-centric viewpoint on the enterprise, capturing data requirements across several layers of abstraction – from high-level business concepts down to implemented data entities. In enterprise modelling, these have been traditionally approached through well-established practices and modelling techniques – i.e., Entity-Relationship models, UML class models and other types of popular data model types. In the current context of digital transformation and agile enterprise relying on distributed information systems, certain technological specifics are lost when employing traditional methods acting on a high level of abstraction. For example, the Linked Data paradigm advocates specific data distribution, publishing and retrieval techniques that would be useful if assimilated on a modelling level - in what could be characterised as *technology-specific modelling methods* (mirroring the field of domain-specific languages, but from a technological perspective). This paper proposes an agile modelling language that provides a diagrammatic and, at the same time, machine-readable integration of several of the Zachman Framework facets. In this language, the "What" facet covers concepts met in a Linked Enterprise Data environment – e.g., graph servers, graph databases, RESTful HTTP requests. These have been conceptualised in the proposed language and implemented in a way that allows the generation of a particular kind of code – process-driven orchestration of PHP-based SPARQL client requests.

Keywords: Zachman Framework · SPARQL orchestration
Resource Description Framework · Agile Modelling Method Engineering

1 Introduction

With respect to data modelling, we are still relying on the traditional, highly abstract modelling techniques based on, e.g., ER diagrams, UML class diagrams. Technology-specific patterns and properties are not in the scope of such languages. This paper makes initial steps towards filling this gap, considering the context of a Linked Data-driven enterprise, where execution of business processes must be supported by orchestrated Linked Data requests. The key categories of resources in such a

© Springer International Publishing AG, part of Springer Nature 2018
R. Matulevičius and R. Dijkman (Eds.): CAiSE 2018 Workshops, LNBIP 316, pp. 197–208, 2018.
https://doi.org/10.1007/978-3-319-92898-2_17

context are graph database servers, graph databases, named graphs, HTTP-based CRUD operations over such graphs - typically performed within a RESTful architecture where combinations of SPARQL queries and HTTP methods, headers and parameters can operate flexibly on the graph storage content [1].

We benefit from methodological enabler such as the Agile Modelling Method Engineering Framework (AMME) [2] and the Resource Description Framework (RDF) [3] – firstly, to customise and extend a business process modelling language with technology-specific concepts and properties included as first-class citizens; secondly, to generate executable PHP-based orchestrations of HTTP requests that could be integrated in scripts supporting various process tasks (e.g., assuming a workflow management system backed by Linked Data resources).

Therefore we hereby propose the notion of "technology-specific modelling languages" (TSML), which reflects the tradition of domain-specific modelling languages (DSML) – however, "domain" is replaced by "technology" since the productivity goal advocated by DSMLs is transferred to a specific technological space (here, Linked Data). Just as in the case of DSMLs, this comes with a trade-off between reusability and productivity, with the second quality being further enhanced by the agility benefits of applying the Agile Modelling Method Engineering Framework (for customising the modelling language and tool). This will further allow the adaptations necessary to extend the proposed modelling tool to generate other kinds of code than the current scope (of PHP scripting). Therefore AMME is a key enabler for the generalisation of the proposal towards other targeted programming environments.

The origins of this work stand in the attempt of establishing an RDF-based approach to representing linked versions of the Zachman Framework enterprise description facets [4] in an agile modelling language [5]. Due to project-based focus [6], only some of those facets have been assimilated in the modelling language – How/When (as processes), Where (as geographical coverage models) and Who (as organisational structures). This paper considers the additional data facet (the "What"), based on the assumption that a Linked Data back-end fuels a business process management system. Data requirements in such a system are not limited to the abstractions allowed by ER or class diagrams – they must also consider the technological context and must be linked to process descriptions in a machine-readable way. Consequently, the mentioned agile modelling language was given the aforementioned TSML quality. This specificity is then further employed by a code generation mechanism that produces PHP-code making use of the EasyRDF library constructs [7] in order to execute orchestrated REST-based SPARQL operations over graph databases.

The Zachman Framework is commonly treated as an ontology, but it is not a formal one in the sense discussed by [8] or [9]. It is also not a modelling method in the sense defined by [10] – we employ it as schema to guide an enterprise metamodel considering the technology-specific definition, design and analysis of architectural information. Our aim is to derive machine-readable knowledge from a technology-specific enterprise architecture design and to query it in order to cross the design-time/run-time bridge with the help of a model-to-RDF transformation plug-in made available for the ADOxx metamodelling platform [11].

The paper is structured as follows: Sect. 2 provides background information about the Zachman Framework, the AMME Framework, the RDF technological space and about the EasyRDF library employed as a target programming environment for code generation. Section 3 comments on related works. Section 4 discusses the design decisions for the proof-of-concept presented in Sect. 5. The paper ends with conclusions.

2 Motivation, Methodology and Enablers

2.1 Motivation: The Zachman Framework

The Zachman Framework (ZF) is an enterprise information systems ontological frame, originating in a business system planning project [4], as a method by which information architecture of organisations can be designed and analysed according to an overarching structure serving multiple perspectives. ZF is a matrix of processes, roles, locations, goals, data structures required by the organisation. A common interpretation of the ZF facets is: (i) What – data requirements/services, (ii) How – processes, (iii) Where – locations, (iv) Who – roles and responsibility assignments, (v) When – timing and (vi) Why – goals; and the abstraction layers typically reflect different stakeholder perspectives: (i) execution perspective (contextual level); (ii) business management perspective (conceptual level); (iii) architect perspective (logical level); (iv) engineer perspective (physical level); (v) technician perspective (as built); (vi) enterprise perspective (functioning). Using these levels and views, an enterprise can be described in different ways for different purposes - this has also been recognised in multi-view enterprise modelling [12, 13]. We employ the Agile Modelling Method Engineering framework to produce modelling tools that can capture in a semantically integrated way the facets of ZF – this paper will focus on the What facet, considering the technological specificity of Linked Data (the "domain-specific" quality is translated to a "technology-specific" viewpoint).

2.2 Methodology: The Agile Modelling Method Engineering

Agile Modelling Method Engineering (AMME) [2] can be considered a Design Science [14] approach specialised for the creation of modelling methods and modelling tools tailored for various kinds of specificity – including the technological specificity hereby discussed. AMME gives methodologists the ability to create and evolve a modelling tool in an agile manner with respect to semantics, syntax and functionality - an environment such as ADOxx [11] is commonly used for prototyping.

The management practices of today's enterprises adopt both the notions of Agile Enterprise [15] and Agile Knowledge Management [16], and the Enterprise Architecture Management is based on an agile form of knowledge representation that is synchronised with software engineering processes. Moreover, the Linked Open Models vision [17] shows that models can be exposed to knowledge-driven information systems using Resource Description Framework (RDF) in order to expose model contents to a code generation framework. In this respect, this paper makes some initial steps targeting a PHP development environment based on the EasyRDF library for Linked Data retrieval.

2.3 Technological Enablers

The Resource Description Framework (RDF) is a standard adopted World Wide Web Consortium (W3C) [3] - a family of specifications originally designed as a metadata data model. It evolved as a technological foundation for the Semantic Web and it can be used to describe Web resources in Linked Data environments. Its constructs are graph structures – most nodes in the RDF graphs are URIs (Uniform Resource Identifier) that identifies a Web resource about which machine-readable statements can be stored as subject-predicate-object triples. In Fig. 1 the key aspects are illustrated: (i) a graphical representation of a graph; (ii) a human-friendly RDF serialisation - the Turtle format [18]; (iii) A SPARQL query example.

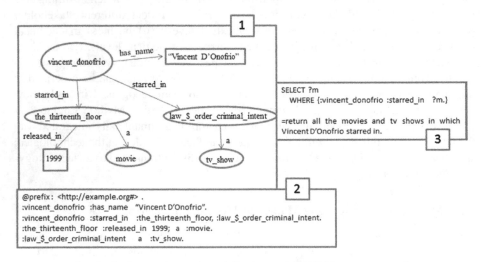

Fig. 1. RDF sample graph, serialisation and SPARQL query example

Another technological enabler is the EasyRDF library [7] which allows PHP scripts to consume and produce RDF based on a series of patterns (that are also captured in our modelling language to support code generation for the use of this particular library). Data is loaded into an EasyRdf Graph object and SPARQL queries can be sent over HTTP using the EasyRdf Sparql Client class providing some object-oriented methods for CRUD operations – some of them executed on full graphs (insert, clear), others sending more granular queries (query, update). The code below exemplifies these CRUD operations.

```php
<?php
require 'vendor/autoload.php';
$client1=new EasyRdf_Sparql_Client("http://localhost:7200/repositories/movies");
$client2=new EasyRdf_Sparql_Client("http://localhost:7200/repositories/movies/statements");
$graph=new EasyRdf_Graph();
$graph->load("http://localhost:7200/movies/resource?uri=".urlencode("http://www.example.org#mymoviegraph"));
$prefix=new EasyRDF_Namespace();
$prefix->set("","http://www.example.org#");
$query1="prefix : <http://www.example.org#> describe :vincent_donofrio";
$result1=$client1->query($query);
print $result1->dump();
$query2="delete {:the_thirteenth_floor :released_in ?x.}  insert {:the_thirteenth_floor  :released_in  2000.} where
{:the_thirteenth_floor  :released_in  ?x.}";
$result2=$client2->update($query2);
$graph->addResource("vincent_donofrio" "lives_in" "Arizona");
$client2->insert($graph,"http://www.example.org#mymoviegraph");
$client2->clear("http://www.example.org#mymoviegraph");
?>
```

The example instantiates two SPARQL clients, one for the read address and one for the write address of a GraphDB query service, which connects to the graph in Fig. 1 with the help of the EasyRdf_Sparql_Client constructor. For the first type of operation (Query) we used a string variable with a DESCRIBE query, for the second (Update) we used another string variable with an update (INSERT/DELETE) query which updates the year of the movie, for the third we directly inserted a new statement using the graph URI and for the last we directly deleted the graph using the Clear() method.

We do not aim to establish an RDF-centric data modelling technique on the level of abstraction of, e.g. ER, but rather to capture in a modelling language the architectural principles of interacting with Linked Data through the EasyRDF library – however, these are common patterns present in other libraries (e.g., rdflib for Python) and further investigation across different programming environments will be necessary to confirm the reusability of these patterns. Moreover, our code generation approach relies on the Linked Open Models vision [17], where several patterns were introduced for converting diagrammatic models into RDF graphs - a plug-in is available for ADOxx in order to achieve this regardless of the type of RDF model. Once models are serialised, they are loaded in GraphDB [19] which is a scalable RDF database to which libraries such as EasyRDF can connect. As we have already discussed, our modelling tool has been extended with a new type of diagram that respects the "What" facet of the ZF considering the technological specificity of Linked Data – i.e., the concepts of graph database, graph, HTTP request.

3 Related Works

The notion of "technology-specific modelling" (TSM) is often mentioned in non-diagrammatic modelling approaches [20], but less so in diagrammatic conceptual modelling, although there is rich a tradition of domain-specific diagrammatic modelling (DSM) [21–23], itself deriving from situational method engineering [24]. DSM was probably intended to subsume TSM, however the distinction is worth discussing especially when model-driven software engineering is considered – i.e., specific technology concepts will benefit from a direct mapping when bridging the design-time and run-time facets. In this work we adopt concepts that are specific to the Linked Data technological space and also have correspondences to the EasyRDF library for PHP, where code must be generated.

Enterprise knowledge can be represented with semantic technology – e.g., RDF graphs coupled with ontologies. Moreover, modelling languages driven by domain-specific requirements are becoming more prominent [23]. The integration of such languages with analytical tools via semantic technology has been discussed before in rather generic terms or decoupled from code generation goals [25, 26]. We think that AMME is a key enabler in adding technology-specific semantics to a modelling language; moreover, we employ it to partition the modelling language with appropriate granularity thus separating modelling concerns pertaining strictly to business views from the technological specificity – at the same time, these models can be linked in meaningful ways so their relations (e.g., from business tasks to HTTP requests to graphs) are traceable for a code generator. This is exploited by the Linked Open Models approach employs the fact that the resulting models/structures are made available to semantic information systems.

The Zachman Framework is used to structure enterprise knowledge according to a two dimensional schema which prescribes six facets and also perspectives for enterprise descriptions but it does not specify neither how to bridge them in machine-oriented ways and make them available to external processing. In time this framework has been extended by other frameworks (e.g., Evernden, The Integrated Architecture Framework) [27]. Moreover, ZF is used to map various processes which are relevant to enterprise architectures (e.g., analysis of the Rational United Process [28], Model-driven architecture [29], TOGAF [30]). Means of bridging the data and process facets have emerged from the process mining community for analytical purposes [31]. A Linked Data-oriented approach focusing on geoprocessing workflows was proposed in [32]. In this context, the contribution of this paper is to describe the data perspective (the What facet of ZF) with means that are amenable to a technology-specific approach to code generation.

4   Design Decisions

The proposed modelling language combines ZF, AMME and RDF to create a multi-perspective conceptual frame available to semantic queries, which also exposes specific Linked Data retrieval concepts characterised by technology-specific properties - e.g., HTTP requests characterised by the CRUD operation that is performed and possibly by the explicitly annotated SPARQL query, as required by some business process task. Such technological details are then queried from models and concatenated in EasyRDF code that can actually execute those queries in the sequence dictated by the business process model to which HTTP requests are linked.

We developed the modelling tool starting from a class diagram which represents the meta-model governing the modelling language which can be changed and evolved using AMME framework as new requirements are adopted. Due to the fact that the

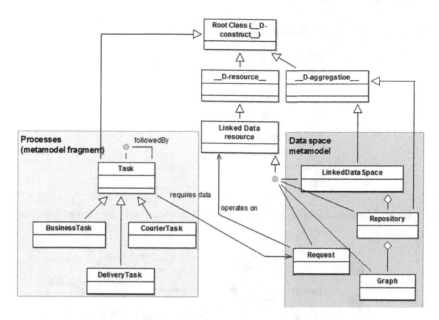

Fig. 2. Metamodel fragment (How and What facets)

work at hand focuses on the What facet of ZF we show in Fig. 2 only a part of the entire meta-model (a fragment which contains the classes for How and What facets).

The metamodelling platform used to develop this agile modelling tool is ADOxx which provides some abstract classes (e.g., __D-construct__, __D-resource__, __D-aggregation__ etc.). __D-construct__ is the root class from which every other class inherits properties and is used in every metamodel. Several types of models have been created to describe transportation processes, locations and participants [5] – however in this paper we only focus on the semantic interface between process tasks and an additional type of model – models of Linked Data resources (the What facet). These have specific symbols that cover ZF facets and in Fig. 3 we emphasised the symbols for the What facet.

Across these types of diagrams hyperlinks are established as depicted in Fig. 4. Different types of links are available: the task Deliver has assigned an employee (Jim) who becomes the responsible person for that task and has as a role Big Car Driver. Moreover the Deliver task has some required data (HTTP) requests, such as Request 2 from the depicted graph which is sent to a REST server that contains a graph database and the graph that we want to query.

All the models can be exported and converted in RDF graphs which are machine-readable ready – i.e., available to queries over the linked models, where certain runtime parameters are stored in the attributes of model elements (e.g., the SPARQL query, the HTTP operation, the address of the graph repository). A graphical representation of the graph which contains the types derived from the meta-model and the links between models is shown in Fig. 4. SPARQL queries can retrieve from these models the overall dependency relations (e.g., which graph is on which database server,

Symbol	ZF facet
task decision 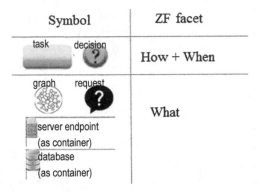	How + When
graph request	What
server endpoint (as container) database (as container)	

Fig. 3. Specific symbols covering How and What ZF facets considering Linked Data concepts

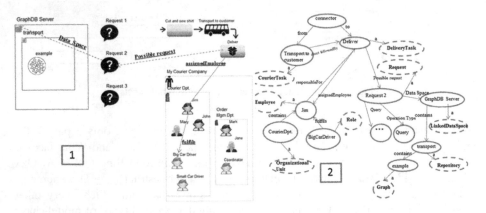

Fig. 4. Linked model fragments (1) and derived RDF graph (2)

which query operates on which graph) – such results are then concatenated in EasyRDF-compatible PHP code to actually execute those queries on those databases, in an order orchestrated according to the process flow linked to those requests.

5   Proof-of-Concept

We adopted the case of a transport company that needs to have its courier processes mapped on human resources and addressable locations. Moreover, we want to obtain information which is necessary to perform some activities (e.g., pieces of information about an invoice, information about clients - retrievable from a Linked Data space encompassing multiple graph servers exposing SPARQL endpoints that follow the typical RESTful recommendations for remote data retrieval). The human resources in the example are described both in terms of roles and instance performers, grouped by departments or organisational units depicted as visual containers, e.g.: Production; Research/Development; Marketing; Finance; Resources.

Figure 5 depicts only two types of diagrams relevant for this work, namely: Model of make-to-order process (M1); Model of linked data space (M2). The first diagram contains a business process made from three types of tasks (i.e., Business Task, Courier Task, Delivery Task) and decisions. These tasks are assigned to user roles (e.g., couriers) and we took into account that at some point in the process the courier needs information about his client in order to deliver the products. The second type of diagram (M2) comprises four major concepts as highlighted in the metamodel: (i) the server concept **(Linked Data Space)**, (ii) the graph database concept **(Repository)**, (iii) the **Graph** itself concept, (iv) the **Request** concept. Thus, the task Deliver is associated with the Request 2 which has as attributes the EasyRDF operation type (Query) and the query itself annotated as a string in the modelling tool. This request is described as being sent to the GraphDB server which contains the graph database where the relevant graph is hosted (with the information about the clients) – the annotations are illustrated in Fig. 6. Containment relations (inspired by the swimlanes in BPMN) establish the hierarchical subordination of graphs to graph repositories, and further to graph servers. Requests can be sent either directly to graphs (for graph-level operations such as a inserting a whole graph) or to graph databases (for granular SPARQL queries).

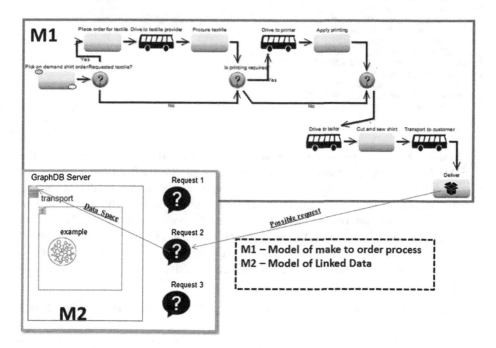

Fig. 5. Samples of business process model (How) and linked data space (What)

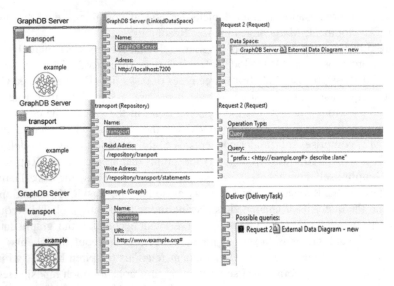

Fig. 6. Example of external data model

```
<?php
require 'vendor/autoload.php';
$graph=new EasyRdf_Graph();
$graph->load("http://localhost:7200/transport/resource?uri=".urlencode("http://wwwexample.org#Business_Process_ Distribute_Shirts");
$prefices=new EasyRDF_Namespace();
$prefices->set("","http://www.example.org#");
$part1=getResource("GraphDB Server","Address");
$part2=getResource("transport", "Read Address");
$runtimeTarget=$part1 . $part2;
$query=getResource("Request 2","Query");
$client=new EasyRdf_Sparql_Client($runtimeTarget);
$client->query($query);
?>
```

In this piece of EasyRDF code we get all parts of the REST target address in the variable $runtimeTarget - those address parts are taken directly from the properties of the modelled concepts. Further, we get the query also from the modelled request annotation and we establish a new REST connection with the EasyRdf_Sparql_Client class – this will actually run the query to retrieve information necessary in the process task that is served by this script. We used the REST address for read operations (http://localhost:7200/repository/transport) and a DESCRIBE query (annotated in Fig. 6) to obtain the information about Jane (client) which is useful for the driver who has to deliver her some shirts. Other examples:

- insert data {graph :example {:Andreea :hasAddress :NewStreetNo23}} – inserts in the graph a new statement of Andreea (client);
- select distinct ?client (count (?client) as ?count) where {graph <http://www.example.org#example> {?client :hasAddress :Street40}   – selects the distinct clients who live at Street40.

6 Conclusions

The paper proposes an agile modelling tool as an enabler for technology-specific model-driven engineering. The proposal illustrates the notion of TSML, relying on agile engineering methodologies to adapt a modelling language for code generation scenarios that do not rely on standards. A current limitation is that code generation is only semi-automated, as certain information is annotated manually – i.e., the SPARQL queries. Only the architectural deployment of those queries is described in a diagrammatic manner. A modelling language for SPARQL queries is a key opportunity for future developments. The current practices of code generation rely on standards and stable model compilers confined to the fixed semantic space established by those standards. With this paper we advocate the idea that agile modelling methods combined with the ability to export arbitrary types of models in RDF knowledge graphs could productively feed a code generation framework based on programming libraries whose constructs can be assimilated as first-class citizens in a TSML. AMME is a key ingredient to ensure the fast reprototyping of such tools, thus contributing to a more agile modelling and code generation paradigm compared to traditional model-driven software engineering approaches.

Acknowledgment. This work is supported by the Romanian National Research Authority through UEFISCDI, under grant agreement PN-III-P2-2.1-PED-2016-1140.

References

1. RDF4J Server REST API. http://docs.rdf4j.org/rest-api
2. Karagiannis, D.: Agile modeling method engineering. In: Proceedings of the 19th Panhellenic Conference on Informatics, pp. 5–10. ACM (2015)
3. RDF - Semantic Web Standards. https://www.w3.org/RDF
4. Zachman, J.A.: Business systems planning and business information control study: a comparison. IBM Syst. J. **21**, 31–53 (1982)
5. Harkai, A., Cinpoeru, M., Buchmann, R.A.: Repurposing Zachman Framework principles for "Enterprise Model"-driven engineering. In: Proceedings of ICEIS 2018, pp. 682–689. SCITEPress (2018). https://doi.org/10.5220/0006710706820689
6. EnterKnow Project Page. http://enterknow.granturi.ubbcluj.ro/
7. EasyRDF Homepage. http://www.easyrdf.org/
8. Smith, B.: Beyond concepts: ontology as reality representation. In: Proceedings of the Third International Conference on Formal Ontology in Information Systems, pp. 73–84. IOS Press (2004)
9. Guarino, N.: Formal ontology, conceptual analysis and knowledge representation. Int. J. Hum Comput Stud. **5–6**, 625–640 (1995)
10. Karagiannis, D., Kühn, H.: Metamodelling platforms. In: Bauknecht, K., Tjoa, A.M., Quirchmayr, G. (eds.) EC-Web 2002. LNCS, vol. 2455, p. 182. Springer, Heidelberg (2002). https://doi.org/10.1007/3-540-45705-4_19
11. BOC-Group GmbH, ADOxx platform page – official website. http://www.adoxx.org/live

12. Bork, D.: Using conceptual modelling for designing multi-view modelling tools. In: Proceedings of the 21st Americas Conference on Information Systems. Association for Information Systems (2015)
13. Kingston, J., Macintosh, A.: Knowledge management through multi-perspective modelling: representing and distributing organizational memory. J. Knowl.-Based Syst. **13**(2–3), 121–131 (2000)
14. Peffers, K., Tuunanen, T., Rothenberger, M.A., Chatterjee, S.: A design science research methodology for information systems research. J. Manag. Inf. Syst. **24**(3), 45–77 (2007)
15. Goldman, S., Naegel, R., Preiss, K.: Agile Competitors and Virtual Organizations: Strategies for Enriching the Customer. Wiley, New York (1994)
16. Levy, M., Hazzan, O.: Agile knowledge management. In: Encyclopedia of Information Science and Technology, pp. 112–117. IGI Global (2008)
17. Karagiannis, D., Buchmann, R.: Linked Open Models: Extending Linked Open Data with conceptual model information. Inf. Syst. **56**, 174–197 (2016)
18. RDF 1.1 Turtle. http://www.w3.org/TR/turtle
19. GraphDB Homepage. http://graphdb.ontotext.com
20. Koehler, A., Peyer, F., Salzmann, C., Saner, D.: Probabilistic and technology-specific modeling of emissions from municipal solid-waste incineration. Environ. Sci. Technol. **45**(8), 3487–3495 (2011)
21. Frank, U.: Domain-specific modeling languages: requirements analysis and design guidelines. In: Reinhartz-Berger, I., Sturm, A., Clark, T., Cohen, S., Bettin, J. (eds.) Domain Engineering, pp. 133–157. Springer, Heidelberg (2013). https://doi.org/10.1007/978-3-642-36654-3_6
22. Kelly, S., Lyytinen, K., Rossi, M.: MetaEdit+ a fully configurable multi-user and multi-tool CASE and CAME environment. In: Constantopoulos, P., Mylopoulos, J., Vassiliou, Y. (eds.) CAiSE 1996. LNCS, vol. 1080, pp. 1–21. Springer, Heidelberg (1996). https://doi.org/10.1007/3-540-61292-0_1
23. Karagiannis, D., Mayr, H.C., Mylopoulos, J.: Domain-Specific Conceptual Modeling. Springer, Cham (2016). https://doi.org/10.1007/978-3-319-39417-6
24. Kumar, K., Welke, R.: Methodology engineering: a proposal for situation-specific methodology construction. In: Cotterman, W.W., Senn, J.A. (eds.) Challenges and Strategies for Research in Systems Development, pp. 257–269. Wiley, New York (1992)
25. Blackburn, M.R., Denno, P.O.: Using Semantic Web technologies for integrating domain-specific modeling and analytical tools. Procedia Comput. Sci. **61**, 141–146 (2015)
26. Nassar, N., Austin, M.: Model-based systems engineering design and trade-off analysis with RDF graphs. Procedia Comput. Sci. **16**, 216–225 (2013)
27. Schekkerman, J.: How to Survive in the Jungle of Enterprise Architecture Frameworks. Trafford, Bloomington (2003)
28. de Villiers, D.J.: Using the Zachman Framework to assess the rational unified process. In: The Rational Edge, Rational Software (2001)
29. Frankel, D.S., Harmon, P., Mukerji, J., Odell, J., Owen, M., Rivitt, P., Rosen, M., Soley, R. M.: The Zachman Framework and the OMG's model driven architecture. White paper. Business Process Trends (2003)
30. The Open Group: ADM and the Zachman Framework (2017). http://pubs.opengroup.org/architecture/togaf8-doc/arch/chap39.html
31. Alizadeh, M., Lu, X., Fahland, D., Zannone, N., van der Aalst, W.M.P.: Linking data and process perspectives for conformance analysis. Comput. Secur. **73**, 172–193 (2018)
32. Yue, P., Guo, X., Zhang, M., Jiang, L., Zhai, X.: Linked Data and SDI: the case on Web geoprocessing workflows. ISPRS J. Photogramm. Remote Sens. **114**, 245–257 (2016)

An Application Design for Reference Enterprise Architecture Models

Felix Timm[(✉)]

Chair of Business Information Systems,
University of Rostock, Rostock, Germany
felix.timm@uni-rostock.de

Abstract. An increasing number of regulations forces financial institutes to implement a holistic and efficient regulatory compliance management (RCM). Since most institutes primarily implement isolated solutions in a deadline-triggered manner, reference enterprise architectures (R-EA) help them to save costs and increase the quality of their RCM approaches, because they reveal implications regulation has on their business, information and IT architecture. The application of such a R-EA to a specific institute is a context-dependent task and requires an intensive knowledge transfer between R-EA constructor and its user. However, the majority of research activities focuses on R-EA construction, while contributions regarding its application are scarce. Thus, this works presents an application design of a R-EA in the context of RCM, which systematically documents in what context the R-EA can be applied and what benefits it offers to its user. Using design science research (DSR), we contribute to research and practice suggesting a framework for R-EA application and apply it in the RCM context.

Keywords: Reference enterprise architecture · Reference model application
Regulative compliance management · Reference compliance organization

1 Introduction

After the global financial crisis in 2007, a significantly increasing number of regulations addressing national, European and international financial markets forced financial organizations to implement a holistic RCM [1]. Kharbili defines RCM as the task *"...of ensuring that enterprises are structured and behave in accordance with the regulations that apply ..."* [2]. Thus, financial institutes need to be aware of the relations among their strategy, processes, applications and infrastructures to be able to rapidly react on complex and changing regulatory requirements. The EA research domain contributes to this purpose by providing methods and tools to establish a more holistic perspective on organizations [3, 4]. EA models represent different architectural layers of an enterprise, such as business, application and technology architecture [5]. Since EA projects are highly time- and resource-consuming, organizations would benefit from reference models for EA. A Reference Enterprise Architecture (R-EA) can be defined as a generic EA for a class of enterprises that is used as foundation in the design and realization of the concrete EA [6]. In prior work we developed a reference compliance

© Springer International Publishing AG, part of Springer Nature 2018
R. Matulevičius and R. Dijkman (Eds.): CAiSE 2018 Workshops, LNBIP 316, pp. 209–221, 2018.
https://doi.org/10.1007/978-3-319-92898-2_18

organization (R-CO), which uses R-EA structures and was developed by adapting methods from the reference modeling (RM) research domain [7]. Since the R-CO aims to be used by financial organizations to improve their RCM, an application design has to be provided to R-CO users. Although there exists research in both fields of RM application [8] and R-EA development [9], IS research lacks in giving guidance how to develop a sufficient R-EA application design. Hence, the research objective of our work is to develop an application design for the R-CO. To reach this aim we deploy a design DSR, which is presented in Sect. 2 and guides this work's structure.

2 Research Design

We structure our work in terms of the DSR methodology suggested by Peffers et al. [10]. Based on discussing literature on RM application we present an application design of the prior developed R-CO as this work's artefact. We define an application design as a framework, which systematically documents in what context the R-CO can be applied and what benefits it offers to its user. Peffers et al. define five activities for DSR projects (i–v). We performed them as follows:

The (i) problem identification revealed the need for a sound application design for the R-CO, since an absence of such was identified in IS literature (see Sect. 1). Consulting related literature in the general RM domain we identified relevant aspects in the RM application domain and clarified the requirements towards the artefact during the DSR process (ii) define the objective for a solution (see Sects. 3.1 and 3.2). During the step (iii) design and development we built a framework for RM application (Sect. 3.3) and elaborated an application design for the R-CO that contains various application scenarios (see Sect. 4). One of these application scenarios is (iv) demonstrated afterwards, which provided a first (v) evaluation of the artefact (see Sect. 5). On this basis, we discuss benefits and drawbacks of the presented artefact and draft future research in this domain (see Sect. 6).

3 Reference Model Application

RMs are information models developed for a certain problem in a certain application domain in order to be reused by a specific enterprise of that domain. RMs are characterized by their universality, recommendation and reusability [11]. The life cycle of RMs can be distinguished between the phase of construction and the phase of application [12]. However, these phases cannot be distinctively delineated from each other. For example, the designer of a RM may have concrete beliefs how the model should be applied. Meanwhile, the user of the RM may have a different perception of the model's value [13]. Therefore, Fettke and Loos suggest a phase that integrates with both and call it "reuse", in which the RM designer prepares the model for its reutilization and the RM user retrieves it [8]. We contribute to a more precisely definition of the reusability attribute of RMs and thereby suggest an artefact that supports the reuse and application phase of the RM lifecycle. Before presenting the RM application framework (Sect. 3.3) and its application the R-CO (Sect. 4), we discuss the value of RMs (Sect. 3.1) and analyze literature that investigates RM application (Sect. 3.2).

3.1 The Value of Reference Models

In order to justify the effort of RM application, the RM user (e.g. an enterprise) has to understand a RM's value. IS researchers do agree that the main value of RMs is to make the design and development of information systems more efficient and effective [14, 15]. Becker and Knackstedt explicitly state metrics that describe the economic effects RM applications offer from a user perspective: a decrease in costs due to the reusability; a decrease of modeling time for enterprise-specific models; an increase of the model quality; a competitive advantage; and, a decrease in modeling risk since reference models are already validated [16]. Other IS researchers agree with these metrics [14, 17].

Despite this consensus, IS research misses to empirically investigate the value of reference models [18]. Only two contributions were identified that conducted a cross-sectional analysis of reference model application benefits. Schütte surveyed 22 RM users and his findings revealed that most RM users applied the RMs primarily for means of cost reduction. Only a minority did so for aspects of proceeds or risk mitigation. In concrete, the majority of RM users stated efficient realization of organizational concepts and the minimization of software lead times as the main reasons for RM application. Interestingly, more than every second RM user stated that they further observed unquantifiable effects. Unfortunately, Schütte did not inquire them explicitly [14]. These findings could imply that both the RM designers and the RM users are not completely aware of the value a RM can generate.

Fettke interviewed users of the Supply Chain Operations Reference Model (SCOR) [18]. The basis of his study was the hypothesis that the success of reference modeling depends on RM application. He operationalized these two variables and interviewed 153 enterprises of the Supply Chain Council. He evaluated how the degree of SCOR application influenced the success of supply chain management. To measure success, he used three of the earlier mentioned metrics (i.e. costs, time, and quality) and added flexibility. His findings show that the SCOR model application had a significant positive influence on the success on supply chain management. Further, he concludes that the RM application enhances the effectivity and efficiency of considered information systems development. Still, his findings are based on cross-sectional data and are yet to be verified by a longitudinal study that analyzes the effects of the SCOR model application in a longer period in certain use cases.

Based on these finding one can derive that the application of reference models offers various advantages to the RM user. Nevertheless, there are also disadvantages a user has to be aware of before applying RMs. First, the application of RMs may negate an already existing competitive advantage since competitors can gather the same knowledge. Second, the maintenance and especially the adjustment to an enterprise-specific context can be time- and resource-consuming. Last, the application of a complex RM requires high knowledge [18]. In consequence, Fettke argues that the sole existence of a RM does imply neither its value nor its success if it is applied. More certainly this depends on the context, in which the RM is applied [18]. For example,

Hars mentions highly regulated domains as a suitable reference models application context [19]. Therefore, the analysis of a RM's intended value is an essential aspect when developing its application design. Such an analysis and its documentation within the RM may mitigate the risk of a diverse value perception between RM designer and user. Thus, we deem it essential to create a shared understanding of a RM's value among RM designer and RM user by documenting its application design by dint of a framework.

3.2   Aspects of Reference Model Application

The majority of research activities focuses on RM construction, while research regarding RM application is scarce [15]. Nevertheless, few methodological works exists.

Fettke and Loos suggest a procedural model that they attach between the construction and application process and name it "reuse". The main processes therein are: (i) design of RM reusability, during which the designer makes the RM accessible; (ii) RM retrieval, during which the user searches, selects and procures the RM; (iii) RM adjustment, where the user might change the RM for his or her specifics; and, (iv) evaluation, where both designer and user change feedback of the process, such as problems or experiences. To support the procedure of reuse the authors characterize RMs by static means: model type, perspective on structure or behavior, and modeling language [8].

Based on his procedure for RM construction, Schütte describes how to apply model in two different application scenarios from the perspective of the RM user [14]. This procedure requires the RM to be already prepared for its application and, thus, may be used after the reuse procedure from Fettke and Loos. Becker and Knackstedt provide a procedure model for the application of configurative RMs [16], which can be seen as an equivalent of their procedure model for configurative RM construction [20].

Further, vom Brocke defines five design principles for both RM construction and application [13]. From the perspective of the RM user, such principles support the RM adjustment during its application. Wolf argues that it is hardly possible to develop scientific methods for RM application. He understands it as a communication task between the RM designer and user, who may not instantly comprehend the RM's value [21]. Thus, he suggests documenting the intention, context, the addressed problem and the suggested value. This is in line with the prior depicted argument that the RM application is context-dependent. We conclude that this may take place in the application preparation of a RM.

In line with Wolf we argue that it is important for both the RM designer and the RM user to explicate possible application scenarios [21]. Analyzing related literature, we identified typical application scenarios presented in Table 1.

3.3   An Application Framework for Reference Models

We understand the application design of a RM to be an important instrument for a successful application process. In consequence, this section summarizes prior depictions using an application framework that contains six application aspects, which

Table 1. Overview on application scenarios in the literature

Application scenario	Description	Source
Construction of specific models	RM user develops specific model	[14, 18, 22]
IS development	RM as a development framework	[16–18, 22, 23]
Consultancy	RM as a consulting artefact	[18]
Knowledge transfer	RM as means for training	[16, 18]
Analysis	RM used to evaluate models	[14, 16, 22]
Software procurement	RM support procurement decisions	[22, 23]
Migration support	RM support migration processes	[23]

should be considered when preparing and conducting RM application. We motivate this with the works by Fettke and Wolf, who agree that the application of a reference model is vague, depends on its context and is full of pitfalls due to implicit knowledge that it requires [18, 21]. Thus, we suggest the presented aspects as a useful tool for the application process of a RM. Not only does it help RM designers after and during the construction process, but further improves the quality of communication with the RM user as well as it concretizes his or her expectations.

The framework for RM application in Table 2 expresses each of the six application aspects by various application items, which we identified in related literature. All aspects can be related to the process steps for RM reusability provided by Fettke and Loos (see Sect. 3.2) [8]. While aspect *(1) RM Specifics* relates to the static characteristics defined in [8], aspect *(2) RM Reuse* addresses the strategy of the model designer how to make the RM available. Both *(1)* and *(2)* relate to the (i) reusability design from [8]. Then, aspect

Table 2. Aspects for reference model application design

Aspect	Item	Description	Source
(1) RM specifics	RM scope	What type of model is the RM?	[8]
	RM perspective	Does the RM address behavior or structure?	[14]
	RM language	What modeling language is used?	[8]
(2) RM reuse	RM marketing	How can the RM be retrieved?	[8, 20]
(3) RM communication	Documentation	Addressed Problem, Intention, Context	[21]
	Addressed stakeholders	Who are addressed RM users?	[16, 18, 21]
(4) RM value	General benefits	What benefits does the RM application offer (costs, quality, risk, time, competitive advantage)?	[16, 18]
	Model specific value	Are there RM specific values (e.g. EA specific benefits)?	[14]
(5) RM application scenarios	Description of scenarios	Different scenarios should be discussed related to the model scope	[14, 16, 18, 22, 23]
	Dimensions of application	Discuss breadth, detail, depth, volume or use of language of RM application	[18]
			[14]

(*continued*)

Table 2. (*continued*)

Aspect	Item	Description	Source
(6) Adjustment strategy	Compositional adjustment mechanisms	The RM should indicate in which cases composition may occur or give identified guidelines	
	Generic adjustment mechanisms	Depending on the RM Scope, design principles for application support the RM user	[13, 14, 16]

(3) RM communication recommends the designer to document the addressed problem and what different stakeholders might be addresses by the RM. This enhances the interface between process (i) and (ii) RM retrieval. In the latter process (ii) the aspects *(4) RM values* and *(5) RM application scenarios* are important for the model user to make an informed choice for an appropriate RM. The value of an RM can both be documented by means of known metrics or model-specific values depending on what model scope is used by the RM at hand. Further, the RM designer should define different application scenarios addressing certain stakeholders and hold different values [18]. For the process (iii) model adjustment the model designer should define an *(6) adjustment strategy*, which – next to undefined compositional adjustments by the user – should include specific design principles appropriate for the problem domain, which need to be elaborated by the model designer during the construction process.

4 Application Design of a Reference Enterprise Architecture

This section uses the framework for RM application design, which is presented in Sect. 3.3 and applies it to the specifics of a prior developed RM. The addressed problem domain of the RM is regulatory compliance in the financial domain. The RM aims to holistically represent all relevant aspects of the financial institute that is affected by regulation. In other words, the RM intends to support institutes to effectively and efficiently implement a RCM that uses an integrated IS approach. Therefore, the RM is based on the structure of EA models. In specific, we developed a "Reference Compliance Organization" (R-CO) using concepts and methods from the EA domain. In the following we present the application design of the R-CO by discussing the six aspects depicted above.

For reasons of comprehensibility we start with aspect *(3) RM communication*, which includes describing the addressed problem, the RM's intention and the context it was developed in. The R-CO addresses the problem that financial institutions currently do not approach a coherent RCM systems and rather implement isolated solutions, which only realize single regulations due to short-term deadline of those [24]. Such isolated compliance solutions typically span organizational structures and processes supported by information systems and IT-based instruments [25]. The intention of the R-CO is to offer financial institutions a holistic model that captures common and best practices of RCM providing insights regarding organizational procedures, their interrelations with necessary information structures and an integrated IS support. At the moment, the R-CO focuses on the context of the German legal sphere and, thus, addresses German financial institutions. The R-CO addresses different stakeholders of the problem domain as RM users. First, (i) financial institutions can use the R-CO to build or improve a holistic RCM. Second, (ii) independent software vendors that focus on compliance systems for financial institutions can use the R-CO to advance their products or broaden their product range. Third, the R-CO is the body of knowledge (iii) business consultancies could use as a foundation in order to analyze their clients. Fourth, (iv) accountancy firms can use this body of knowledge as well as an auditing framework. And last, one day a complete, sound and thorough R-CO could be an instrument for (v) the Financial Supervisory Authority that represents a RCM standard.

Based on these considerations the R-CO has the following *(1) RM Specifics*. Using the categorization by Fettke and Loos for RM scope the R-CO represents an enterprise model, capturing the RCM division of financial institutions and focusing on both business and IS concepts [8]. Thus, the R-CO represents both behavioral and structural perspectives, i.e. it defines compliance processes but also necessary information structures. In this context, the R-CO uses the modeling language ArchiMate in its current version 3.0 [5]. It is based on The Open Group Architecture Framework and divides an EA model into a business layer, an application layer and a technology layer [26]. The R-CO utilizes the business (RCM structures and procedures) and application layer (information structures and IS utilized in RCM), because the infrastructural realization of the RCM is out of the problem domain's scope. Further, the R-CO is structured by several architecture views that address certain concerns regarding the R-CO, like process responsibilities or application usage. On the one hand, the decision to use EA is sufficiently motivated from the perspective of the problem domain [24, 25]. On the other hand, it is in line with EA research findings, since EA models can be used as a regulative instrument (i.e. to guide enterprises in certain aspects) or an informative instrument (i.e. to enable decision making by sharing knowledge) [27].

The development of the R-CO was funded by a group of nine companies organized in a committee of the German IT-association Bitkom [28]. The companies' representatives are experienced in the field of IT-based compliance as they operate as consultants and software vendors in this domain. In consequence, the *(2) Approach for RM Reuse* was developed within this committee. To date, the RM model is not publicly accessible and managed by both the Bitkom association and the participating companies. Potential RM user can retrieve the R-CO by contacting the right holders.

In general, the *(4) RM Value* of the R-CO is that it addresses a prevalent problem in the practice of RCM in the financial sector. As discussed in prior work both research and practice highlight the absence of reference models for RCM, which holistically offer insights from a business as well as an IS perspective and base on real-life scenarios and actual organizational behavior [1, 25, 29]. Depending on the different stakeholders that are addressed as potential RM users and further depending on the application scenario the value of R-CO application to the user may vary. With regards to the metrics described in [16] the R-CO designers claim the following advantages when applying the R-CO:

- a *decrease in costs* since a correct R-CO helps institutes to avoid penalty charges when applied or a reduction of development costs for regulation-specific software development;
- an *improvement in quality* due to transforming isolated RCM solutions into an integrated and IS supported RCM approach by applying best practice approaches;
- the application of the R-CO *mitigates the risk* of the institute's reputational and financial damage in case of an unidentified case of money laundering or fraud;
- a *decrease in expenditure of time* from implementation of regulatory requirements.

The stated advantages are neither complete—since it highly depends on the application context—nor are the effects validated so far. However, they reflect the experiences made during the construction process and were elaborated together with the domain experts of the Bitkom committee. Although we do not completely exclude competitive advantage as a benefit of R-CO application, we do not specifically claim that an enterprise will gain a competitive advantage from it. The R-CO rather addresses a domain that financial institutes consider as a cost driver. However, an inefficient and ineffective RCM may result in a competitive disadvantage due to the damage regulatory violations cause. Next to these RM value metrics, the R-CO holds model-specific values. Since the R-CO uses EA structures, general benefits of EA are valid for the R-CO as well. For certain regulatory domain like money laundering or fraud prevention, the R-CO does not only capture necessary organizational processes, but further relates certain process steps to the demanded information and data structures and presents automation potentials due to integrated IS landscapes. The R-CO can be used as a TO-BE model and be compared to the AS-IS model of a certain financial institute [3, 27]. On this basis, migration paths can be derived in order to reach a state of holistic RCM implementation.

The R-CO holds various possible *(5) RM Application Scenarios*. They can be related to the above mentioned stakeholder and further to a value they create. The following Table 3 summarizes five R-CO application scenarios and documents addressed stakeholders as well as created values. The scenarios were developed together with the Bitkom committee and their potential was confirmed in interviews we conducted during the R-CO construction. While there are various scenarios how to use the R-CO, the extent to which the model is used may also vary. Fettke defines five dimensions of RM application, which can be transferred to the R-CO: breadth, detail, depth, volume and use of language [18]. The R-CO covers different regulations like anti-money laundering (AML) or prevention of other criminal acts. They can be applied altogether or separately as R-CO modules (breadth). Further, the R-CO consists of several level of details. While in one application context an aggregated model may be sufficient, another may require the detailed R-CO application (detail). Then, financial institutes or other RM users may intend to extend the application to their business partners in order to trigger some synergy effects (depth). Still, the RM user could also just realize certain segments of the R-CO (volume) or use another terminology for the phenomena described in the R-CO (use of language).

In line with vom Brocke, we understand the construction process of the R-CO as "design for reuse", which constructs the RM, but simultaneously considers mechanisms that support the RM user during the application [13]. Therefore, the R-CO uses the

Table 3. Application scenarios of the R-CO

#	Application scenario	Stakeholder	Related RM value
(I)	GAP analysis with individual models	Institutes	• Risk mitigation • RCM quality improvement
(II)	Development of compliance software	IS Vendors (ISVs)	• Decrease of development time • Product quality improvement
(III)	Analysis of new regulations	Institutes, ISV, consultancy, auditing	• Decrease time of implementation • Improve integration quality
(IV)	Building a coherent RCM	Institutes	• Cost and time reduction of R-CO • Risk mitigation • RCM quality improvement
(V)	Personnel training	Institutes, ISV, consultancies, auditing	• Knowledge transfer • Risk mitigation

principles of aggregation and specialization. The different regulatory domains (e.g. AML) can be applied as modules or also be aggregated in order to utilize synergy effects when expanding the model scope. Moreover, the R-CO does not intend to cover the plethora of enterprise specifics for a single RM user. Thus, the model documents, where RM users have to specialize certain aspects (e.g. certain processes or application landscapes). Next to these design principles the R-CO user most likely will require adjustments, we did not consider during the construction (compositional adjustments). Based on our experience in applying the model we identified the need to mark compulsory R-CO elements (e.g. aspects that are definitely required by regulations) and optional elements, which may include best practices that improve the RCM but may not be necessary to comply with the law.

5   Results of a First Application Use Case

In order to demonstrate the application of the R-CO in more detail, this section illustrates one application scenario that is stated in Sect. 4. In the context of a two-day workshop we applied the R-CO at a German financial thrift institute using application scenario *(I) Gap Analysis with Individual Models*.

Next to the workshop facilitator and EA modeler, two employees from the thrift institute participated for the whole course of the workshop: the institute's chief compliance officer and anti-money laundering manager, who holds this position for more than twenty years; his deputy, who is employed there for twenty years and also worked for more than five years in customer advisory. The overall objective of the R-CO application was to identify gaps between the institute's as-is situation and the R-CO regarding two specific segments of the model: the onboarding process of business clients and the processing of suspected cases in the anti-money laundering (AML).

The workshop agenda was divided into six parts, while each day had a distinct focus. On the first day the as-is situation of the institute was examined. In the first part, the participants were surveyed regarding the general RCM approach of the institute. This aimed to understand how the participants understand and structure the field of RCM and its related tasks. Further, RCM domains were discussed and the two topics AML and onboarding were related to other domains. In the second part, we interviewed the participants about the AML process in detail. Therefore, we utilized the method of participative modeling using a facilitator's toolbox, a whiteboard and a bulletin board [30]. While the facilitator worked together with the participants and asked questions, the EA modeler took notes of the spoken word and simultaneously structured the results in a first structure using an EA modeling tool—still, he asked questions at times. For this task, the team used a prior developed catalogue of questions that related to the aspects captured in the R-CO. Nevertheless, also additional questions were raised and answered during the session. In summary, they addressed organizational processes, used information structures and supporting information systems. Similar to this approach the third part focused on the onboarding process. After these sessions, the facilitator and EA modeler reviewed the results and developed an as-is EA model based on the gathered material. This institute's EA model was constructed using the same structure and ArchiMate views as the R-CO is based on. It captured AML and onboarding processes, information structures and application landscapes.

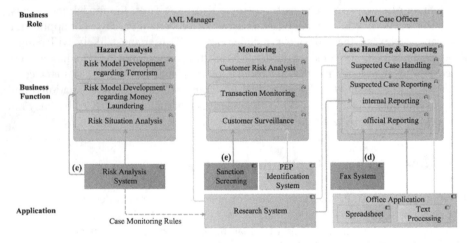

Fig. 1. GAP analysis of the AML case handling IS support (red element indicate elements the institute did not implement) (Color figure online)

The objective of the second workshop day was to identify similarities and differences between the institute and the R-CO. After a short introduction of the R-CO and the ArchiMate modeling language, we performed a gap analysis using a professional modeling tool. The tool helped us to visualize the similarities and differences of the models and proofed to be a very conducive approach to trigger reasoning about them. Different reasons for such differences emerged: (a) parts were missing in the institute EA model because it wasn't discussed on during the modeling sessions; (b) there was a misunderstanding between the participants and the workshop team; (c) aspects captured in the R-CO did not apply to the institute; (d) the institute applied processes that were not captured by the R-CO yet, since they were just implemented after the R-CO construction; and, (e) the R-CO unveiled room of improvement of the institute's compliance approaches. While case (a) and (b) are often observed in modeling sessions [30], cases (c) and (d) confirm claims by vom Brocke—saying that RM application also should integrate a feedback loop to the RM designer [13]. Nevertheless, the most interesting discussions emerged in case (e). Without any further input, both participants directly started thinking whether missing elements should be implemented in their compliance division and why. In Fig. 1 a simplified model view illustrates the gap analysis for the IS support of the AML case handling process. While the institute by the time of the workshop already used a new system for the official reporting instead of a fax system (case d), discussion arose whether the support of a risk analysis system and sanction screening should be implemented in the institute's process (case e). At the end of the workshop the participants were asked for consultation to completely understand the process or data set at discussion and whether they should integrate it in their organization. Later, the participants especially assessed the visualization of the models from the first day and its transparent comparison as very helpful. Further, they never felt lost or misunderstood. In addition, the participants agreed with our overall approach for using EA structures for the R-CO and pointed out that the R-CO together with the application scenario helps institutes to understand their current state in RCM.

6 Discussion and Conclusion

Using a DSR methodology, we develop a structured application design for the Reference Compliance Organization (R-CO). After discussing the problem at hand, we analyze related literature from the reference modeling domain to derive a basic application framework that can be understood as an interface between R-CO designers and R-CO users. It depicts the value of the R-CO and describes different aspects of the application – such as addressed stakeholders, application scenarios or adjustment mechanisms. For demonstration purposes, a concrete application scenario is presented. We contribute to the IS research community by deducing relevant aspects of RM application, present their application to R-EA specifics and elaborate application scenarios for R-EA application. Further, practitioners from the financial domain gain insights how the R-CO support their regulatory compliance management (RCM). From the perspective of validity, we already evaluated one application scenario in detail as depicted in the demonstration use case. Further, scenario *(II) development of compliance software* was also verified since one IS vendor of the Bitkom committee expanded his product range based on the R-CO. Nevertheless, the remaining scenarios are still to be evaluated. To date, they are based on expert's experiences from the RCM domain. The main direction of future research is to further evaluate and expand the application scenarios. For example, to use the R-CO to build a coherent RCM for a certain institute (scenario IV). This may result in a more advanced adjustment mechanisms of the R-CO according to [13]. This will also raise detailed conclusions regarding the R-CO's value.

References

1. Syed Abdullah, N., Sadiq, S., Indulska, M.: Emerging challenges in information systems research for regulatory compliance management. In: Pernici, B. (ed.) CAiSE 2010. LNCS, vol. 6051, pp. 251–265. Springer, Heidelberg (2010). https://doi.org/10.1007/978-3-642-13094-6_21
2. Kharbili, M.E.: Business process regulatory compliance management solution frameworks: a comparative evaluation. In: Conferences in Research and Practice in Information Technology Series, vol. 130, pp. 23–32 (2012)
3. Ahlemann, F., Stettiner, E., Messerschmidt, M.: Strategic Enterprise Architecture Management: Challenges, Best Practices, and Future Developments. Springer, Heidelberg (2012). https://doi.org/10.1007/978-3-642-24223-6
4. Lankhorst, M.: Enterprise Architecture at Work: Modelling, Communication and Analysis. Springer, Heidelberg (2017). https://doi.org/10.1007/978-3-662-53933-0
5. ArchiMate 3.0 specification. Open Group standard (2016)
6. ten Harmsen van der Beek, W., Trienekens, J., Grefen, P.: The application of enterprise reference architecture in the financial industry. In: Aier, S., Ekstedt, M., Matthes, F., Proper, E., Sanz, J.L. (eds.) PRET/TEAR -2012. LNBIP, vol. 131, pp. 93–110. Springer, Heidelberg (2012). https://doi.org/10.1007/978-3-642-34163-2_6
7. Timm, F., Sandkuhl, K.: Towards a reference compliance organization in the financial sector. In: Drews, P., Funk, B., Niemeyer, P., Xie, L. (eds.) MKWI 2018, Lüneburg (2018)
8. Fettke, P., Loos, P.: Methoden zur Wiederverwendung von Referenzmodellen-übersicht und Taxonomie. Referenzmodellierung 2002, Multikonferenz Wirtschaftsinformatik (2002)
9. Sanchez-Puchol, F., Pastor-Collado, J.A.: A first literature review on enterprise reference architecture. In: MCIS Proceedings, vol. 15 (2017)
10. Peffers, K., Tuunanen, T., Rothenberger, M.A., Chatterjee, S.: A design science research methodology for information systems research. JMIS 24, 45–77 (2007)
11. Vom Brocke, J.: Referenzmodellierung. Gestaltung und Verteilung von Konstruktionsprozessen. Logos, Berlin (2003)
12. Fettke, P., Loos, P.: Referenzmodellierungsforschung. Wirtschaftsinf 46, 331–340 (2004)
13. Vom Brocke, J.: Design Principles for reference modeling. In: Fettke, P., Loos, P. (eds.) Reference Modeling for Business Systems Analysis, pp. 47–76. Idea Group, Hershey (2006)
14. Schütte, R.: Grundsätze ordnungsmäßiger Referenzmodellierung. Konstruktion konfigurations- und anpassungsorientierter Modelle. Gabler Verlag, Wiesbaden (1998)
15. Fettke, P., Loos, P.: Referenzmodellierungsforschung. ISYM, Mainz (2004)
16. Becker, J., Knackstedt, R.: Konstruktion und Anwendung fachkonzeptioneller Referenzmodelle im Data Warehousing. In: Uhr, W., Esswein, W., Schoop, E. (eds.) Mit 60 Tabellen, pp. 415–434. Physica-Verlag HD, Heidelberg (2003)
17. Fettke, P., Loos, P.: Perspectives on reference modeling. In: Fettke, P., Loos, P. (eds.) Reference Modeling for Business Systems Analysis, pp. 1–21. Idea Group, Hershey (2006)
18. Fettke, P.: Empirisches Business Engineering. Grundlegung und ausgewählte Ergebnisse, Saarbrücken (2008)
19. Hars, A.: Referenzdatenmodelle. Gabler Verlag, Wiesbaden (1994)
20. Becker, J., Delfmann, P., Knackstedt, R., Kuropka, D.: Konfigurative Referenzmodellierung. In: Becker, J., Knackstedt, R. (eds.) Wissensmanagement mit Referenzmodellen: Konzepte für die Anwendungssystem- und Organisationsgestaltung, pp. 25–144. Physica-Verlag, Heidelberg (2002)
21. Wolf, S.: Wissenschaftstheoretische und fachmethodische Grundlagen der Konstruktion von generischen Referenzmodellen betrieblicher Systeme. Shaker, Aachen (2001)

22. Fettke, P., Loos, P.: Referenzmodelle für den Handel. HMD - Praxis 235 (2004)
23. Höhnel, W., Krahl, D., Schreiber, D.: Lessons Learned in Reference Modeling. In: Fettke, P., Loos, P. (eds.) Reference Modeling for Business Systems Analysis, pp. 355–371. Idea Group, Hershey (2006)
24. Gozman, D., Currie, W.: Managing governance, risk, and compliance for post-crisis regulatory change. a model of IS capabilities for financial organizations. In: HICSS (2015)
25. Cleven, A., Winter, R.: Regulatory compliance in information systems research – literature analysis and research agenda. In: Halpin, T., Krogstie, J., Nurcan, S., Proper, E., Schmidt, R., Soffer, P., Ukor, R. (eds.) BPMDS/EMMSAD -2009. LNBIP, vol. 29, pp. 174–186. Springer, Heidelberg (2009). https://doi.org/10.1007/978-3-642-01862-6_15
26. TOGAF Version 9. Van Haren Publishing, Zaltbommel (2010)
27. Greefhorst, D., Proper, E.: Architecture Principles: The Cornerstones of Enterprise Architecture. Springer, Heidelberg (2011). https://doi.org/10.1007/978-3-642-20279-7
28. Bitkom: Forschungsprojekt: IT gestützte Compliance im Finanzsektor. https://www.bitkom. org/Themen/Digitale-Transformation-Branchen/Banking-Finance/Forschungsprojekt-IT-gestuetzte-Compliance-im-Finanzsektor-2.html. Accessed 27 Feb 2018
29. Akhigbe, O., Amyot, D., Richards, G.: Information technology artifacts in the regulatory compliance of business processes: a meta-analysis. In: Benyoucef, M., Weiss, M., Mili, H. (eds.) MCETECH 2015. LNBIP, vol. 209, pp. 89–104. Springer, Cham (2015). https://doi. org/10.1007/978-3-319-17957-5_6
30. Stirna, J., Persson, A., Sandkuhl, K.: Participative enterprise modeling: experiences and recommendations. In: Krogstie, J., Opdahl, A., Sindre, G. (eds.) CAiSE 2007. LNCS, vol. 4495, pp. 546–560. Springer, Heidelberg (2007). https://doi.org/10.1007/978-3-540-72988-4_38

Towards an Agile and Ontology-Aided Modeling Environment for DSML Adaptation

Emanuele Laurenzi[1,2,3]([✉]), Knut Hinkelmann[1,3], Stefano Izzo[1],
Ulrich Reimer[2], and Alta van der Merwe[3]

[1] FHNW University of Applied Sciences and Arts Northwestern Switzerland,
Riggenbachstrasse 16, 4600 Olten, Switzerland
{emanuele.laurenzi,knut.hinkelmann}@fhnw.ch, stefano.izzo.fhnw@gmail.com
[2] IPM-FHSG, Institute of Information and Process Management, University of
Applied Sciences St. Gallen, Rosenbergstrasse, 59, 9001 St. Gallen, Switzerland
ulrich.reimer@fhsg.ch
[3] Department of Informatics, University of Pretoria,
Lynnwood Rd, Pretoria 0083, South Africa
alta.vdm@up.ac.za

Abstract. The advent of digitalization exposes enterprises to an ongoing transformation with the challenge to quickly capture relevant aspects of changes. This brings the demand to create or adapt domain-specific modeling languages (DSMLs) efficiently and in a timely manner, which, on the contrary, is a complex and time-consuming engineering task. This is not just due to the required high expertise in both knowledge engineering and targeted domain. It is also due to the sequential approach that still characterizes the accommodation of new requirements in modeling language engineering. In this paper we present a DSML adaptation approach where agility is fostered by merging engineering phases in a single modeling environment. This is supported by ontology concepts, which are tightly coupled with DSML constructs. Hence, a modeling environment is being developed that enables a modeling language to be adapted on-the-fly. An initial set of operators is presented for the rapid and efficient adaptation of both syntax and semantics of modeling languages. The approach allows modeling languages to be quickly released for usage.

Keywords: Agile modeling environment
Domain-specific adaptation
Enterprise modeling language engineering
Ontology-aided modeling environment
Domain-specific modeling language

1 Introduction

With the advent of digitalization, model-driven approaches are receiving more attention in Enterprise Modeling [1]. Enterprises are exposed to an ongoing

© Springer International Publishing AG, part of Springer Nature 2018
R. Matulevičius and R. Dijkman (Eds.): CAiSE 2018 Workshops, LNBIP 316, pp. 222–234, 2018.
https://doi.org/10.1007/978-3-319-92898-2_19

transformation with the challenge to quickly and efficiently capture relevant aspects of changes. Burlton et al. [2], in their Business Agility Manifesto argue that it is not sufficient to overcome this challenge with a faster software development - "once operational, such software is likely to prove difficult to continuously and rapidly change without unintended consequences". The current *Knowledge Age* has shifted the purpose of modeling from software development to the creation of knowledge bases through models. Hence, models are becoming more and more means of representing relevant knowledge about business models, business processes, organization structure or resources, which can be used for automation and operations. These models have the ultimate objective to support decision makers. For instance, Enterprise Architecture models support decision makers in business transformation [3]. Models are built using modeling languages, which in turns should enable accommodating evolving requirements, ideally in a way that can be easily understood by experts and stakeholders within a targeted domain. However, existing modeling languages might not be expressive and concise enough to address a specific application domain and therefore may need to be adapted, i.e. extend modeling constructs (i.e. concepts and/or relations), remove unnecessary ones, integrating constructs from different languages or assigning predefined value types as well as concrete values. In this context model-driven domain-specific modeling language adaptation is still a time consuming and complex engineering effort. Namely, it requires numerous iterative phases until a modeling language is rolled out. Some (or all) phases most of the times are still performed sequentially, recalling the rigid waterfall methodology of software engineering. In particular, a modeling language can be validated only after it is implemented and, in turn, the latter starts after the design phase has taken place. That means, some modeling requirements conceptualized in early phases may become outdated while validating the modeling language in the final phases. Although some agile modeling engineering approaches were introduced to allow intertwining phases (e.g. in [1]), a modeling requirement still needs to go through all the engineering phases sequentially in order to be solidly embedded in the modeling language. Additionally, the complexity of domain-specific adaptation goes at the expenses of the duration of the engineering phases. This complexity mainly resides on the lack of development support, i.e. scarce availability of guidelines and best practices [4] as well as the required domain expertise that the knowledge engineer (i.e. developer of the modeling language) should have but rarely has [5].

This engineering effort reclaims supportive modeling approaches that fosters agility along the engineering life-cycle. In contribution to that, this work proposes an agile and ontology-aided modeling environment for domain-specific modeling language adaptation, which enables knowledge engineers accommodating new requirements in a timely and efficient manner. The rest of the paper is structured as follows: Sect. 2 presents the theoretical background supporting the derivation of requirements for an agile modeling environment allowing for domain-specific modeling adaptation. Next, Sect. 3 presents the main idea of the modeling environment and motivates the adoption of ontologies as means to support agility. This section also address the previously derived requirements, and the first set of operators for the domain-specific adaptation is introduced. Finally, Sect. 4 presents the validation of our approach (1) by developing a modeling environment that meets the requirements discussed in the previous section and (2) by implementing the introduced operators on our modeling environment, which are in turn validated in a research project use case.

2   Background

Domain-Specific Adaptation: With the need to address particular application domains, existing modeling languages might not be expressive and concise enough to be adopted. This can lead to the need of adapting existing modeling languages through a domain-specific conceptualization [6,7]. In result, a domain-specific modeling language (DSML) [8,9] is created. Conversely to a general-purpose modeling language (GPML), concepts of a DSML are tailored to a specific domain and are represented by graphical notations familiar to the user of the models. Hence, complexity shifts from the model (i.e. level one) to the meta-model (i.e. level two) to ease the design and understanding of models by domain experts or modelers. Additionally, DSMLs foster the creation of uniform models, and thus support producing quality models. Developing a DSML can be done from scratch or through domain-specific adaptation of existing modeling languages. The latter approach provides the benefit of considering established experience and lessons learned from existing modeling languages or notations. This in turn fosters the reusability (total or partial) of the modeling constructs within the modeling community or across projects. The domain-specific adaptation includes the possibility of (a) introducing new modeling constructs, (b) removing, modifying, replacing existing ones, or borrowing constructs from other application domains and provided with a new semantics. (c) integrating modeling constructs that belong to different modeling languages. In [1], these actions are defined as extensibility, adaptability and integrity, respectively.

Benefits of a domain-specific adaptation come, however, at the expenses of a higher engineering effort for the knowledge engineer, who has to embed domain aspects in the modeling language. Namely, she/he is demanded to understand both (1) the semantics of the modeling language(s) to adapt and (2) the domain knowledge that needs to be covered by the adapted language. This requires a significant experience in modeling and numerous meetings with domain experts [10] to gain domain knowledge. A further complexity lies in (3) expressing the modeling language on right level of abstraction, which leads to complex trade-off decisions between productivity and re-usability of modeling elements [5].

Providing support to the knowledge engineer to perform a domain-specific modeling language adaptation is the first requirement of our modeling environment (*Requirement(1)*).

Meta-Modeling as Means for Domain-Specific Adaptation: In model-driven approaches, the way DSMLs are defined is often rooted to the meta-modeling hierarchy [11]. Meta-modeling is a model-driven technique adopted to ease the development of a modeling language and, thus applicable for DSMLs too. It is a common practice to specify a modeling language in Level two (see Fig. 1). For example, standard modeling languages like ArchiMate, BPMN, CMMN, DMN are typically modeled as UML class diagrams in Level two. Thus, Level two (L2) contains the meta-model, which defines the modeling language to create models in Level one (L1) (see the two levels in Fig. 1).

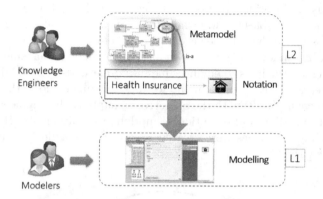

Fig. 1. Meta-model in level two (L2) and Model in level one (L1) [12]

A modeling language comprises *abstract syntax, notation* and *semantics* [13]. Abstract syntax corresponds to the class hierarchy of modeling constructs, which consist of modeling elements and properties (i.e. relations and attributes). Modeling constructs are typically expressed through notations (e.g. graphical or textual), also known as concrete syntax, which should be cognitively adequate to ensure user's understanding of models [12]. The semantics reflects the meaning of the syntactic elements of a modeling language. It can be divided into *structural* and *behavioral* semantics. While structural semantics reverts to the meaning of the class-instance representation, the behavioral one relates to model execution. In this paper we use the term semantics to refer to the structural semantics only. This can be expressed formally (i.e. through mathematics or ontologies) or informally (i.e. through natural language). The abstract syntax of a language is commonly mapped to domain semantics concepts. Constraints (or rules) over the modeling constructs are needed, for example to specify cardinality restrictions or to express that two classes are disjoint. The modeling environment has to embrace a model-driven approach to perform domain-specific modeling language adaptation (*Requirement(2)*).

Agility on the DSML Engineering Process: Developing a modeling language is an engineering task (see [14]), so it is the domain-specific modeling language adaptation. In modeling method engineering (which includes modeling languages) the OMiLab Lifecycle [15] defines the cycle of five phases: create, design, formalize, develop and deploy/validate (see Fig. 2). In general terms, the engineering process that embraces the meta-modeling technique follows the iterative phases (a) conceptualizing the meta-model, (b) implementing it in a meta-modeling tool (e.g. ADOxx[1] or MetaEdit+[2]), and finally (c) validating the modeling language. The latter generates feedback, and determine language amendments. Obviously, the modeling language can be evaluated only after its meta-model is implemented. Hence, abstract syntax, constraints and graphical notations should be conceptualized, implemented and then used for evaluation purposes. This engineering process can be characterized by a sequential design approach, which resembles the waterfall-style approach of software development, where previous phases have to be accomplished before moving forward. To avoid this, the AMME framework [1] was introduced as an agile management approach that follows agile principles to engineer modeling methods. The OMiLab Lifecycle instantiated AMME by introducing feedback channels along the five phases (see black arrows in Fig. 2) with the objective to support the engineering process during the propagation and evolution of modeling requirements [16]. In result, various modeling languages were created following this agile modeling method engineering, e.g. [7,17].

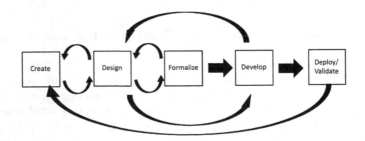

Fig. 2. The OMiLab lifecycle for modeling method engineering [16]

Although this approach allows intertwining most of the phases (e.g. create-design, design-formalize and design-develop) from the point of time a new requirement is accommodated until it is validated it has to go through all or most of the phases in a subsequent manner. For instance, if a new requirement arises while validating the modeling language, it needs to be captured and represented in the form of modeling requirement in the creation phase. Next, the latter is designed such that it fits other modeling constructs. At some point it might be formalized, then it is embedded in the prototype during the development phase and finally the modeling language is ready to be validated again. This sequential approach become problematic with the long duration of each engineering phase as the longer it takes the higher the risk to have outdated requirements. This risk can be avoided by eliminating as much as possible sequential phases in the case when new requirements arise. Hence, the modeling environment should foster

---

[1] https://www.adoxx.org/live/home.
[2] http://www.metacase.com/products.html.

agility by enabling the knowledge engineer to accommodate new requirements by avoiding as much as possible sequential phases (*Requirement(3)*).

Accommodation of Evolving Requirements: A DSML is subject to evolve over time. This is due to new modeling requirements or result from a better understanding of the domain [18]. Therefore, the knowledge engineer is continuously demanded to adapt the meta-model. Moreover, amendments of the meta-model are continuously required due to pitfalls related to inappropriate constraints, abstraction issues, or ambiguity of modeling elements. Also, decisions on whether to promote productivity rather than reusability of the modeling language [19] are subject to continuous changes. The more specific the concepts are (i.e. higher specificity level of the modeling language and thus higher productivity), the lower the possibility to reuse the modeling language across domains or even in different areas, processes or projects of the same domain. Within this context, it becomes even more relevant to support the knowledge engineer with a modeling environment that quickly allows accommodating modeling requirements, ideally on-the-fly. Modeling tools like Visual Paradigm[3] address this challenge by implementing the UML mechanisms *stereotype* and *tagged values*. Hence, the user is enabled on-the-fly to customize modeling constructs. However, adapting a modeling language may lead to a change in the semantics. For instance, specializing an existing modeling construct requires a new interpretation of the new inserted modeling construct. The same applies when editing an existing modeling construct or adding a new one. The new interpretation has to be specified as the semantics of the modeling construct to avoid ambiguous interpretation and non-sense constructs. It is also important that the adaptation of the modeling language does not lead to side effects. For example, adding or removing modeling constructs should not lead to unwanted results or consistency issues. The modeling environment should foster both agility and model quality by enabling the knowledge engineer to accommodate new requirements on-the-fly and efficiently (*Requirement(4)*).

3   The Agile and Ontology-Aided Modeling Environment

Merging Engineering Phases in a Single Integrated Modeling Environment: Different engineering phases can address different expertise. For instance, while conceptualization and implementation are tasks of knowledge engineers, validation often requires the involvement of modelers. This often leads to the adoption of different tools: one for the development of a DSML (occurring in Level 2) and one for using and validating the language and thus creating models (occurring in Level 1). The adoption of two separate tools reflects per se an implementation of the sequential engineering process introduced in Sect. 2. In order to foster agility by avoiding sequential phases (see *Requirement(3)*), we propose a single environment which integrates Level one with Level two. This implies that

---

[3] https://www.visual-paradigm.com/.

the different engineering phases are being merged in the same environment and performed in parallel. The integrated environment places knowledge engineers and modelers in the center of our approach (Fig. 3) by creating conditions for the two roles to provide feedback to each other in a timely manner. *Requirement(1)* and *Requirement(2)* are full-filled as domain-specific modeling language adaptation is allowed within model-driven context. Section 4 shows how the domain-specific adaptation takes place in the modeling environment. Performing the engineering phases in parallel means that while the knowledge engineer adapts modeling languages, the implementation and validation can occur at the same time. For this, a formalization of the knowledge that results from all changes that occur in the modeling language is required. Hence, the formalization has the purpose to automate the execution of engineering phases in parallel. For instance, assuming a new modeling element is inserted (see "Acute Hospital" concept in Fig. 3), its formalization and validation should occur automatically. According to Bork and Fill in [4] a formal specification is necessary to provide unambiguous understanding of models and to foster the interoperability between different computer systems. The same can be applied to modeling languages with the advantage that a formal specification of a modeling language can be automatically propagated on models. A well-known approach to formally define semantics of modeling languages and models is by means of the semantic lifting [20]. Modeling elements and their instances are associated with ontology concepts, which are represented in logic-based languages [17,21]. The problem of this approach, however, is to ensure consistency between the modeling language and related ontology concepts. If a change occurs in the language or any of the models, the ontology should be adapted accordingly. To avoid this problem the modeling environment is fully ontology-based. Namely, modeling constructs are formally defined through ontology concepts and tightly coupled with the respective graphical notations, which avoids the consistency problems caused by the semantic lifting. Knowledge engineers and modelers can rely on customizable graphical notations for increasing clarity of models. Having a modeling language that is ontology-based allows to build ontology-based models. Hence, both modeling languages and models can then be used for reasoning services (like in [22]). This fulfills *Requirement(4)* as new requirements can be accommodated on-the-fly and efficiently.

This approach builds on the semantic meta-model idea introduced in [12]. We take a step forward by distinguishing between the *Domain Ontology* and the *Language Ontology*.

Domain Ontology: The Domain Ontology refers to what Atkinson [23] calls the Ontological meta-modeling View. The Domain Ontology contains classes, properties and instances that describe a domain of discourse. For example, in the health domain there are concepts like patient, disease, physician or hospital, which are structured in a class hierarchy (see right-hand side of Fig. 3). The domain ontology can be contain standards to represent domain knowledge like the International Classification of Functioning, Disability and Health (ICF)

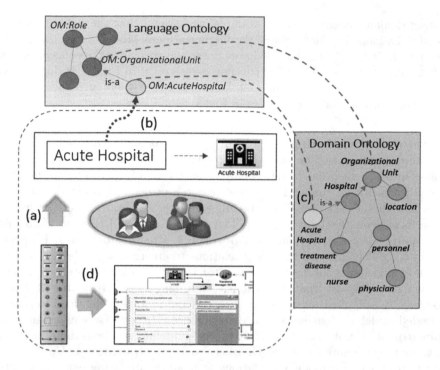

Fig. 3. Conceptualization of the Agile and Ontology-aided Modeling Environment

ontology[4]. Concepts in the Domain Ontology represent the semantics of language constructs, which intends to be independent from a particular modeling language. For instance, the semantics of a modeling construct like "Gateway" from BPMN can be the same as the "Sentry" from CMMN, i.e. both can express the same condition. For this, concepts of the Domain Ontology are mapped to modeling constructs that reside in the Language Ontology.

Language Ontology: The Language Ontology refers to what Atkinson [23] calls the Linguistic meta-modeling View. The Language Ontology contains classes, properties and instances that describe the syntax elements of a modeling language, i.e. modeling elements and modeling relations with respective taxonomy, object properties can occur between the modeling elements and modeling relations (e.g. for the specification of source and target from a modeling relation to a modeling element). Each modeling element and relation is linked to a graphical notation through a data type property (i.e. attribute). Instances can represent types of modeling constructs, e.g. see task types like user task, service task etc. in [24]. The Language Ontology can contain one or more modeling languages, which are separate from each other or integrated [25]. The Language Ontology supports the adaptation of the modeling language (see vertical arrow of Fig. 3). In the modeling environment, new modeling elements can be added for

---

[4] https://bioportal.bioontology.org/ontologies/ICF.

existing domain concepts. As an example, we assume that the palette contains already the modeling elements of the Organizational Model. From the palette (see step (a) in Fig. 3), the knowledge engineer can specialize the concept organizational unit to an acute hospital concept (see step (b) in Fig. 3). If this concept is not yet defined in the Domain Ontology, it is added there as a specialization of the concept hospital (see step (c) in Fig. 3).

Operators for Adapting a Modeling Language: The adaptation of a modeling language can be done by applying a set of operators on the Language Ontology. In order to determine an initial set of operators, we build on lessons learned from the work of recent research projects, Patient-Radar [6,26] and CloudSocket[5] [27,28]. Thus, the following set of operators were derived to be performed on the Language Ontology, which implies a theoretical foundation based on ontology formalism. **Operator 1**. Create sub-class: It is applied on modeling elements and modeling relations to create new modeling elements and new modeling relations. This operator is also applied to integrate modeling elements (classes) from different modeling languages. **Operator 2**. Delete sub-class: It is applied on modeling elements and modeling relations to remove unneeded modeling elements and modeling relations from the modeling language. **Operator 3**. Create relation: It connects modeling elements and modeling relations to the related Domain Ontology concept. **Operator 4**. Update relation: It is applied on modeling relations as it allows updating existing connections between modeling elements/relations and the related Domain Ontology concepts. **Operator 5**. Delete relation: It allows deleting existing connections between modeling elements/relations and the related Domain Ontology concepts. **Operator 6**. Create attribute: It allows adding new attributes to modeling elements and modeling relations. **Operator 7**. Update attribute: It allows updating existing attributes. **Operator 8**. Delete attribute: It allows deleting existing attributes. **Operator 9**. Assign attribute type: It allows assigning value types String, Integer, Boolean to attributes of modeling elements. **Operator 10**. Update attribute types: It allows updating types that are assigned to attributes of modeling elements.

4   Validation

The validation took place (a) by developing the modeling environment such that the four requirements introduced in Sect. 2 were met as discussed in Sect. 3 and (b) by implementing the derived list of operators on the modeling environment. The operators were also validated by applying them on a use case of the Patient-Radar research project. The BPMN modeling language was adapted on-the-fly with modeling elements from the patient transferal domain [6]. Figure 4 shows the screen-shot of **Operators 1 and 2** as illustration. Namely, a subclass of the User Task is created by right-clicking on the User Tasks element in the palette.

---

[5] https://site.cloudsocket.eu/.

The pop-up window in screen-shot number 2 allows the user to (a) assign a name to the new element, (b) specify whether the graphical notation element must be shown in the palette, (c) assign the image for the graphical appearance and (d) map the element to its semantics in the Domain Ontology. The new element is then stored in the Language Ontology as a new class. The screen-shot number 3 of Fig. 4 shows the hierarchy of the modeling elements. The new added element "Prepare KoGu" is shown in the last tier as a sub-concept of "User Task". **Operators from 3 to 8:** By right-clicking on an element in the palette, a context menu is shown, which enables the user to edit the element. A pop-up window provides the possibility to add, modify or delete a relation or an attribute. **Operators 9 and 10:** By right-clicking on an element in the palette, the user can select "create new property". For a new data type property the user is able to assign attribute types as well as assigning predefined values.

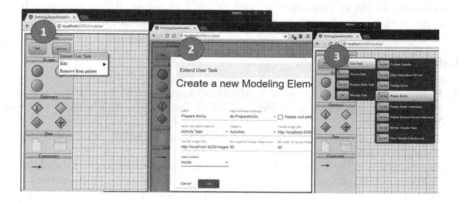

Fig. 4. Operators 1 and 2

5   Conclusion

In this paper the first set of requirements for an agile modeling environment was derived. This emerged from the need to rapidly and efficiently create and adapt domain-specific modeling languages in the context of Enterprise Model-ing. Hence, we addressed the main hinder: the subsequent modeling language engineering phases, which prevents a domain-specific modeling language to be quickly rolled out. The new approach allows to perform engineering phases such as conceptualization, implementation and validation all at once in a single mod-eling environment. The latter integrates Level two and Level one, where the meta-model and model are created, respectively. Thus, the knowledge engineer is enabled to adapt the meta-model and create models from the same modeling environment. The grounding of modeling contructs with ontology concepts sup-ports the agile approach (i.e. on-the-fly accommodation of new requirements) by ensuring that operations on the modeling language are reflected in the Lan-guage Ontology. A first set of operators to apply on the Language Ontology was derived. This allowed the quick propagation of a modeling requirements: from its implementation, to its formal representation, which makes it ready to be validated by applying reasoning services on the Language Ontology. The formalism of the ontology also removes ambiguity on the meaning of language constructs. These benefits are propagated to the models which are built with the formally grounded modeling language. A distinction between Language Ontology and Domain Ontology was also introduced. While the Language Ontology is strictly related to the structure of modeling languages, the Domain Ontology contains the (language-independent) semantics of language constructs. Hence, the Domain Ontology is highly portable as it can be mapped to various modeling languages. The approach was validated by developing the modeling environment with respect to the discussed requirements. Additionally, the set of operators was implemented on the modeling environment and validated in a project's use case. Future work goes towards the improvement of our prototype, which comprises an extension of set of operators as well as applying reasoning services such as consistency checking on both Language and Domain Ontology.

References

1. Karagiannis, D.: Agile modeling method engineering. In: Proceedings of the 19th Panhellenic Conference on Informatics - PCI 2015, pp. 5–10. ACM Press, New York (2015)
2. Burlton, R.T., Ross, R.G., Zachman, J.A.: The Business Agility Manifesto. https://busagilitymanifesto.org
3. Zachman, J.A.: The Concise Definition of The Zachman Framework by: John A. Zachman (2008). https://www.zachman.com/about-the-zachman-framework
4. Bork, D., Fill, H.G.: Formal aspects of enterprise modeling methods: a comparison framework. In: 2014 47th Hawaii International Conference on System Sciences, pp. 3400–3409. IEEE (2014)
5. Frank, U.: Domain-specific modeling languages: requirements analysis and design guidelines. In: Reinhartz-Berger, I., Sturm, A., Clark, T., Cohen, S., Bettin, J. (eds.) Domain Engineering, pp. 133–157. Springer, Heidelberg (2013). https://doi.org/10.1007/978-3-642-36654-3_6
6. Laurenzi, E., Hinkelmann, K., Reimer, U., van der Merwe, A., Sibold, P., Endl, R.: DSML4PTM - a domain-specific modelling language for patient transferal management. In: ICEIS 2017 - Proceedings of the 19th International Conference on Enterprise Information Systems, Porto, Portugal, pp. 520–531 (2017)
7. Karagiannis, D., Buchmann, R.A., Burzynski, P., Reimer, U., Walch, M.: Fundamental conceptual modeling languages in OMiLAB. Domain-Specific Conceptual Modeling, pp. 3–30. Springer, Cham (2016). https://doi.org/10.1007/978-3-319-39417-6_1
8. Clark, T., van den Brand, M., Combemale, B., Rumpe, B.: Conceptual model of the globalization for domain-specific languages. In: Combemale, B., Cheng, B., France, R., Jézéquel, J.M., Rumpe, B. (eds.) Globalizing Domain-Specific Languages. LNCS, vol. 9400, pp. 7–20. Springer, Cham (2015). https://doi.org/10.1007/978-3-319-26172-0_2
9. van Deursen, A., Klint, P., Visser, J.: Domain-specific languages: an annotated bibliography. SIGPLAN Not. **35**(6), 26–36 (2000)

10. Nikles, S., Brander, S.: Separating Conceptual and Visual Aspects in Meta-Modelling, pp. 90–94 (2009)

11. Strahringer, S.: Metamodellierung als Instrument des Methodenvergleichs: Eine Evaluierung am Beispiel objektorientierter Analysenmethoden. Publications of Darmstadt Technical University, Institute for Business Studies (BWL) (1996)

12. Hinkelmann, K., Laurenzi, E., Martin, A., Thönssen, B.: Ontology-based meta-modeling. In: Dornberger, R. (ed.) Business Information Systems and Technology 4.0. SSDC, vol. 141, pp. 177–194. Springer, Cham (2018). https://doi.org/10.1007/978-3-319-74322-6_12

13. Karagiannis, D., Kühn, H.: Metamodelling platforms. In: Bauknecht, K., Tjoa, A.M., Quirchmayr, G. (eds.) EC-Web 2002. LNCS, vol. 2455, pp. 182–182. Springer, Heidelberg (2002). https://doi.org/10.1007/3-540-45705-4_19

14. Hölldobler, K., Roth, A., Rumpe, B., Wortmann, A.: Advances in modeling language engineering. In: Ouhammou, Y., Ivanovic, M., Abelló, A., Bellatreche, L. (eds.) MEDI 2017. LNCS, vol. 10563, pp. 3–17. Springer, Cham (2017). https://doi.org/10.1007/978-3-319-66854-3_1

15. Laboratory Open Models - OMILab: Idea and Objectives (2015)

16. Efendioglu, N., Woitsch, R., Karagiannis, D.: Modelling method design. In: Proceedings of the 17th International Conference on Information Integration and Web-based Applications and Services - iiWAS 2015, pp. 1–10. ACM Press, New York (2015)

17. Buchmann, R.A.: Modeling product-service systems for the internet of things: the ComVantage method. Domain-Specific Conceptual Modeling, pp. 417–437. Springer, Cham (2016). https://doi.org/10.1007/978-3-319-39417-6_19

18. Götzinger, D., Miron, E.-T., Staffel, F.: OMiLAB: an open collaborative environment for modeling method engineering. Domain-Specific Conceptual Modeling, pp. 55–76. Springer, Cham (2016). https://doi.org/10.1007/978-3-319-39417-6_3

19. Frank, U.: Multilevel modeling toward a new paradigm of conceptual modeling and information systems design (2013)

20. Azzini, A., Braghin, C., Damiani, E., Zavatarelli, F.: Using semantic lifting for improving process mining: a data loss prevention system case study (2013)

21. Emmenegger, S., Hinkelmann, K., Laurenzi, E., Martin, A., Thönssen, B., Witschel, H.F., Zhang, C.: An ontology-based and case-based reasoning supported workplace learning approach. In: Hammoudi, S., Pires, L.F., Selic, B., Desfray, P. (eds.) MODELSWARD 2016. CCIS, vol. 692, pp. 333–354. Springer, Cham (2017). https://doi.org/10.1007/978-3-319-66302-9_17

22. Walter, T., Parreiras, F.S., Staab, S.: An ontology-based framework for domain-specific modeling. Softw. Syst. Model. **13**(1), 83–108 (2014)

23. Atkinson, C., Kuhne, T.: Model-driven development: a metamodeling foundation. IEEE Softw. **20**(5), 36–41 (2003)

24. Rospocher, M., Ghidini, C., Serafini, L.: An ontology for the business process modelling notation. In: 8th International Conference on Formal Ontology in Information Systems (2014)

25. Hinkelmann, K., Pierfranceschi, A., Laurenzi, E.: The knowledge work designer-modelling process logic and business logic. In: Proceedings - Series of the Gesellschaft fur Informatik (GI). Lecture Notes in Informatics (LNI), vol. P255 (2016)

26. Reimer, U., Laurenzi, E.: Creating and maintaining a collaboration platform via domain-specific reference modelling. In: EChallenges e-2014 Conference: 29–30 October 2014, Belfast, Ireland, pp. 1–9. IEEE (2014)

27. Hinkelmann, K., Laurenzi, E., Lammel, B., Kurjakovic, S., Woitsch, R.: A semantically-enhanced modelling environment for business process as a service. In: 2016 4th International Conference on Enterprise Systems (ES), pp. 143–152. IEEE (2016)
28. Kritikos, K., Laurenzi, E., Hinkelmann, K.: Towards business-to-IT alignment in the cloud. In: Mann, Z.Á., Stolz, V. (eds.) ESOCC 2017. CCIS, vol. 824, pp. 35–52. Springer, Cham (2018). https://doi.org/10.1007/978-3-319-79090-9_3

Towards a Risk-Aware Business Process Modelling Tool Using the ADOxx Platform

Rafika Thabet[1,2(✉)], Elyes Lamine[3,4], Amine Boufaied[1],
Ouajdi Korbaa[1], and Hervé Pingaud[2,4]

[1] MARS Laboratory, University of Sousse,
ISITCom Hammam Sousse, Sousse, Tunisia
rafika.thabet@gmail.com, boufaied.amine@gmail.com,
ouajdi.Korbaa@centraliens-lille.org
[2] Laboratory of Chemical Engineering, CNRS, INP Toulouse,
University of Toulouse, Toulouse, France
herve.pingaud@univ-jfc.fr
[3] Industrial Engineering Center, IMT Mines-Albi,
University of Toulouse, Albi, France
elyes.lamine@mines-albi.fr
[4] ISIS, INU Champollion, University of Toulouse, Castres, France

Abstract. Business Process modelling is a key element in the management of organizations. It allows to build an analytical representation of 'as-is' processes in an organization and compared it with 'to-be' processes for improving their efficiency. Besides, although, risk is an element that can affect business process negatively, it is still managed independently. A necessary link is missing between business process and risk models. To better manage risk related to business process, it should be integrated and evaluated dynamically within the business process models. Currently, there are different meta-models allowing business process modelling. Nevertheless, there are few meta-models allowing risk modelling and even fewer ones that integrate both concepts related to risks and business processes. Based on this need and these observations, we propose, in this work, a risk-aware business process modelling tool using the ADOxx meta-modelling platform.

Keywords: Modelling method · R-BPM · BPRIM · ADOxx
Medication use system

1 Introduction

The Business Process Management (BPM) is a business process-engineering paradigm that consists of designing, monitoring, evaluating and continuously improving processes. This paradigm promotes responsiveness and flexibility of the organization while ensuring the satisfaction of stakeholders' requirements [1]. A process is a holistic structure of activities organized in time and space in order to achieve a goal [2]. Particularly, a business process is characterized by the integration of different business areas of the organization into a vision of value creation for stakeholders. However, these processes are exposed to uncertain and unexpected events, which could be

© Springer International Publishing AG, part of Springer Nature 2018
R. Matulevičius and R. Dijkman (Eds.): CAiSE 2018 Workshops, LNBIP 316, pp. 235–248, 2018.
https://doi.org/10.1007/978-3-319-92898-2_20

inherent for the achievement of process objectives and, consequently, affect the process value. Hence, in order to preserve the value created by its processes, the organization needs to identify and assess such events through risk management practices [3]. Indeed, risk management has developed into a mature discipline in management and decision sciences. However, risk problems are traditionally separated in these disciplines from operational business concerns [4].

To face this need, a new paradigm named Risk-aware Business Process Management (R-BPM) has recently emerged [2, 5]. It aims to integrate the two traditionally separated fields of risk management and business process management. The R-BPM promotes risks consideration in the stages of BPM and enables a robust and efficient business process management within an uncertain environment. In this context, several R-BPM approaches were proposed in literature, in particular, that proposed by Sienou in [2], called "Business Process-risk management - Integrated Method (BPRIM)", which constitutes a promising method that proposes a theoretical basis for the coupling of these two paradigms.

Risk-aware business process modelling represents an essential and crucial task in the R-BPM lifecycle. In this context, business process models need to be enriched with risk-related information. Currently, a large number of business process modelling languages are available such as Petri nets, Event-driven Process Chain (EPC), UML activity diagrams, Business Process Model and Notation (BPMN), Yet Another Workflow Language (YAWL) and many others [1]. Although some of these languages are very broad and cover a variety of aspects, none of them can sufficiently integrate both risk and business process aspects [3]. Indeed, efforts are underway to incorporate risk into process models so that process performance can be determined in a global sense [2, 4, 6]. Nevertheless, the research and practice of risk-aware business process modelling is still very limited and requires further exploration.

To advance the theory of risk in the business process context, this study proposes a risk-aware business process modelling method based on BPRIM [2] and the corresponding modelling tool for risk modelling and management of the process-based organizations. For this purpose, we used the ADOxx meta-modelling platform.

This paper is structured as follows: the Sect. 2 presents the R-BPM paradigm and a comparative study of existing approaches in this context. Section 3 proposes the adopted approach and methodology. In the Sect. 4, we present an overview of the first results obtained after the implementation of our modelling method. In Sect. 5 our case study is presented. The document ends with a conclusion and some perspectives.

2   Risk-Aware Business Process Management

2.1   The R-BPM Importance

During these last years, a major research interest is given to integrate and treat risk in the process perspective. Two study streams have emerged: the management of risk in business processes [2, 5, 7], called Risk-aware Business Process Management (R-BPM), and process-based risk management. In any case, this convergence of risk management and process management is a positive development to maximize the process value. The R-BPM promotes risks consideration in the stages of business processes management and enables a robust and efficient business process management within an uncertain environment. Indeed, The importance of this integration has been confirmed in the research community [4, 8], in the industry guidelines, and in many studies [5].

2.2 Classification of R-BPM Approaches

Generally, the R-BPM approaches are classified according to the integration level of the risk concept in the life cycle of the BPM [5]. So two categories are underlined:

- **R-BPM approaches at the design level:** consists of approaches that focus on risk management during the design-time phase of business processes;
- **R-BPM approaches at the operational level:** consists of approaches that focus on risk management during and after the execution of business processes.

In this work, we are interested in the design-time R-BPM approaches. These approaches can be classified into two categories: those that introduce new risk-related constructs in order to incorporate risk information into the business process model and those that attempt to reason risks using risk analysis methods or techniques without the introduction of new constructs [5]. In our case, we focus on the first category, as related approaches do not provide enough support for design activities, because they do not introduce new risk concepts supporting users to design an R-BPM model.

In order to study the formalization degree of design-time R-BPM approaches, we propose to classify them according to several criteria. This investigation was inspired by the generic concepts of modelling methods as presented in [9, 10] and the work of Suriadi et al. [5]. The result of this investigation is illustrated in Table 1. According to [9], a modelling method consists of three components: (1) a modelling language, which contains the elements with which a model can be described, (2) a modelling procedure, which describes the steps applying the modelling language to create models, and (3) mechanisms & algorithms provide functionalities to use and evaluate models described by a modelling language.

The presented approaches mainly concentrate on the concrete syntax definition of constructs proposed for the risk. For instance, the approach proposed in [2] introduces new graphical notations to represent the risk elements (such as risk factor, risk events, risk situation, value, impact, etc.) by extending the EPC language. In addition, the approach proposed in [11], proposes a set of graphical notations to represent the risk elements being able to be associated to business process activities. However, few approaches tried to formalize the abstract syntax of proposed risk constructs. Among these approaches, we find the works of Cope et al. [6, 7], Strecker et al. [12], Betz et al. [13], and Sienou et al. [2] which design a Meta-model using the UML language to define the abstract syntax of their constructs, and the approach proposed by Weiss and Winkelmmann [14] which rather used the Entity Relationship (ER) diagrams. In addition, with the exception of the work of Sienou et al. [2], Pittl et al. [15] and that of Weiss and Winkelmmann [14], the majority of these approaches are not guided by any existing standards of risk. However, few of these approaches have been implemented. Which led to a gap in this research area.

Table 1. Formalization degree analysis of Design-time R-BPM approaches (with: - Not supporting the concept, + largely supporting the concept and ± partially supporting the concept)

Design-time R-BPM Approaches	Risk components characterization	Risk standard	Risk Formalization			Risk analysis	Modelling language risk-process	Meta-model Risk-process	Implementation
			Abstract syntax	Notation	Semantic				
Tjoa, Jakoubi et al. [11, 16],	±	−	−	+	−	−	−	−	±
Sienou et al. [2],	+	+	+	+	−	−	+	+	−
Cope et al. [6, 7],	±	−	+	+	−	±	±	−	−
Weiss and Winkelmann [14],	+	+	+	+	−	−	±	+	−
Rotaru et al. [17],	+	−	+	+	±	−	±	±	−
Betz et al. [13],	±	−	+	+	−	−	±	+	+
Strecker et al. [12],	−	−	+	+	−	−	±	+	−
Panayiotou et al. [18],	−	−	−	+	−	±	−	−	+
Pittl et al. [15],	±	+	+	+	+	+	+	+	+
Lhannaoui et al. [19],	±	−	−	+	−	±	±	−	−
Shah et al. [3]	+	±	+	−	−	+	−	±	−

As illustrated in Table 1, the Sienou's method, called BPRIM [2], seems a very promising approach. This is a method that has been developed in our research laboratory and has received our full attention. We will detail it in the following section.

3   Adopted Approach

The BPRIM method [2] is the only one that offers a complete conceptual methodological framework. It consists in the BPRIM lifecycle, the BPRIM conceptual models and the BPRIM modelling language.

3.1   BPRIM Lifecycle

The BPRIM lifecycle is the process integrating risk management concept into the business process design. Indeed, it focuses on risk driven business process design. As shown in Fig. 2, it consists of the following four phases:

- **Contextualization:** In this phase, the process models are defined. The information, organization, resource and functional aspects of the process models will allow establishing the context of risk.
- **Assessment:** In this phase, first, risks are identified. Then processes are analysed. Qualitative and quantitative evaluation of risks is subsequently launched. The process models must be enriched with risks models.
- **Treatment:** Based on information from the previous phase, this phase defines a set of treatment options, and then triggers a new iteration of the assessment phase in order to understand their possible effects. This phase can lead to a reframing that would imply the implementation of treatment actions by adjusting models or defining alternatives.
- **Monitoring:** It is a control phase, which provides guidance for refinement of the models or the transition to the implementation phase.

3.2   BPRIM Conceptual Models

In the context of risk-aware business process modelling, the links between the concepts of business process and risk are insufficient. The BPRIM conceptual models offers a conceptual unification of risks and processes into a common meta-model in order to fill this missing link. The latter is based on the standard ISO 19440 and it is compatible with the standard ISO 31000. Figure 1 illustrates an excerpt of the meta-model showing the relationship between the concepts of risks and business processes.

3.3   BPRIM Language

The BPRIM language is a common graphical modelling language of business processes and risks. It based on the extension of the EPC language. This language is designed to support the BPRIM lifecycle and must enable to extend the process models with risk models. The BPRIM language offers: an abstract syntax and a concrete syntax (also called notation). The abstract syntax is represented by the meta-model of Fig. 1. This

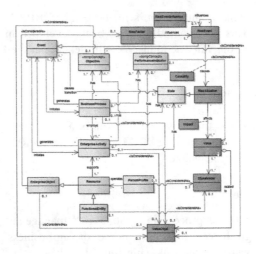

Fig. 1. Excerpt of the risk-aware business process meta-model [2]

syntax constitutes the grammar of the BPRIM language, with a set of predefined to apply. The notation that defines the graphical representation of the BPRIM language is detailed in [2]. In Fig. 2, a detailed overview of the BPRIM approach is summarized using a mapping between BPRIM diagrams and BPRIM lifecycle.

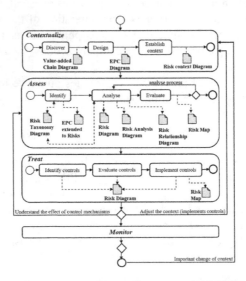

Fig. 2. Mapping between BPRIM diagrams and BRIM lifecycle [2]

3.4 BPRIM Weaknesses

After studying the formalization degree of design-time R-BPM approaches, we have seen some limitations of the BPRIM method:

- It is a rich conceptual method, but it does not yet integrate mechanisms and algorithms allowing to analyse constructed models;
- The validity of the formalization of the proposed constructs was not verified;
- There is no tool, which supports the approach.

To advance the theory of R-BPM context, we propose to consolidate the BPRIM method and to fill its gaps in order to design and to implement a complete modelling method. Our first objective is thus to equip the BPRIM method with a modelling tool able to edit several diagrams as advocate by this method and to integrate new algorithms able to (1) verify and validate the models according defined rules, and (2) evaluate risks related to business processes.

4 Preliminary Results

4.1 Design of the BPRIM Modelling Method

In order to design the BPRIM modelling method and realize the tool supporting it, several meta-modelling environments are available, and can be used [20] like Eclipse Modelling Framework (EMF) [21], MetaEdit+ [22], and ADOxx platform [23]. They are an integrated development environments for defining and using modelling methods and graphical modelling languages. However, we should select the most appropriate one for our BPRIM language. In order to do this, we try to understand the advantages and disadvantages of these meta-modelling environments (see Table 2).

Table 2. Comparison of some meta-modelling environments

	License	Multi-user	Required knowledge	Repository provision	Specific functionalities
MetaEdit+	Commercial	No	None	Yes	Code generation, model analyses, reports creation
EMF (GEF, GMF)	Open source	No	Java programming language	No	Code generation
EMF (Sirius)	Open source	No	None	No	Multi-view modelling
ADOxx	Open use	Yes	None	Yes	Process simulation, process evaluation, process cost calculation, multi-view modelling, query language
Oryx	Open source	No	None	Yes	Web-based process modelling

Compared to the other environments, ADOxx platform is a multi-user platform that provides a repository based on a relational database for meta-models and models. To specify these meta-models, the ADOxx platform does not require any knowledge of a programming language, in contrast to the use of the EMF with the Graphical Editing Framework (GEF) and the Graphical Modelling Framework (GMF) that requires a deep knowledge of the Java programming language [24]. In addition, the ADOxx platform provide broader functionalities than a code generation. It provides a number of business related functionalities such as process simulation, evaluation, and so on.

Based on these observations, we choose to use the ADOxx platform to conceptualize the BPRIM modelling method and realize the tool supporting it. Indeed, ADOxx is applied in several academic and industrial projects. It supports: (1) modelling languages using modelling concepts from a meta-model to define abstract syntax, concrete syntax, and semantics, (2) modelling procedures applying the modelling steps to create models, and (3) modelling mechanisms and algorithms by providing functionalities to use and evaluate models described by a modelling language. These functionalities enables the structural analysis and the simulation of models [25].

For the conceptualization of the BPRIM modelling method on ADOxx, the BPRIM diagrams were represented as model types. Figure 3 illustrates the modelTypes, classes, relationClasses, and mechanisms of the BPRIM modelling method. The classes and relationClasses are grouped by model types. To support the risk analysis, BPRIM modelling method provides a set of some specific algorithms for conducting graphical analyses.

4.2   Realization of the BPRIM Modelling Method Using ADOxx

We designate our modelling method as ADoBPRIM which corresponds to the implementation of the modelling method BPRIM using the ADOxx meta-modelling platform. The corresponding tool provides a risk-driven business process design. The first results obtained by ADoBPRIM are presented in Fig. 4. As already presented, the BPRIM lifecycle consists of three phases: Conceptualization, Assessment and Treatment.

Currently, our tool supports:

- A set of nine BPRIM diagrams corresponding to the BPRIM lifecycle phases. These diagrams are presented in Fig. 2. They are diagrams of: value-added chain, EPC, risk context, risk taxonomy, EPC extended to risks, risk, risk analysis, risk map and risk relationships;
- A modelling palette consisting of a set of seventeen constructs and twelve corresponding relationships, related to those proposed in BPRIM language;
- A set of algorithms using the ADOscript programming language. These algorithms allow to check the validity of the models (or diagrams) constructed and to qualitatively analyse and evaluate the Risk Analysis Diagrams.

The implementation of the BPRIM approach enabled us to verify the validity of the constructs and the models proposed in the BPRIM language and lifecycle, and to extend it in order to build an entire modelling method.

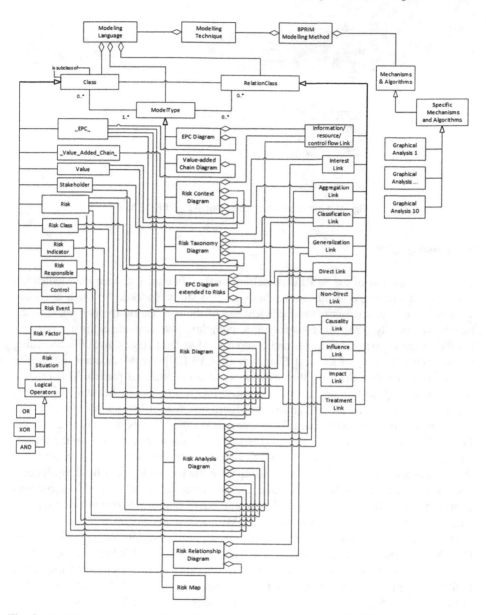

Fig. 3. Model types, classes, relationClasses, and mechanisms of the BPRIM modelling method

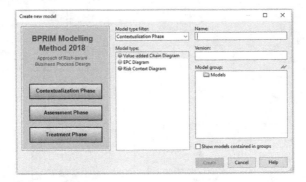

Fig. 4. Graphical interface of our ADoBPRIM tool

5 Case Study

To illustrate the use of the BPRIM modelling method, we have chosen the Medication Use System within the healthcare facilities as case study. Indeed, the Medication use system is the safe, appropriate and efficient use of the medication by the patient in the healthcare facility [26]. It consists in a complex and multidisciplinary process, involving numerous professionals and composed of several stages. In 2006, according to the French Society of Clinical Pharmacy (FSCP) [27], the Medication use system was used to mention the drug therapy process of a hospitalized patient. This process included the stages of ordering, dispensing, administration and medication monitoring. The complexity of this process causes an occurrence risk of Medication Errors (ME), which can involve serious clinical consequences on the patients. Indeed, in 2015, the French National Authority for Health (FNAH) [26] considers that 40% of the serious adverse events are of medication origin. For this reason, the safety of this process is in the heart of the concerns of the guardianships and the healthcare facilities [26]. Indeed, this process safety needs in particular the implementation of a risk management approach. The latter aims to insure the patient safety and the delivered treatments, in particular, to limit the risk occurrence of ME, which are potential sources of preventable adverse drug events. Therefore, we suggest studying the potential of the BPRIM modelling method to manage the ME risks related to Medication use system.

Figure 5 illustrates some instantiated diagrams using our ADoBPRIM modelling tool for the management of the Medication use system extended to ME risks. We present, in Fig. 5-(1), a description of sub-processes of the Medication use system by using the EPC diagram. The sub-processes and the activities were inspired by the macro-process presented in the French National Authority for Health (FNAH) report in 2013 [26]. In Fig. 5-(2), we describe the ME risks context within the Medication use system by using the Risk context diagram. The ME taxonomy is presented in Fig. 5-(3) by using the Risk taxonomy diagram. The Medication use system extended to ME risks is presented in Fig. 5-(4) using the EPC diagram extended to risks. For each ME risk related to the Medication use system must correspond an analysis diagram. In Fig. 5- (5), we have taken the Overdose risk as an example and we have described its corresponding analysis diagram. At diagram's level, some specific algorithms are available for checking validity of the built diagram, qualitatively analyzing and evaluating the risk modeled. These analysis and evaluation algorithms are specific to our application domain of the Medication use system exposed to risk of ME.

To instantiate these diagrams, we performed a deep analysis of the literature concerning the ME risks to which are exposed the activities of the medication use system.

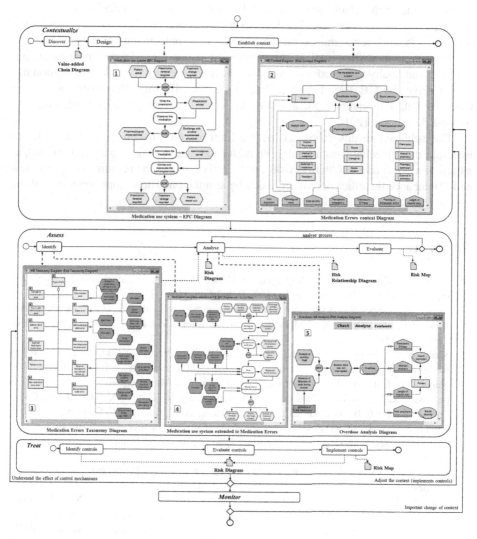

Fig. 5. Some instantiated diagrams using ADoBPRIM modelling tool for the Medication use system

The application of the proposed method to model risks of ME related to the Medication system, allowed us to verify the validity and the correct formulation of the constructs and the diagrams proposed in the BPRIM language and the BPRIM process.

6 Conclusion

The integration of BPM disciplines and risk management is an innovative research topic that has launched many challenges in the BPM field. This research aims to address some of the challenges considered in these areas as embedding risk concept into business process models. To develop a risk-aware business process modelling method, this work relies mostly on the research accomplishments of Sienou [2]. The corresponding modelling tool is then proposed using the ADOxx meta-modelling platform and finally validated by a real case study for the design of the Medication use system driven by ME risks. The modelling tool is available through a project within the Open Models Laboratory [28], a worldwide community of modelers and modeling method developers [29].

The achieved results motivated us for improve our modelling tool in order to integrate more mechanisms and algorithms for (1) analyse the impact and the propagation of a priori and a posteriori risks on the activities and the resources of processes, and (2) enhance the efficiency of processes by simulation. These improvements will be the subject of future publications.

References

1. Weske, M.: Business Process Management: Concepts, Languages, Architectures. Springer, Heidelberg (2012). https://doi.org/10.1007/978-3-642-28616-2
2. Sienou, A.: Proposition d'un cadre méthodologique pour le management intégré des risques et des processus d'entreprise. Methodol. Framew. Integr. Manag. Risks Bus. Process. INP Toulouse (2009)
3. Shah, L.A., Etienne, A., Siadat, A., Vernadat, F.: Process-oriented risk assessment methodology for manufacturing process evaluation. Int. J. Prod. Res. **55**, 4516–4529 (2017)
4. Neiger, D., Churilov, L., zur Muehlen, M., Rosemann, M.: Integrating risks in business process models with value focused process engineering. In: ECIS, pp. 1606–1615 (2006)
5. Suriadi, S., Weiß, B., Winkelmann, A., ter Hofstede, A.H., Adams, M., Conforti, R., Fidge, C., La Rosa, M., Ouyang, C., Rosemann, M.: Current research in risk-aware business process management: overview, comparison, and gap analysis. Commun. Assoc. Inf. Syst. **34**, 933–984 (2014)
6. Cope, E.W., Kuster, J.M., Etzweiler, D., Deleris, L.A., Ray, B.: Incorporating risk into business process models. IBM J. Res. Dev. **54**, 1–4 (2010)
7. Cope, E.W., Deleris, L.A., Etzweiler, D., Koehler, J., Kuester, J.M., Ray, B.K.: System and Method for Creating and Expressing Risk-Extended Business Process Models (2014)
8. Rosemann, M., Zur Muehlen, M.: Integrating risks in business process models. In: ACIS 2005 Proceedings, vol. 50 (2005)
9. Karagiannis, D., Kühn, H.: Metamodelling platforms. In: Bauknecht, K., Tjoa, A.M., Quirchmayr, G. (eds.) EC-Web 2002. LNCS, vol. 2455, p. 182. Springer, Heidelberg (2002). https://doi.org/10.1007/3-540-45705-4_19

10. Bork, D., Fill, H.-G.: Formal aspects of enterprise modeling methods: a comparison framework. In: 47th Hawaii International Conference on System Sciences (HICSS), 2014, pp. 3400–3409. IEEE (2014)
11. Jakoubi, S., Tjoa, S., Goluch, S., Kitzler, G.: A formal approach towards risk-aware service level analysis and planning. In: ARES 2010 International Conference on Availability, Reliability, and Security, 2010, pp. 180–187. IEEE (2010)
12. Strecker, S., Heise, D., Frank, U.: RiskM: a multi-perspective modeling method for IT risk assessment. Inf. Syst. Front. **13**, 595–611 (2011)
13. Betz, S., Hickl, S., Oberweis, A.: Risk-aware business process modeling and simulation using XML nets. In: IEEE 13th conference on Commerce and enterprise computing (cec), 2011, pp. 349–356. IEEE (2011)
14. Weiss, B., Winkelmann, A.: Developing a process-oriented notation for modeling operational risks-a conceptual metamodel approach to operational risk management in knowledge intensive business processes within the financial industry. In: 44th Hawaii International Conference on System Sciences (HICSS), 2011, pp. 1–10. IEEE (2011)
15. Pittl, B., Fill, H.-G., Honegger, G.: Enabling Risk-Aware Enterprise Modeling using Semantic Annotations and Visual Rules (2017)
16. Tjoa, S., Jakoubi, S., Goluch, G., Kitzler, G., Goluch, S., Quirchmayr, G.: A formal approach enabling risk-aware business process modeling and simulation. IEEE Trans. Serv. Comput. **4**, 153–166 (2011)
17. Rotaru, K., Wilkin, C., Churilov, L., Neiger, D., Ceglowski, A.: Formalizing process-based risk with value-focused process engineering. Inf. Syst. E-Bus. Manag. **9**, 447–474 (2011)
18. Panayiotou, N., Oikonomitsios, S., Athanasiadou, C., Gayialis, S.: Risk assessment in virtual enterprise networks: a process-driven internal audit approach. In: Managing Risk Virtual Enterprise Networks Implementing Supply Chain Principles, pp. 290–312. IGI Global, Hershey (2010)
19. Lhannaoui, H., Kabbaj, M.I., Bakkoury, Z.: Analyzing risks in business process models using a deviational technique. In: 9th International Conference on Software Engineering and Applications (ICSOFT-EA), 2014, pp. 189–194. IEEE (2014)
20. Kern, H., Hummel, A., Kühne, S.: Towards a comparative analysis of meta-metamodels. In: Proceedings of the Compilation of the Co-Located Workshops on DSM 2011, TMC 2011, AGERE! 2011, AOOPES 2011, NEAT 2011, & VMIL 2011, pp. 7–12. ACM (2011)
21. McNeill, K.: Metamodeling with EMF: Generating concrete, reusable Java snippets. Extend Eclipse Ecore Metamodel IBM. 21 (2008)
22. Tolvanen, J.-P., Rossi, M.: MetaEdit + : defining and using domain-specific modeling languages and code generators. In: Companion of the 18th annual ACM SIGPLAN conference on Object-oriented programming, systems, languages, and applications, pp. 92–93. ACM (2003)
23. Efendioglu, N., Woitsch, R.: Modelling method design: an Adoxx realisation. In: Enterprise Distributed Object Computing Workshop (EDOCW), 2016 IEEE 20th International, pp. 1–8. IEEE (2016)
24. Fill, H.-G., Karagiannis, D.: On the conceptualisation of modelling methods using the ADOxx meta modelling platform. Enterp. Model. Inf. Syst. Archit. J. Concept. Model. **8**, 4–25 (2013)
25. Visic, N.: Language-Oriented Modeling Method Engineering (2016)
26. HAS, de S, H.A.: Outils de sécurisation et d'auto-évaluation de l'administration des médicaments. St.-Denis Plaine HAS (2013)
27. Schmitt, E., Antier, D., Bernheim, C., Dufay, E., Husson, M.C., Tissot, E.: Dictionnaire français de l'erreur médicamenteuse. Société Fr. Pharm. Clin. (2006)

28. Karagiannis, D., Mayr, H.C., Mylopoulos, J.: Domain-Specific Conceptual Modeling. Springer, Cham (2016). https://doi.org/10.1007/978-3-319-39417-6
29. Bork, D., Miron, E.-T.: OMiLAB-An open innovation community for modeling method engineering. In: 8th International Conference of Management and Industrial Engineering (ICMIE 2017), Bucharest, Romania, pp. 64–77 (2017). ISSN 2344-0937

FAiSE – Flexible Advanced Information Systems

First Workshop on Flexible Advanced Information Systems – FAiSE

Preface

The recent developments in information systems, Internet of Things (IoT) technologies, and the uptake of the digitalization wave in industries have led to the availability of a continuous flow of massive amounts of data and events. These data can be used by organizations to provide smarter and personalized services and products to people and organizations, as well as to improve the efficiency of their work and the value of their business models. The new challenges that information systems are facing in this context are related to both being able to exploit the data stemming from the IoT and the ability to react fast to the changes notified by the data and events.

The main purpose of the Workshop on Flexible Advanced Information Systems is to provide a forum for discussions of the synergies between the IoT, innovative technologies, and advanced information systems, and thus encourage exchanges between researchers and practitioners toward identifying concepts and approaches supporting the exploitation of advances in IoT toward enabling flexible information systems.

One distinguishing characteristic of the workshop is its special focus on publications and presentations that report on fundamental or applied research toward the reconciliation of the divide among several disparate areas in research and practice. The main areas we identified are the use of IoT for digitalization and provisioning of smarter and personalized services to people and organizations; the research in flexible information systems that allow organizations to maintain control and react to constant changes in competitive, rapidly changing environments; and the growing acceptance and integration of data analytics into information systems facilitating data-driven process performance improvement.

This first edition of FAiSE attracted four submissions. Each submission was reviewed by three to four members of the Program Committee (PC). Of these submissions, the PC selected two high-quality articles for publication in the workshop proceedings. Our half-day workshop program also featured a keynote by Pierluigi Plebani (Politecnico di Milano) on *"Orienteering in the Fog: An Information Systems Perspective."* Furthermore, presentations were given of real-world scenarios reporting on significant contributions, and evidence of the successful application of flexible advanced information systems and IoT in combination.

The workshop took place on June 12, 2018, in conjunction with the 30th International Conference on Advanced Information Systems Engineering (CAiSE 2018). More information and our workshop program is available at https://bpt.hpi.uni-potsdam.de/FAiSE18.

We would like to thank the workshop chairs of CAiSE 2018 for their support, the authors of all submitted articles for their courage to work in a new research direction, and the members of the PC for the timely and valuable reviews of the submissions.

April 2018

Dimka Karastoyanova
Luise Pufahl

FAiSE Organization

Organizing Committee

Luise Pufahl   Hasso Plattner Institute, University of Potsdam, Germany
Dimka Karastoyanova   University of Groningen, The Netherlands

Program Committee

Vasilios Andrikopoulos   University of Groningen, The Netherlands
George Azzopardi   University of Groningen, The Netherlands
Marcin Hewelt   Hasso Plattner Institute, University of Potsdam, Germany
Maria-Eugenia Iacob   University of Twente, The Netherlands
Agnes Koschmider   Karlsruhe Institute of Technology, Germany
Patricia Lago   Vrije Universiteit Amsterdam, The Netherlands
Barbara Pernici   Politecnico di Milano, Italy
Pierluigi Plebani   Politecnico di Milano, Italy
Estefanía Serral Asensio   Katholieke Universiteit Leuven, Belgium
Andreas Weiß   University of Stuttgart, Germany
André Ludwig   The KLU, Germany
Manfred Reichert   University of Ulm, Germany
Fabrizio Maria Maggi   University of Tartu, Estonia
Andreas Metzger   University of Duisburg-Essen, Germany

A Reference Framework for Advanced Flexible Information Systems

Paul Grefen[✉], Rik Eshuis, Oktay Turetken, and Irene Vanderfeesten

School of Industrial Engineering, Eindhoven University of Technology,
Eindhoven, The Netherlands
{p.w.p.j.grefen, h.eshuis, o.turetken,
i.t.p.vanderfeesten}@tue.nl

Abstract. The nature of information systems is currently going through a major transition. In the past, information systems managing 'physical processes' and systems managing 'administrative processes' would usually be separated in two different 'worlds'. Now, we see that these worlds need to be tightly coupled or even integrated to deal with developments like the transformation of supply chains to demand chains, just-in-time logistics, servitization and mass-customization of products and services. This causes confusion, as positioning systems and approaches underlying these systems with respect to each other is not easy. Improper positioning may in turn lead to blind spots in system functionality - resulting in the inability to properly support the entire spectrum of business functionality - or replication of functionality - usually resulting in inconsistency of functionality and data. To address this issue, this paper presents a reference framework for advanced flexible information systems, in which existing systems and approaches can be positioned, analyzed and compared. The framework is based on a concept of multi-layer, bimodal flexibility. We apply this framework on a small but representative set of research and development efforts for advanced flexible information systems.

1 Introduction

Driven by both changes in the business world and revolutions in information technology, the nature of information systems is currently going through a major transition. In the past, information systems managing 'physical processes' and systems managing 'administrative processes' would usually be separated in two different 'worlds'. As an example, in a typical factory the manufacturing shop floor is managed by a manufacturing execution system (MES), whereas customer details are managed in a customer relationship management system (CRM) - with often very little structural linkage of the two. In a logistics context, typically there are systems managing customer orders and different systems physically tracking the whereabouts of transport vehicles (like trucks). In modern industrial practice, we see that these worlds need to be tightly coupled or even integrated to deal with developments like the transformation of supply chains to demand chains, just-in-time logistics, servitization and mass-customization of products and services – some of which under umbrella developments like Industry 4.0 [8]. In research, this is reflected for instance, in a recent interest in the combination of

© Springer International Publishing AG, part of Springer Nature 2018
R. Matulevičius and R. Dijkman (Eds.): CAiSE 2018 Workshops, LNBIP 316, pp. 253–264, 2018.
https://doi.org/10.1007/978-3-319-92898-2_21

business process management and the internet-of-things (IoT) [11], and business models and IoT [4].

This transition causes confusion, as positioning systems and approaches underlying these systems with respect to each other is not easy. Concepts and terminologies are different, architectures are different, people are different – both in designing and in managing the systems. Improper positioning may lead to problems when 'physical' and 'administrative' systems are linked or integrated. These problems can be of two kinds – if the linking or integration succeeds at all. The first kind shows as blind spots in system functionality - resulting in the inability of the resulting system to properly support the entire spectrum of business functionality. The second kind shows as replications of functionality - usually resulting in inconsistency of business function-ality and business data (and the obvious unnecessary investment of double functionality).

To address this issue of positioning, this paper proposes a reference framework for advanced flexible information systems (AFIS), in which existing systems and approaches can be positioned, analyzed and compared. We label a system as AFIS if it is built to support advanced business functionality (i.e., crossing functional boundaries) in a flexible way (i.e., reacting to changes in its environment on various time horizons). We apply our reference framework on a small but representative set of research and development efforts for advanced flexible information systems.

This paper is organized as follows. In Sects. 2 and 3, we present the ingredients of the new reference framework: perspectives and layers, respectively functions and control loops. Section 4 discusses the framework. The application of the framework is discussed in Sect. 5. In Sect. 6, we discuss related work and compare it to our framework – we do this at the end of the paper because this enables clearer positioning for the reader. We conclude the paper in Sect. 7.

2   The Perspectives and Layers

In designing the reference framework, we aim at covering the complete functionality spectrum of an AFIS. This has implications for the system *perspectives* and the system *layers* that the framework covers.

From a perspective point of view, we distinguish between the *design time* and the *execution time* perspectives. In the design time perspective, we cover support for the conception, design and analysis of models that define the desired behavior of the system. In the execution time perspective, we cover support for the execution of these models, including the (real-time) collection of data from this execution.

From the point of view of system layers, we make sure to have a set of meaningful layers in the abstraction dimension of real-time information processing in AFIS. To do so, we distinguish four layers. The *physical layer* is at the lowest level of abstraction: this is where the physical 'work' is executed, i.e., the hardware-oriented layer that is controlled by the upper layers and that generates data about its state. One layer up in the abstraction dimension, we find the *event layer*: this is where events from the physical layer are processed and commands are passed down to the physical layer. On top of the event layer, we find the *process layer*, where events are interpreted in the context of business processes. In this layer, the emphasis is on the sequencing of events – or in other words: on the control flow between tasks. The highest layer is the *business layer*, where the effect of process execution is interpreted in the context of business goals – or in other words: where the mapping of the *how* of business to the *what* of business is made [6].

When we combine the two perspectives and the four layers, we get eight areas of possible attention, as shown in Table 1. From the viewpoint of AFIS, we are interested in the interaction with the physical layer (i.e., the execution time), but not in the design of the physical layer, as this concerns hardware design. So we place the design time perspective of the physical layer out of scope for our reference framework.

Table 1. Overview of perspectives and layers of the reference framework

		Perspectives	
		Design time	Execution time
Layers	Business layer	*Business model design*	*Business model enactment*
	Process layer	*Process model design*	*Process model enactment*
	Event layer	*Event model design*	*Event model enactment*
	Physical layer	*<Out of scope>*	*Physical work execution*

3 The Functions and Loops

In our reference framework, we place a set of abstract information system function-alities that are made concrete per layer of the framework. We have chosen a set of seven functionalities – knowing that many variations on this set are possible, but that these do not change the essence and purpose of the resulting framework. The seven functionalities are shown in Fig. 1 with a few example concretizations. *Model* includes designing or redesigning an enactable model for the behavior of a layer of an AFIS. *Adapt* covers making a model fit for enactment, e.g. by parameterization (with may also be labeled *Deploy*). *Control* supervises the enactment of a model, i.e., select the order and timing of enactment and assigning resources. *Perform* physically enacts the model, i.e., performs the individual steps as dictated by the *Control* function. *Measure* covers obtaining the relevant characteristics of the enactment of a step. *Record* covers storing the measurements of the *Measure* function for subsequent use. Finally, *Analyze* covers processing a set of measurements to make them fit for decision making.

To support flexibility, we require a reactive capability in our framework, i.e., means to adapt to changing circumstances. We cover this with the principle of a control (or feedback) loop. We recognize the need for direct, automatic reactions (real-time flexibility, i.e., readjustment of a model) and for reactions that require a redesign of a model (i.e., non-automatic and indirect in execution). This leads to the inclusion of a bimodal pair of control loops in our framework (shown in the left of Fig. 1), supporting both tactic/strategic business (process) redesign and operational (real-time) business (process) readjustment. These loops are shown more explicitly in Fig. 2, in which we distinguish between *prescriptive data flows* (informing other modules what to do) and

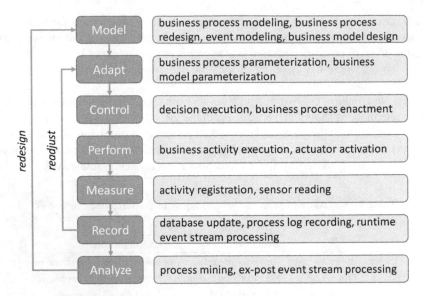

Fig. 1. Reference framework functions with bimodal control loops (left) and example concretizations (right)

descriptive data flows (informing other modules what has been done). We choose the term 'bimodal' as the control loops have similar characteristics as bimodal information system development [13]. Bimodal control loops enable bimodal flexibility (on dual time horizons) in advanced information systems.

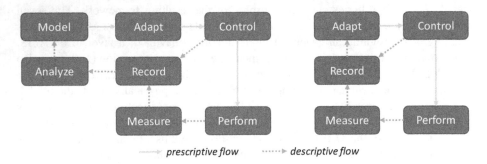

Fig. 2. Bimodal control loops: redesign (left) and readjust (right) as in Fig. 1

4   The Reference Framework

We combine the notion of bimodal control loops and the contents of Table 1 to arrive at the structure (or conceptual architecture) of a *multi-layer, bimodal flexibility reference framework* for AFIS. This framework is shown in Fig. 3. The framework has eight interconnected cells, corresponding with the cells of Table 1, of which one has been declared out of scope as discussed before. We have placed the *model* and *analyze* functions in the *design time perspective*, as these require intelligent, time-consuming activities (often with human involvement) that have a slower processing cycle (shorter 'clock tick') than the execution time perspective. The other five functions are placed in the *execution time perspective*, as these take place in the same processing cycle and with the same 'clock tick' – preferably in an automated fashion. In the physical layer, we have placed the *perform* and *measure* functions, as these have a physical semantics. In the upper three layers, 'measurements' are provided by the *adapt* function of the layer below and activities are 'performed' by the *control* function of the level below – these abstract the execution time interface of the level below (as in a strictly layered architecture).

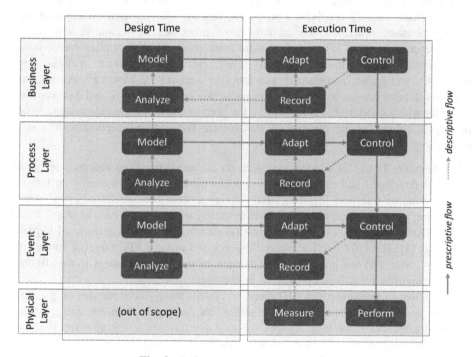

Fig. 3. Reference framework for AFIS

The reference framework is an abstract structure for a complete AFIS covering the spectrum from business goal to physical activity execution from both the design and execution perspectives, putting the emphasis on the data flows between the layers and the functions within the layers, operationalizing both descriptive flows for business intelligence and prescriptive flows for operations control. To use the framework in practice, concrete system frameworks (or system architectures) are mapped to it. This mapping has three steps:

1. *Trim:* remove the functions (or entire layers) from the reference framework that are not covered by the concrete system.

2. *Complete:* add specific data flows that are not covered by the reference framework (examples are included in Sect. 5).
3. *Concretize:* replace the abstract function labels in the framework by more concrete function labels that suit the application domain of the concrete system.

Note that steps 2 and 3 represent proper *specialization* of the reference framework to a concrete case.

5   Application of the Framework

To illustrate the use of the AFIS reference framework, we map a set of large, contemporary system development efforts to it. We pick a set of three recent European projects (from the FP7 and H2020 programs) that all have the characteristics of integrating physical processes and administrative processes in a context with strong real-time characteristics. These projects are from three different application domains: international, synchro-modal logistics (GET Service), high-tech manufacturing (HORSE), and traffic management and mobility services (C-MobILE). As we have been involved or are involved in these projects, we know them well and can provide a mapping with a good deal of certainty - so the precise choice of concrete systems is of a pragmatic nature for the purpose of this paper. We end this section with a short discussion.

GET Service. In the GET Service project, an advanced planning and control system has been developed and prototyped for synchro-modal logistics, focusing on international container transport [2]. The GET Service system uses advanced event stream processing to process real-time event data from logistics sources (such as ships, trucks and roads) into information used for decision making in inter-organizational logistics processes [3]. The GET Service approach is mapped to the AFIS reference framework in Fig. 4. Note that we have specialized some of the function labels in this figure - correspondence to Fig. 3 is by location in the figure.

As shown in the figure, the GET Service system mainly concentrates on the three bottom layers. The physical layer contains the transport vehicles and transport infrastructure, which are both sources for IoT measurements, but also receive commands for the execution of physical logistics steps. An example of the latter is the instruction to drive a truck from A to B or to unload a container from a ship. As such, the physical logistics entities can be seen as complex sensors and actuators in an IoT context. The processing of real-time, low-level logistics event streams takes place in the event layer. Here, a complex event engine filters, aggregates and combines events into high-level events that can be used for decision making (the *process event stream* function in the figure).

High-level events can be used to adapt a logistics task that is currently being managed – in the real-time control loop – or be used to redesign the event processing model (such as aggregation or combination rules) – in the redesign loop. High-level events are also passed to the process layer, where they are used to trigger replanning of logistics processes – in the (near) real-time loop – or to remodel logistics processes

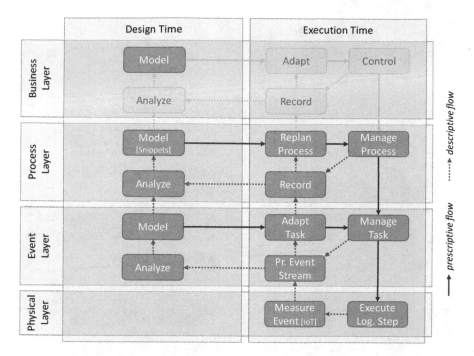

Fig. 4. GET Service approach mapped to AFIS reference framework

from process snippets – in the redesign loop. The GET Service approach clearly supports the bimodal flexibility perspective in its control loops.

The GET Service framework includes business models that explain why several parties collaborate in inter-organizational business processes to achieve which business goals. This implies the model function in the business layer. This function is not explicitly connected to the process layer, however – making this an isolated element in the framework. Consequently, the GET Service system explicitly supports real-time, agile business processes, but not agile business models.

HORSE. The HORSE project focuses on the development of an integrated manufacturing control system that integrates manufacturing process management with real-time control of hybrid manufacturing tasks [7]. Here the term 'hybrid' indicates that tasks can be executed by robots, humans, or combinations of these. The HORSE approach is mapped to the AFIS framework in Fig. 5.

In the physical layer, we find the physical work cells in factories in which robots and/or humans perform manufacturing steps that are part of tasks. What happens in these work cells is measured by various sensors and controlled by a step supervisor software module. The tasks and steps in work cells are controlled in the event layer. In this layer, the real-time control loop is used to manage exceptions in the execution of tasks (such as possible collisions between humans and robots) in the context of the work cell. The execution of the event layer is driven by a local execution model that is constructed in design time – but there is no general-purpose explicit data feed from

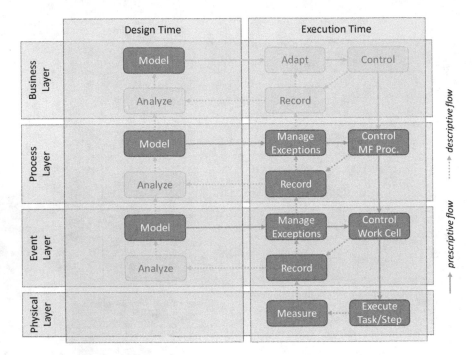

Fig. 5. HORSE approach mapped to AFIS reference framework

execution time to design time for this purpose (there are some specific exceptions, though, such as teaching a step to a robot by instruction, i.e., designing a script by physically manipulating a robot). Events about the execution of tasks are sent to the process layer, where a manufacturing process is executed. The real-time control loop is used to manage exceptions at the global level, i.e., across a set of work cells that form a manufacturing line. Like in the event layer, a process model is designed for this purpose, but without explicit feedback from the execution time environment. Like in the GET Service case, collaborative business models are included in the HORSE approach, but they are isolated with respect to data feeds.

The analysis in the AFIS framework clearly shows that the HORSE approach supports flexibility, but focuses strongly on the real-time loop in the bimodal perspective.

C-MobILE. The C-MobILE project focuses on the development of an approach and system framework for the support of integrated mobility services [12]. The addressed mobility services focus on automotive transport, but also include public transport. The mapping of the C-MobILE approach to the AFIS framework is shown in Fig. 6. Note that this mapping includes data flows that are not included in the reference model – this is a case of specialization as explained in Sect. 4.

As shown in Fig. 6, the C-MobILE system has a focus on the physical and event layer of our framework. In the physical layer, we find vehicles with on-board units (OBU) and infrastructure (roads) with road-side units (RSU) that function as IoT

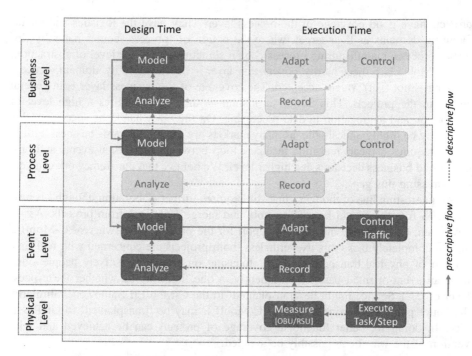

Fig. 6. C-MobILE approach mapped to AFIS reference framework

objects – they are event sources. Commands are sent to the physical layer either through these OBUs or RSUs, or through mobile devices (typically smartphones) to vehicle drivers using mobile networks. On the event layer, traffic management and mobility management services perform traffic control operations to orchestrate vehicles – this has a strong real-time character. The way this is done is modeled in the design time aspect – recorded traffic information can be used to redesign the control models.

Like in the previous two cases, there is attention for collaborative business models in the C-MobILE approach, but this is not covered by technical systems. They are analyzed, however, and used as a basis for modeling business processes – for which no automated execution support is covered, however. These business process models can be related to event processing models, mainly for designing sequencing issues.

The focus on the lower levels of our framework is typical for the application domain, which currently is rather device-centric (as in OBUs, RSUs and interface devices). The non-automated coverage of functionality in the top-left corner of our framework shows an increase of interest for the higher levels as well. The C-MobILE approach covers a bimodal control approach, but at a low level of abstraction from the application domain point of view (concentrated in the physical and event layers).

Discussion. From the above analysis of the three example projects, we see that none of the research efforts cover the entire field of functionality covered by the AFIS reference framework. They are all strongly 'rooted in technology', i.e., they mostly cover the functionality in the lower two layers of the framework. The GET Service and HORSE projects have good coverage of the process layer. They have the logistics and manufacturing domains as their target, where the notion of 'process' comes naturally (logistics process, manufacturing process) - be it sometimes at a low level of abstraction. The C-MobILE project hardly covers this layer - in the mobility domain, process thinking is not (yet) widely accepted. The coverage of the business layer is in general sparse in the projects. This is not surprising, as this layer requires a high level of abstraction and aggregation in data processing. On the other hand, the sparsity of this level may be highly undesirable, as many markets are moving towards business agility, which requires a (near) real-time feedback loop between operational events and processes and business decisions at a higher level. We believe that our framework can help in addressing this gap.

An interesting line of thought - that still requires further elaboration, though - is how the AFIS framework can be used to 'mix and merge' solutions from projects. As we have seen, GET Service has proper support for the process layer, whereas C-MobILE almost completely lacks this. Nevertheless, both projects are concerned with real-time support of physical transport services - focusing on goods respectively people - and have an event-oriented basis. Consequently, a question may be whether the process layer of GET Service might be 'transplanted' to the C-MobILE framework. Similarly, the better populated business layer of C-MobILE may be 'transplanted' to GET Service. In doing so, better functional coverage of projects can be achieved and reinvention of the wheel can possibly be avoided.

6 Related Work

The need for reference models to manage complexity and interoperability has been acknowledged widely in the information systems domain. We find them in the form of conceptual reference models, reference architectures and reference frameworks. We discuss related work in these three classes of reference models below.

A well-known reference model from the business process management domain is the Workflow Management Coalition (WfMC) Reference Model [15]. The model has some characteristics of a reference architecture, but is incomplete as an architecture specification. Though it has partially the same objectives as the framework of this paper, i.e. positioning functionality, its scope is much smaller: it is limited to the process layer only.

Reference architectures for information systems have been proposed in many 'forms and colors'. A more architectural counterpart of the WfMC model is for example the Mercurius reference architecture [5]. This reference architecture can also be positioned in the framework we propose, but like the WfMC model, it is limited to the process layer. A reference architecture for traffic management – related to the C-MobILE case discussed in Sect. 5 – was developed in the USA [10]. This reference architecture is domain-specific and focuses on the event layer and physical layer of our framework. A reference architecture for the Internet of Things also addresses the bottom two layers of our framework – a comparison of four competing architectures is presented by the Open Group [14]. An approach for the analysis and design of reference architectures [1] allows for the general classification of individual architectures.

It does, however, not provide a tool to position concrete systems and approaches with respect to the functionality they cover in a spectrum.

In the field of reference frameworks, we find for example business frameworks that do not describe the structure of information systems, but of the business organization that should be served by these systems. A nice example is the IEC hierarchy for manufacturing [9], which defines a set of organizational aggregation levels in a manufacturing company, which can be mapped to specific types of information systems. It can be used in structuring systems, but only in an indirect way. A different kind of framework can be found in an overview of benefits and challenges for the combination of the IoT and business process management [11]. This overview contains a control model that has similarities with our redesign control loop (see Fig. 2) – and partly inspired our thinking. This control model is not layered, however, and does not make an explicit distinction between design time and execution time aspects. Its main purpose is to be the 'anchor' for a list of research problems and opportunities.

7 Conclusion

Positioning systems and approaches in the turbulent world or advanced flexible information systems (AFIS) is not an easy thing – given many concurrent developments like IoT, Industry 4.0, servitization, etcetera. Improper positioning hinders integration of approaches, exchangeability of parts of approaches, or simply interfacing between modules of different approaches.

In this paper, we have shown the design of a reference framework for AFIS that helps in proper positioning. We think that it is essential to both cover multiple abstraction layers in such a framework and include a bimodal control loop mechanism. The abstraction layers allow for a separation of concerns in complex decision making – and hence a separation in concerns towards business intelligence functionality. The bimodal character supports a separation between real-time, on-line reacting and non-real-time, potentially off-line redesign.

The practical application of the framework to a small set of complex AFIS cases in this paper shows that the framework is a proper tool for the analysis of these cases. The three case studies show that the business layer is sparsely covered in general - certainly where it comes to structured (automated) linking with the layers below. We expect this to be the case in many other projects as well. Given the attention to the business layer (both from practice and from research programs), we consider this an omission in current practice and an opportunity for future research in AFIS.

We plan to use the framework to position a larger set of cases to obtain a more complete overview of the developments in AFIS from a technical point of view and the match to application domain requirements. In other words, we aim at using the framework as a tool for analyzing technology push and requirements pull forces in the AFIS domain.

References

1. Angelov, S., Grefen, P., Greefhorst, D.: A framework for analysis and design of software reference architectures. Inf. Softw. Technol. **54**(4), 417–431 (2012)
2. Baumgraß, A., Dijkman, R., Grefen, P., Pourmirza, S., Völzer, H., Weske, M.: A software architecture for transportation planning and monitoring in a collaborative network. In: Camarinha-Matos, L.M., Bénaben, F., Picard, W. (eds.) PRO-VE 2015. IAICT, vol. 463, pp. 277–284. Springer, Cham (2015). https://doi.org/10.1007/978-3-319-24141-8_25
3. Baumgraß, A., et al.: Towards a methodology for the engineering of event-driven process applications. In: Reichert, M., Reijers, H.A. (eds.) BPM 2015. LNBIP, vol. 256, pp. 501–514. Springer, Cham (2016). https://doi.org/10.1007/978-3-319-42887-1_40
4. Fleisch, E., Weinberger, M., Wortmann, F.: Business models and the internet of things (extended abstract). In: Podnar Žarko, I., Pripužić, K., Serrano, M. (eds.) Interoperability and Open-Source Solutions for the Internet of Things. LNCS, vol. 9001, pp. 6–10. Springer, Cham (2015). https://doi.org/10.1007/978-3-319-16546-2_2
5. Grefen, P., Remmerts de Vries, R.: A reference architecture for workflow management systems. Data Knowl. Eng. **27**(1), 31–57 (1998)
6. Grefen, P.: Service-Dominant Business Engineering with BASE/X - Practitioner Business Modeling Handbook. Amazon CreateSpace (2015)
7. Grefen, P., Vanderfeesten, I., Boultadakis, G.: Supporting hybrid manufacturing: bringing process and human/robot control to the cloud. In: Proceedings of the 5th IEEE International Conference on Cloud Networking, pp. 200–203. IEEE (2016)
8. Industrie 4.0: Smart Manufacturing for the Future. Germany Trade & Invest (2014)
9. Enterprise-Control System Integration - Part 1: Models and Terminology, 2nd edn. The International Electrotechnical Commission (IEC), Geneva (2013)
10. Connected Vehicle Reference Implementation Architecture. www.iteris.com/cvria. Inspected 2018
11. Janiesch, C., et al.: The internet-of-things meets business process management: mutual benefits and challenges. arXiv:1709.03628 (2017)
12. Lu, M., et al.: Cooperative and connected intelligent transport systems for sustainable European road transport. In: Proceedings of the 7th Transport Research Arena (2018)
13. Mingay, S., Mesaglio, M.: How to Achieve Enterprise Agility with a Bimodal Capability. White Paper, Gartner (2015)
14. Reference Architectures and Open Group Standards for the Internet of Things – Four Internet of Things Reference Architectures. http://www.opengroup.org/iot/wp-refarchs/p3.htm. Inspected 2018
15. Reference Model - The Workflow Reference Model. White Paper WFMC-TC-1003. Workflow Management Coalition (1995)

Integrating IoT Devices into Business Processes

Christian Friedow, Maximilian Völker, and Marcin Hewelt(✉)

Hasso Plattner Institute, University of Potsdam, Potsdam, Germany
marcin.hewelt@hpi.de

Abstract. The Internet of Things (IoT) has arrived in everyday life, controlling and measuring everything from assembly lines, through shipping containers to household appliances. Thus, IoT devices are often part of larger and more complex business processes, which might change their course based on events from these devices. However, when developing IoT applications the process perspective is often neglected and coordination of devices is realized in an ad-hoc way using custom scripts. In this paper we propose to employ process model to define the process layer of IoT applications and enact them through a process engine. Our approach thus bridges the gap between physical IoT devices and business processes. The presented implementation shows that those two can be combined without in-depth programming expertise or extensive configuration, without restricting or strongly coupling the components.

Keywords: Business processes · Business event processing
Process automation · Process execution · BPMN · Internet of Things
IoT · Fragment-based case management · Case management · Events

1 Introduction

Business Processes are operated in increasingly complex environments and have to take into account external events that influence the course of the process execution [1]. The complexity is further exacerbated through the rapid growth of devices in the "Internet of Things" (IoT). These devices are used to automate, measure, and control large parts in different environments, starting from industrial facilities up to lighting and radiators in private homes. However, when developing IoT applications, the process perspective is often neglected and devices are coordinated in an ad-hoc way using a different app for each device or custom scripts that realize the integration logic.r Thus, understanding and adapting IoT applications developed this way becomes a burden. There is a mismatch between business processes that include manual tasks, integrate legacy applications, or call webservices, and the ad-hoc logic of the IoT.

Several web-based services like zapier [2] and IFTTT [3] offer an event-based way to integrate different systems and services, including some IoT devices. However, they are limited to simple event-condition-action rules linking a trigger

© Springer International Publishing AG, part of Springer Nature 2018
R. Matulevičius and R. Dijkman (Eds.): CAiSE 2018 Workshops, LNBIP 316, pp. 265–277, 2018.
https://doi.org/10.1007/978-3-319-92898-2_22

event from one system or service to an action in another one [4]. Meyer et al. [5] propose to integrate IoT devices as resources into business processes, but do not address the execution of such processes. Serral et al. [6] suggest a model-driven solution to integrate pervasive services which interact with sensors and actuators. It allows to create context-specific tasks models and execute them in an engine. However, [6] does not consider business tasks, but rather focuses on supporting behavioral patterns of users.

We propose to employ BPMN process models to define the process layer of IoT applications and enact them through a process engine. This extends the framework of [7] with IoT devices. Technically, this contribution provides a way to bidirectionally integrate low-level, physical IoT devices into business processes, in a way that the execution of process instances is influenced by events, e.g. sensor values, and in return, process instances can send commands to those devices. To simplify this connection and to abstract from the concrete physical device, the Bosch IoT Things service is used. By this means, the process engine and the device do not need to share much knowledge about each other and the implementation of each is encapsulated.

The presented implementation is based on several existing systems: the Gryphon process modeling tool, the Unicorn event processing engine, and the Chimera case engine, all introduced in Sect. 2. Section 3 describes in detail how these systems work together to realize IoT applications with a process layer. Afterwards, in Sect. 4, we demonstrate the feasibility of our approach by realizing an usecase that involves several devices, manual tasks, and webservice calls. We summarize and discuss our approach in Sect. 5, pointing out how it could be improved upon in future work.

2   Foundations

The approach presented in this work is built on a few software systems, which will be briefly introduced in the following.

2.1   Bosch IoT Things Service

The Bosch IoT Things service[1] provides an interface for managing so-called "digital twins" in the cloud. For each connected device, e.g. a Raspberry Pi, a digital representation (the "twin") is stored in the cloud. This counterpart, referred to as "Thing", consists of several static attributes and features (attributes the value of which change over time), reflecting values of the physical device.

The example in Fig. 1 shows an abbreviated, possible configuration of a Thing, monitoring a truck. A geolocation sensor connected to the device can be represented as a feature comprising properties for longitude and latitude. Now, each time the sensor measures a location change, the device would update the geolocation feature of its digital representation with the new sensor data.

---

[1] https://www.bosch-iot-suite.com/things/.

```
{"thingId": "truck104",
  "attributes": {
    "no-of-trailers": "2",
    "driver": "51843"},
  "features": {
    "geolocation-sensor": {
      "properties": {
        "latitude": "52.393787",
        "longitude": "13.131836"}},
    "temperature": {
      "properties": {
        "out": "31",
        "in": "24"}}}}
```

Fig. 1. Shortened configuration of an exemplary Thing

Services interested in the device's data can subscribe to changes and get notified each time the digital equivalent is updated. This way, the Bosch IoT Things service abstracts from concrete device particularities and offers a unified interface to access the device's data. The service also offers backwards communication: services can send data and messages back to the device, for example, to give commands. The communication follows a specified format based on JSON, and Things themselves are also represented in this format. To access a Thing, a Rest API, as well as a WebSocket connection can be used.

2.2 Unicorn

Unicorn[2], an event processing platform, was developed within a logistics project for planning for more efficient transport and was presented by Baumgrass et al. [8] and first described in [9]. As an event processing platform, Unicorn gathers events from event producers, processes, e.g. aggregates, filters or enriches them, and distributes them further to event consumers. The processing is done by Esper[3], a Java library based on the event processing language (EPL).

Event producers can publish events to Unicorn using its Rest API, or events can be fetched using so-called event adapters, which actively poll event sources, like web services. Event consumers can subscribe to event queries and are notified by Unicorn each time a relevant event occurred or a query matched, through REST endpoints. In addition, events can be viewed in a provided web-interface.

2.3 Gryphon

Gryphon[4] is a web-based modeler for process models, build on NodeJS and connected to a MongoDB to persist the models. Next to common process mod-

---

[2] https://bpt.hpi.uni-potsdam.de/UNICORN.
[3] http://www.espertech.com/esper/.
[4] https://github.com/bptlab/gryphon.

els, fragment-based case models can be created, as described by the fragment-based case management (fCM) approach [10]. Additionally, object life cycles can be defined for data objects and their possible transitions used within the case models.

Models can then be transferred directly to connected Chimera instances (see below) for deployment, or exported as JSON to reuse them in other services.

2.4 Chimera

Chimera[5] is a case engine for executing fragment-based case models (fCM). To accomplish that, Chimera takes a fragment-based case model as an input, analyzes it and enables activities, gateways and events based on their data-flow and control-flow dependencies. Running cases and their current state can be viewed in a web-based interface, which also allows for manual execution of activities and data entry.

Important parts of Chimera for the approach presented in this paper are webservice tasks, data-based gateways, receiving events and manual tasks. As the name suggests, webservice tasks are able to call webservices predefined in the model. Data-based gateways are gateways, whose decisions are based on data-objects and their state or their attribute values, and which therefore can be executed (i.e. decided) automatically by the engine. Receiving events are start or intermediate events, that, in order to be executed, register event queries to Unicorn and wait for the fulfillment of these queries. Data from the event notification can be stored in data object. These three model elements are executed without manual intervention, which enables case models that only consist of these types to be executed completely automatically by Chimera.

3 Approach and Implementation

In this section, we present an exemplary approach and implementation to allow physical devices and event processing services to interact with each other. The practical realization is based on the foundations introduced in Sect. 2. A Raspberry Pi is used as a physical device and the Bosch IoT Things service operates the digital twin. The event processing platform Unicorn registers changes of Things and provides events, which are used by the case engine Chimera to start and influence business processes, modeled in Grpyhon beforehand.

In the following, a general, architectural overview is presented, followed by more specific explanations for each component.

3.1 Overview

Figure 2 provides an overview of the overall structure and components involved. The Raspberry Pi communicates with the Bosch IoT Things service, which in

---

[5] https://bpt.hpi.uni-potsdam.de/Chimera.

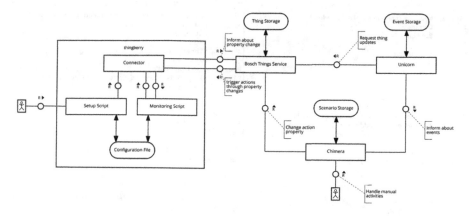

Fig. 2. Fundamental modeling concepts (FMC) model

turn is requested by Unicorn for event processing. Chimera, subscribed to Thing related events, gets notified each time a new, relevant event occurs and performs its activities accordingly. In case an action should be performed, Chimera communicates with the Bosch IoT Things service, which then notifies the Raspberry Pi about the change.

3.2 Creating a Digital Representation for an IoT Device

This section describes the process of connecting a physical device to the Bosch IoT Things service and keeping the device synchronized with its digital twin. The thingberry[6] software responsible for this is written in Python and runs on the physical device, in our case a Raspberry Pi. It contains three main software components. First, a setup component that allows to create and store a description of the device, which defines connected sensors, actuators, and attributes. Second, a monitoring component, that observes the connected sensors for value changes. Third, a connector component that, (a) uses the description provided by the setup component to create the digital twin in the Bosch IoT Things service, and (b) connects to the Bosch IoT Things service updating the state of the digital twin, whenever the state of the physical device changes. These components are described in more detail in the following subsections.

Setting up the Representation. The setup component is a command-line tool, used to gather meta information about the device, e.g. the device name, as well as context information, e.g. sensors and the pins they are connected to. An excerpt from an exemplary setup process is given in Fig. 3, which shows the setup for a connected Pi camera and a button. After finishing the setup process, this information is stored locally as a configuration file in JSON format. Thus, configurations can be easily shared and reused for similar device setups.

---

[6] https://github.com/MaximilianV/thingberry.

```
Please choose a component to be added to your thing:   Please choose a component to be added to your thing:
1       Camera                                         1       Camera
2       Button                                         2       Button
3       NFC                                            3       NFC
4       Vibration                                      4       Vibration
5       Display                                        5       Display
Please select an entry:1                               Please select an entry:2
Please name the new Action:                            Please select a feature to insert the component:
camera                                                 1       New entry
Configuring Camera Action:                             Please select an entry:1
Delay until photo is taken (def. 2): 3                 Please name the new Feature:
Destination to save image: /var/www/html/images        Buttons
What's the current IP address? 192.168.0.123           Please name the new Property:
Completed setup for Camera component.                  LoginButton
                                                       Configuring Button Property:
                                                       Which pin is the button connected to? 12
Add another component? (y/n)                           Completed setup for Button component.
y
```

Split side by side for clarity.

Fig. 3. Excerpt from an exemplary setup process

In order to reduce the effort and time involved in setting up the digital representation, the user is guided through the process. This eliminates the need to manually write a complex configuration file based on documentation. So far, the setup component offers support for five physical components, commonly used with the Rasperry Pi – buttons, the Pi camera, segment displays, NFC-chips, generic binary components. These can be used in the setup process without any further programming effort or in-depth knowledge about the component. All these components can be configured using the textual interface of the setup component. More components can be added by extending the provided architecture inside the repository, which are also automatically integrated into the setup script.

Two different types of components can be distinguished:

Observers "listen" to changes of the system, like a button press or other sensor values. They are organized in features and properties, and often need to be configured, e.g. which physical pin the button is connected to.

Actions can be triggered externally, e.g. by business process activities. They provide a way to interact with the device or with the environment using the device, like sending a signal or taking a photo. All actions provided by a device, and therefore by the Thing, are grouped as properties within an artificial Thing-feature called "actions" (see the explanation of Thing terminology in Sect. 2.1).

A physical component can be of one or both of the described types. For example, the button component is an observer, which monitors the pin of the (push) button, but the button itself cannot be operated automatically by an action. In contrast, the NFC component serves as an observer, which reads an NFC-chip, as well as an action, which writes to an NFC-chip.

Connecting to the Cloud Service. The connector component takes care of any communication between the physical device and the Bosch IoT Things service. To connect to the service, the provided Rest API[7] is used. Working with the configuration file created by the previous step, the connector component creates a new Thing instance in the Bosch IoT Things service and configures it according to the file. Thing features and properties are instantiated with the provided names and initialized with default values.

During operation of the IoT application, the connector component also updates the digital twin with the latest device state, e.g. sensor values. Due to the fine-grained structure, each change of information can be addressed and processed individually. If a sensor reports a new value, only this specific value can be updated and there is no need to refresh the whole Thing.

Monitoring the Device and Its Components. The third component manages the device at "runtime": Each connected physical component, like a button, is monitored in its own thread, according to the configuration. The decoupled structure of the implementation allows to supervise different components simultaneously, whilst being more error resistant, as each component operates in an own thread. In case a change is registered, e.g. the button is pressed or the measured temperature increases, the new value is assigned to the corresponding feature and property of the Thing. Then, the updated value is provided to the connector component, which updates the digital twin in the Bosch IoT Things service. By comparing the previous value with the updated one, unnecessary calls and updates to the Rest API are avoided.

The monitoring component also manages the return path from the Bosch IoT Things service to the Raspberry Pi and its connected components. On startup, a WebSocket connection to the cloud service is established and within this connection, the script registers for events about changes to the Thing. Thus, every time a Thing changes, an event is received containing information about the affected Thing entity, the changed feature and property, as well as the new value. Since so-called actions are organized in a separate "actions"-feature, action related events can be identified by filtering firstly according to the configured Thing name and secondly, the change must concern an action. Most actions can be triggered by setting the corresponding property-value in the "actions"-features to *true* (i.e. enabling it). Now, each time a property within the "actions"-feature of the current Thing is set to *true*, an event passes the filter and can be processed further. Based on the event's information, the monitoring component determines the requested action and executes it in an additional thread. After completing the action's task, the corresponding property in the twin is reset to allow another execution. A more abstract view is provided in Sect. 3.5 below.

---

[7] https://things.s-apps.de1.bosch-iot-cloud.com/documentation/rest/.

3.3 Receiving Events from "Digital Twins"

Every time a Thing in the Bosch IoT Things service is updated, an event should be registered inside Unicorn. In order to receive the updates, which we created earlier through the Python script, we developed an event adapter for Unicorn[8]. This event adapter requests the Bosch IoT Things service Rest API for all Things in regular intervals. Afterwards, it calculates the JSON difference between the last two requests according to RFC 6902[9] and converts the updates into events in Unicorn.

Table 1. Mapping from target of change to corresponding event type

Target of change	Event type
Thing was created	ThingAdded
Attribute was changed	AttributeChanged
Feature was changed	FeatureChanged
Property was changed	PropertyChanged
Thing was deleted	ThingRemoved

Events created by this adapter will have different event types based on the target of the change. Table 1 shows the change made to the Thing and the event type of the corresponding event. The events created by the Bosch IoT Things adapter can now be either processed further using EPL or used directly by other services that subscribed accordingly to Unicorn.

3.4 React Flexibly to Events

In order to react to events using fragment based case models, the case model execution engine Chimera is introduced to the workflow. Chimera already implements a configurable connection which connects to the Rest API provided by Unicorn. If a case model containing message receive or send events is deployed to Chimera, the engine will register the specified queries in Unicorn. Message receive events will additionally register a callback to Chimera, which is called by Unicorn each time the registered EPL query is matched. The implementation of the connection between Unicorn and Chimera has been described in [11] and conceptually extended in [7].

Bringing together the events created in Unicorn when the digital twin is changed and a case model using the mentioned message receive events, opens up the possibility to drive a case model using events from IoT devices. That enables case model execution engines like Chimera to automatically decide gateways or

---

[8] https://github.com/bptlab/Unicorn/tree/dev/EapEventProcessing/src/main/java/de/hpi/unicorn/adapter/BoschIot.

[9] https://tools.ietf.org/html/rfc6902.

change the state of objects, based on sensor values or real life events measured by IoT devices. The next challenge was to trigger actions, like taking a photo or displaying some text on a IoT device, using certain activities inside the case model.

3.5 Sending Commands from Business Activities

As mentioned before, the communication between cloud service and device is bi-directional. Thereby, e.g. business process instances can trigger actions on physical devices and affect the environment. In Sect. 3.2, "actions" were introduced and how they can be triggered on devices. To accomplish the required property-change, so-called webservice-activities are used inside Chimera. Those activities can be enriched with a URL that is called as soon as the activity is executed. In this case, the webservice-activities are configured to perform a request to the Bosch IoT Things service Rest API, which changes the desired property in the digital twin.

> Example: A business process requires a device (the Raspberry Pi) to take a photo. During the modeling process, a webservice-activity is inserted at the desired point and configured with a request to enable the "camera"-property in the "actions"-feature on the correct Thing. The Raspberry Pi configured for this Thing, now receives an event for this change through its WebSocket connection to the Bosch IoT Things service. It determines that the "camera"-property was connected to the configured Pi-Camera-component during the setup process and executes the logic behind it (taking a photo). As it is very likely that the image needs to be viewed at some point later, the component also updates the "camera"-feature with the path of the last photo taken. In addition, the value of the "camera"-property in the "action"-feature is reset (i.e. disabled) and therefore ready to be triggered again.

4 Evaluation

In order to evaluate the approach presented above to connect Internet of Things devices to business processes, we realize an exemplary use case. The use case should not only combine different physical components or only be of theoretical or abstract use, but should also demonstrate, how the combination of IoT and business processes can simplify and enhance our everyday lives.

The Idea is a simple coffee machine billing system. The system aims to automate the process of counting the coffee amount for each user, as well as detecting potential coffee theft, to simplify the billing for a shared coffee machine. In a successful execution of the process, a user should be identified before using the coffee grinder and the amount of consumed coffee in the corresponding user account should increase. If the coffee grinder is used without previous identification the action should be treated as theft and should be documented.

Starting from this informal description, we determined the sensors and actors necessary to implement the use case. In order to ease the authentication process for users, we connected an NFC sensor module to a Raspberry Pi. We also connected a vibration sensor attached to the coffee grinder, in order to detect when it is used. Finally, we connected a display and a camera to the Raspberry Pi, to visualize process progress and take photos of potential thieves.

Creating a Digital Representation for the Raspberry Pi. After connecting all sensors and actors the Raspberry Pi, a digital representation needs to be created. We implemented the scripts for all components in Python and executed the setup script, introduced in Sect. 3.2, which initialized the digital representation of the Raspberry Pi, afterwards. As the initialization finished, the Raspberry Pi was ready to be monitored by the daemon script, which pushes changes of sensor values and receives execution commands for actions.

Receiving Events from Digital Twins. The Thing inside the Bosch IoT Things service already receives updates from the Raspberry Pi and to get these updates into Unicorn too, the Bosch IoT event adapter inside an existing Unicorn instance needs to be started. No additional customization or configuration was required at this step.

ID	Timestamp	EventType	Values
161	2018-01-29 10:24:19.000	PropertyChanged (8)	feature=actions, property=display, propertyValue=BPT meets IoT, thingId=com.friedow:thingberry
160	2018-01-29 09:53:05.000	PropertyChanged (8)	feature=vibration, property=lastTriggered, propertyValue=2018-01-29 09:53:01.118664, thingId=com.friedow:thingberry

Fig. 4. Events concerning the Raspberry Pi

Figure 4 shows a vibration event that was successfully pushed to Unicorn from the the Raspberry Pi, as well as an action event which will show a message on the display.

React Flexibly to Events. Now that the updates of sensor values are available in Unicorn, they can be used by other systems like Chimera. But before actually using Chimera to receive and work on the basis of events, we had to model our exemplary use case as a fragment-based case model. Therefore, we captured our example in eight fragments, modeled them in Gryphon and deployed the case model to Chimera. Figure 5 shows the case fragment in which a user is able to use the coffee grinder if he is currently authenticated.

In order to receive event notifications from Unicorn, Chimera registers EPL queries for each event-receiving model element. From this point on, every time Unicorn receives an event which matches the query, Chimera is notified and the process model is powered by this event.

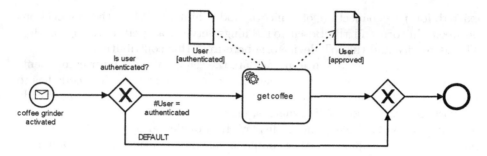

Fig. 5. Exemplary case fragment "Get Coffee"

Sending Commands from Business Activities. After the exemplary show-case successfully received events and powered fragment based case model instances with it, the last task was to trigger actions like taking a photo or show-ing some text on the Raspberry Pi's display. As already described in Sect. 3.5, actions are triggered by setting certain properties on the Thing inside the Bosch IoT Cloud. To achieve this, we defined webservice tasks inside the case model, changing the corresponding property. These can then be automatically executed by Chimera, if they were enabled. That opened up the possibility to take a photo or display some text using just the executed case model itself.

Wrap-Up. The small use case clearly demonstrates the level of abstraction and the capabilities of the underlying implementation. Whereas the Raspberry Pi just sends its data to the Bosch IoT Things service, having no knowledge about other connected systems, Chimera and Unicorn do not need any detailed information about the device and its physical characteristics. Therefore, it furthermore shows the power of the connection between Internet of Things and business process management and how manual tasks can be automated.

5   Conclusion

The approach presented in this contribution allows to coordinate the devices used in an IoT application using a process engine for the process logic. It can also be used to extend existing business process or case models by integrating external events produced by IoT devices. Thus, with our approach, business pro-cesses can make use of real-world sensor data, while on the other hand changing the physical state of the world, by triggering actions. By using a defined and documented interface, the physical world and its model representation can be kept decoupled, allowing to reuse device data in various instances and to access data from multiple different devices from within a single instance.

The presented implementation provides an uncomplicated way to connect small and inexpensive devices with business processes via a cloud service. For the implementation we combined several existing systems. While previous work existed for the connection of Unicorn and Chimera [7,11], the connections between Unicorn and the Bosch IoT Things service, as well as the Bosch IoT Things service and the IoT device originate from this contribution.

One limiting factor of our approach are the sensor and actuator components connected to the Rasberry Pi. For each of these components custom code has to be written to read sensor values or trigger actions. Our implementation already supports several sensors and actuators, like buttons, binary sensors, the camera module, the NFC reader, and a display. It provides also templates that can be sub-classed to support further components, thus reducing the programmatic effort to realize future use cases.

Further the specification of webservice tasks in the case models requires a lot of knowledge about the setup; concrete names of Things, as well as their feature and property names must be available at modeling time and the corresponding Rest API call needs to be assembled manually. In future work we want to examine, how this step can be made more flexible by allowing to define the webservice tasks at deploy or run time. This kind of flexible late binding has already been implemented for email tasks which can be configured on a per-case basis at runtime. Another approach would be to specify Things as well as their features and properties as part of the data model in Gryphon. This is already done for event types that are modeled in Gryphon and registered with Unicorn when the case model is deployed.

References

1. Baumgraß, A., Botezatu, M., Di Ciccio, C., Dijkman, R., Grefen, P., Hewelt, M., Mendling, J., Meyer, A., Pourmirza, S., Völzer, H.: Towards a methodology for the engineering of event-driven process applications. In: Reichert, M., Reijers, H.A. (eds.) BPM 2015. LNBIP, vol. 256, pp. 501–514. Springer, Cham (2016). https://doi.org/10.1007/978-3-319-42887-1_40
2. Zapier: Zapier documentation (2018). https://zapier.com/developer/documentation/v2/. Accessed Mar 2018
3. IFTTT: IFTTT documentation (2018). https://platform.ifttt.com/docs. Accessed Mar 2018
4. Rahmati, A., Fernandes, E., Jung, J., Prakash, A.: IFTTT vs. Zapier: a comparative study of trigger-action programming frameworks. CoRR **abs/1709.02788** (2017)
5. Meyer, S., Ruppen, A., Magerkurth, C.: Internet of Things-aware process modeling: integrating iot devices as business process resources. In: Salinesi, C., Norrie, M.C., Pastor, Ó. (eds.) CAiSE 2013. LNCS, vol. 7908, pp. 84–98. Springer, Heidelberg (2013). https://doi.org/10.1007/978-3-642-38709-8_6
6. Serral, E., Valderas, P., Pelechano, V.: Context-adaptive coordination of pervasive services by interpreting models during runtime. Comput. J. **56**(1), 87–114 (2013)
7. Mandal, S., Hewelt, M., Weske, M.: A Framework for Integrating Real-World Events and Business Processes in an IoT Environment. In: Panetto, H., et al. (eds.) On the Move to Meaningful Internet Systems. OTM 2017 Conferences, OTM 2017. LNCS, vol. 10573, pp. 194–212. Springer, Cham (2017). https://doi.org/10.1007/978-3-319-69462-7_13

8. Baumgrass, A., Di Ciccio, C., Dijkman, R.M., Hewelt, M., Mendling, J., Meyer, A., Pourmirza, S., Weske, M., Wong, T.Y.: GET Controller and UNICORN: event-driven process execution and monitoring in logistics. In: BPM Demo Session, pp. 75–79 (2015)
9. Herzberg, N., Meyer, A., Weske, M.: An event processing platform for business process management. In: EDOC. IEEE (2013)
10. Hewelt, M., Weske, M.: A hybrid approach for flexible case modeling and execution. In: La Rosa, M., Loos, P., Pastor, O. (eds.) BPM 2016. LNBIP, vol. 260, pp. 38–54. Springer, Cham (2016). https://doi.org/10.1007/978-3-319-45468-9_3
11. Beyer, J., Kuhn, P., Hewelt, M., Mandal, S., Weske, M.: Unicorn meets Chimera: integrating external events into case management. In: BPM Demo Track, vol. 1789, CEUR-WS (2016)

Author Index

Printed in the United States
By Bookmasters